WATERING THE SAHARA:

Recollections of Paul Green
from 1894 to 1937

WATERING THE SAHARA:

Recollections of Paul Green from 1894 to 1937

James R. Spence

Edited by Margaret D. Bauer

Margaret D. Bauer

Office of Archives and History
North Carolina Department of Cultural Resources
Raleigh
2008

Printed by Edwards Brothers

Contents

Illustrations

Editor's Preface

In the fall of 2001 I was fortunate to have come into my hands a manuscript by North Carolina native James R. Spence, author of *The Making of a Governor: The Moore-Preyer-Lake Primaries of 1964* (Winston-Salem: John F. Blair Publishers, 1968) and *Portrait of a Place and Time: Recollections of a Farmer's Son* (Winter Park, Fla.: Discovery Publishing House, 1991). The almost three-hundred-page typescript, then titled "Young Paul Green, The Years 1894-1937," is based on interview conversations the author conducted with Paul Green and members of his family; other recorded interviews with Green by Green's administrative assistant Rhoda Wynn (the first director of the Paul Green Foundation), photographer Billy E. Barnes (director of the North Carolina Fund in the 1960s), and historian Jacquelyn Hall (now director of the Southern Oral History Program); excerpts from Green's diaries; quotations from letters and telegrams in the Paul Green Papers; and various biographical sources—from Elizabeth Lay Green's biography of her husband, *The Paul Green I Know*, to actress Bette Davis's autobiography, in which she talks about her first role as a vixen, which happened to be in the first movie that Paul Green worked on.

At the recommendation of Winston-Salem public relations executive Carroll H. Leggett, former North Carolina attorney general and U.S. senator Robert B. Morgan (for whom Mr. Leggett had served as chief of staff) sent me Mr. Spence's manuscript. Senator Morgan

Paul Green and Rhoda Wynn, ca. 1975. This and all subsequent photographs are provided courtesy of the Paul Green Foundation and the Paul Green Papers, Southern Historical Collection, Wilson Library, University of North Carolina at Chapel Hill, unless otherwise noted.

had received a copy from James Spence himself before Spence's death in 1995. As editor of the *North Carolina Literary Review* (*NCLR*), I was recommended as someone who might be interested in excerpting from it for publication in the *NCLR* and/or in helping the manuscript find its way into book form. I elected to try to find a publisher for the entire manuscript, for reasons I will explain later.

The bound typescript I first saw had no documentation for the author's sources, without which, of course, the idea of editing the manuscript for book publication was daunting. Still, I wrote to Mrs. Marilyn Younce Spence, the author's widow, regarding her husband's manuscript and received a call from her brother, Greensboro attorney Charles P. Younce, giving me permission to pursue publication. While helping his sister move, Mr. Younce eventually found among her belongings first, in 2003, a shoebox full of cassette tapes of the author's interviews, and later, in 2004, the original typescript, with note reference numbers marked on it (and including pages that were missing from the copy I had), as well as the corresponding source notes. With this information I could more easily imagine preparing the manuscript for publication, although my editorial duties and a book on which I was already working kept me from making any significant progress until 2006. During the interim, however, I was able to share the manuscript and then meet with preeminent Green scholar Laurence G. Avery, editor of both *A Southern Life: Letters of Paul Green, 1916-1981* and *The Paul Green Reader*; Betsy Green Moyer, daughter of Paul Green; Marsha Warren, then executive director of the Paul Green Foundation; and Charles P. Younce, brother of and attorney for Mrs. James R. Spence, all of whom endorsed the idea of turning it into a book—and all of whom have shown great patience with how long it has taken me to find the time necessary to do so.

Upon receiving the manuscript in 2001, I initially read it with an eye toward excerpting from it for the *NCLR*, but my first impression was that I was reading a *book* manuscript. *Our State* magazine did excerpt effectively from the author's preface and Spence's coverage of Green's World War I experience for a story titled "The Poet Soldier," by James R. Spence, which appeared in the periodical's March 2005 issue in a special feature section called "A Soldier's Story: From Colonial Days to the Present." Otherwise, the material here is, to my knowledge, previously unpublished. As I proceeded through the various editing stages—listening to the Spence tapes (which Marilyn Younce Spence donated to the Southern Historical Collection [SHC], Wilson Library, University of North Carolina at Chapel Hill) to find and document the excerpts from those recorded interviews, then checking the passages quoted from other recorded interviews with Green against the transcripts of those recordings, which are collected in the Southern Oral History Program Collection (likewise held by the SHC); and checking quotations and documentation of all the print sources, including books and articles, as well as the diaries and letters and other materials from the Green Papers—I found that

James Spence did rely heavily on Paul Green's own words for this biography. He quotes most extensively from interviews with the writer—his own, as well as those of Rhoda Wynn and Billy Barnes—and from Green's diaries and letters. He also excerpts from Green's writing about his life and about his writing in his own essays and sketches collected in his books *The Hawthorn Tree*, *Home to My Valley*, *Drama and the Weather*, and *Words and Ways*.

At the time that Spence conducted his interviews for this manuscript (1974-1979), there was as yet no scholarly biography of the playwright; indeed, noted Green scholar Laurence G. Avery was then still editing the letters of dramatist Maxwell Anderson. Avery's volume of Green's letters did not appear until twenty years after Spence's first interview session, and John Herbert Roper's biography, *Paul Green: Playwright of the Real South*, followed the interviews by almost thirty years. Besides Green's own words, then, Spence consulted (and sometimes drew heavily from) such monographs on Green as Agatha Boyd Adams's *Paul Green of Chapel Hill* and slim volumes by the playwright's wife, Elizabeth Lay Green's *The Paul Green I Know*, and his best friend, Barrett H. Clark's *Paul Green*, as well as an article by North Carolina literary historian Richard Walser, "Paul Green Undergraduate." Spence also read and cited autobiographies and biographies of those who worked with Green—producer Cheryl Crawford, actresses Bette Davis and Lotte Lenya, professor Frederick Henry Koch, and writers Thomas Wolfe and William Faulkner—as well as books on the various groups with which Green was involved—Campbell College, the University of North Carolina, the Carolina Playmakers, Broadway, the Group Theatre, and the Federal Theatre (all of which sources are cited more fully in the chapters to follow). And, of course, Spence also read Green's plays and fiction and the reviews of his plays and novels. Finally, he read the newspaper coverage—national, state, and local—of Green's social activism.

As editor, I have gone through and fully documented all of the published sources referenced in Spence's manuscript; I've set up a consistent documentation style for distinguishing and documenting the unpublished recorded interviews and the diary excerpts; I've documented the material from the Paul Green Papers as per the instructions of the Southern Historical Collection at Chapel Hill; and I've inserted bibliographic endnotes for all of Green's titles, in order to direct readers in finding them in his numerous books. I have proofread every excerpt, quotation, and citation, making corrections and providing further documentation as needed. All of this source checking and editing required numerous readings of the manuscript, particularly when listening for passages from recorded interviews but also to find and document all the print sources referenced (not all of which were completely cited). The repeated readings led me to realize that the manuscript was still in draft stage. It appears to me that the author died before he finished polishing the chapters, including going back to make connections between the events he chose to record. Thus, one of my duties as editor of this manuscript was to compose these transitions, but that is the extent of the actual *writing* I did within the chapters (and some of these transitions were accomplished by simply moving Spence's own material around).

I did also change the author's title, but the title is still Spence's. H. L. Mencken's well-known essay "The Sahara of the Bozart" came up a few times in Spence's interviews with Green, and Spence (who seems to have agreed with Mencken's characterization of the South) addressed Green's achievement of "watering" the South's artistic desert with his own work. Indeed, Spence even told Green that he was "tempted to call this book 'Watering the Sahara' because . . . that's what you've been doing all these years . . . you've been involved in watering the Sahara down here." He continued, "A thread that runs through this whole thing . . . is that when you started, it was a Sahara just like Mencken said it was, and just look how it has flowered since then." Spence is among those who continued to appreciate Green's contribution to southern letters past the playwright's heyday. Spence's manuscript (and listening to his recorded interviews, many of which were not used in this book) reminds us of Green's reputation in his own day—that his early Pulitzer Prize brought him national attention from Broadway to Hollywood, in both of which places he found work (or rather, work sought him out) for years to come, including numerous requests of him to write screenplays of movies; a commission to adapt Richard Wright's *Native Son* for the stage; and offers to teach from his own alma mater in Chapel Hill, as well as from Harvard and Princeton.

Ironically, although Green's value was widely recognized while he lived, since his death southern literary scholars have largely overlooked him—with, of course, the notable exceptions of Laurence Avery and John Roper. And though Avery and Roper certainly recognized Paul Green's greatness and published scholarly works appropriate for such a writer, there is still relatively little scholarship on Green's individual works (including his Pulitzer Prize-winning play), and the biennial meeting of the Society for the Study of Southern Literature rarely includes a single paper on this major southern playwright. Paul Green is still well known in his own state, but largely because of his symphonic drama *The Lost Colony*, which has been performed continuously in Manteo every summer since 1937 (except for the years of World War II when blackouts were ordered along the eastern coast). Except for the content of *The Paul Green Reader*, a recent edition of *The Lost Colony* (both edited by Laurence Avery and published by the University of North Carolina Press) and a limited reprint edition of the novel *This Body the Earth* (published by the Paul Green Foundation), Green's works are out of print.

If not for my role as editor of the *NCLR*, I would probably have to count myself among those scholars who have overlooked this major figure of the Southern Renascence, the very heyday of southern writing that produced the likes of Green contemporary William Faulkner, as well as Zora Neale Hurston. While Hurston (like Green a folklorist) has long since been rediscovered and even canonized, Paul Green continues to remain largely unknown beyond North Carolina. Living in North Carolina and regularly teaching North Carolina literature, I would likely be aware of Green's authorship of *The Lost Colony* and *In Abraham's Bosom*; but while preparing the *NCLR*'s tenth anniversary issue some years back, I read most of Green's short fiction in search of a story we might reprint, which then led me to learn of his work on *Native Son* and to discover photographs of Green with Richard Wright in Chapel Hill. But Spence's manuscript and the recorded interviews that inspired it have introduced me to the vast Green canon—the numerous plays and screenplays, the novels, and the poetry, in addition to the short fiction I'd already read.

There is much in Green's body of work to be explored in scholarly studies of the period, the region, and the various genres in which

Margaret D. Bauer, 1998.

Green wrote. And there is much as yet untouched material in the recorded interviews with the writer—those conducted by James Spence, as well as the others—that literary scholars, film studies scholars, historians, folklorists, and sociologists would find of value. I am already exploring the Richard Wright material in these interviews as 2008 marks the year of Wright's 100th birthday. I invite those who are motivated by this book to listen to the Spence recordings and to read the other Green interview transcripts yourselves—and I hope you will contact me, in my capacity as editor of the *NCLR*, to talk about what you hear (or read in the transcripts) that inspires an idea for an article on Paul Green.

Margaret D. Bauer

Author's Preface

My first interview with Paul Green took place on October 24, 1974, at his home on Old Lystra Road, west of Chapel Hill, North Carolina. We sat in his library beneath a large fireplace and were warmed by a fire he had built himself. Green knew that I was coming to talk about Harnett County history. His father's farm and my grandfather's farm had been separated by less than five miles, and both had a Lillington, North Carolina, address. His father's first wife had been a Spence, although not closely related to our family. When Paul Green, as a young man, had been a schoolteacher in our area, he had taught two of my father's brothers (Dwight M. and Kendall Spence) in a three-room schoolhouse (he was only five years older than Kendall).

I had met Mr. Green in 1947 when I was a student at the University of North Carolina and we had briefly talked of Harnett County. I had spoken to him again at the Harnett County centennial celebration in 1955, at which time I was practicing law in Lillington. When we met again in 1974 Mr. Green had passed his eightieth birthday. As we shook hands at the door, I was struck by how young and vigorous he looked. He was tall, about six feet, and not overweight. His hair was still dark, though with some gray, and was combed straight back with no part. His facial profile, as distinctive as John Barrymore's, had not changed. His voice was somewhat high-pitched, but with a great amount of range, and had a musical quality. His movements were never those of an old man.

His assistant, Rhoda Wynn, helped us prepare for the interview. His tape recorder and my tape recorder operated side by side. We liked each other immediately. We were soon discussing rural life in

Harnett County, mutual acquaintances, and Buies Creek Academy, where he went to high school, which was known as Campbell College by the time I enrolled for my sophomore year (and which would later become Campbell University, with a law school and a pharmacy school).

When my time was up (a man from Texas was waiting to talk about music for one of Mr. Green's outdoor historical dramas), he said, "Maybe we can continue this sometime." I took the cue. I later came up from Florida on vacation from my job at a bank and spent two days with him. Sometimes we talked in the house, and sometimes we went out to his study, which was a converted tobacco barn. We were diligent, taking a break only for lunch. That noontime meal was often prepared by Mrs. Green, who was approximately her husband's age, with major assistance from a servant who arrived each morning. The food was country in substance and preparation, the kind I would get when I visited my aunts in Harnett County—no tossed salads, Brussels sprouts, or broccoli but plenty of field peas, corn, sweet potatoes, fried chicken, and roast pork. I noticed that Mr. Green had

Paul Green, 1975.

an affinity for pie, and in the years that followed it began to show under his belt.

My conversations with Mr. Green (he asked me to call him "Paul" but I never could) revealed that he had been severely scarred in his youth by at least four occurrences: an incident with his grandfather Byrd when he was three, which I relate in the opening paragraphs of chapter 1 of this book; his rejection of the fundamentalist religion that was a part of the fabric of his early life; the sudden death of his mother when he was nearing his fourteenth birthday (he said he believed, in retrospect, that he had had a nervous breakdown at that time); and his battlefield experience in Belgium in World War I. The scars seemed totally healed, however. I found a man who was at peace with himself.

Paul Green was still a liberal when I spoke with him (and he remained a liberal). He had actively fought capital punishment all his life, had actually visited prisoners on death row, and had been a leader on small committees that had saved men from being executed—at least one of whom had been totally innocent of the crime. He had opposed racial segregation all of his post-college life; had written extensively about the plight of black people; and had advocated integration of public schools, Chapel Hill theaters, and the University of North Carolina long before any of these actions took place. When Harnett County Native Americans appealed to him because their children had been denied entrance to Dunn High School, he appeared in court on their behalf.

I believe I once saw the outer limits of his liberalism. One of his young granddaughters came in and introduced a black university student she was dating. What could he say, this philosophy teacher who understood logic and was keenly aware of his own preachings about the brotherhood of man? After the couple left, he said, "I think she's trying to test me."

He was opposed to organized religion, and yet as a young man in Harnett County he taught Sunday School, and he had read the Bible at age ten (although he admitted to skipping over a lot of "begats"). He was still trying to sort out his beliefs when he came back from World War I, but after he had completed studying philosophy under Prof. Horace Williams and had begun his own teaching career—and certainly by the time he wrote his play *The Field God*, which was produced in New York in 1926—he was fixed in his anti-religion stand.

He told me of sometimes bitter discussions with his brothers about religion. One said, "I told you if you went to school in Chapel Hill you would lose your soul, and you have." Mr. Green indicated to me that in his later years he had toned down his anti-religion statements and tried not to get into such discussions. He had made some accommodations to the society in which he functioned. His wife's father was an Episcopal minister who wanted to baptize his grandchildren. Green went along with it when Mrs. Green appealed to him. His sister Mary Green Johnson was a deeply religious person. He loved her dearly and did not want to hurt her. He never made anti-religious statements around her.

His stand against religions extended to all religion-based violence and wars throughout the world. He had visited India and had seen the conflict between Hindu and Muslim. He was appalled at the fighting between Christians in Ireland. His logic in this matter led to his opposition to Zionism and to the establishment of the state of Israel because he thought the result would be more suffering and death. That opposition did not, however, interfere with his admiration of, friendship with, and love of Jewish people with whom he had worked, some of whom had been instrumental in his success.

Mr. Green furnished me with numerous items from his personal files, such as a copy of the poem he wrote to a French girl who was his close friend in Paris just after the end of World War I, and the original of a telegram he received from Chicago in 1936 telling him that his play *Hymn to the Rising Sun* had been closed because of its "moral character." He directed me to his family correspondence. Over a period of more than forty years he had kept every card and letter from all members of the family and carbon copies of his correspondence to them. He helped me find everything that had been published about him and all of his published writings, including his two out-of-print novels. He had kept a diary continuously from the day he enlisted in the army during World War I. He had copies made for me. I also met with three of his sisters—Caro Mae Green Russell, Erma Green Gold, and Mary Green Johnson, who helped me check the dates and accuracy of information about family-related events.

Paul Green, 1976.

I found Paul Green to be a humble man. His plays had been on Broadway, and he had won a Pulitzer Prize. He had written for Samuel Goldwyn and Darryl F. Zanuck in Hollywood. He had "invented" the outdoor historical drama with the writing of *The Lost Colony*. But he was never satisfied with what he had written and often pointed to flaws. He seemed genuinely grateful that he had been able to get through life without making some terrible mistake that would have changed everything for him. He thought a lot about times when disaster had been close: the time when he had his pistol in his hand and told a rebellious soldier that if he did not get back in line he would shoot him; the time he was billeted in a French home in which there was a girl his age, and he wanted so badly to slip into her bedroom in the middle of the night. Some of his humility had come from poverty—poverty on the farm in Harnett County, poverty as a teacher in the Department of Philosophy at the University of North Carolina for an annual salary of $2,500, poverty in Germany and England on a Guggenheim Fellowship just before the Great Depression, poverty when his automobile was repossessed several years after he had had two plays produced in New York. Now he was just happy to have enough for a comfortable existence and to provide for his wife when he was gone.

In recent years I have read biographies of writers and persons associated with Broadway and Hollywood in which the subjects are revealed to have been unprincipled and unlikable people. I found nothing of this sort to reveal about Mr. Green. There was no hint of a mean streak, no shadow of a dishonest attitude. Once I turned off the tape recorder and talked to him about sex life in Hollywood. I could imagine that a tall, handsome playwright and former semi-pro baseball player would have been aggressively pursued. He denied that he was involved in any extramarital affairs, and I am inclined to believe him. During the 1930s he always rushed back to his family in Chapel Hill after each brief writing assignment. During World War II, when travel became a problem, he took his wife and children to California for the duration. All that I discerned of him indicated a genuine family man who remained devoted to his wife during their entire married life.

I have already said enough to convey to you that my book about Paul Green is not a critical biography. There are a couple of points I want to make about his work, however. Much of his writing is not in fashion now. His Pulitzer Prize-winning play *In Abraham's Bosom* is not produced anymore and was never produced south of the Mason-Dixon Line. Many of his "folk" plays (as they were called when they were written) and his short stories are about black people of another era and do not appeal to modern readers, black or white. His two novels are so accurate in recording the Harnett County grammar and accents of rural people that they may be found offensive to today's readers. (Once a New York producer asked him to modify the local speech in a play because "we're having trouble reading it.")

A few years before Paul Green's death in 1981, *Reader's Digest* ran an article about him, which stated that more people had seen the live performances of his outdoor historical dramas than had seen the plays of Tennessee Williams and Arthur Miller. With all the little-theater productions of Williams's and Miller's plays, that may no longer be true, but the statement still reminds us of the number of people Green's work reached. Green certainly would not have compared his outdoor dramas with *The Glass Menagerie* or *Death of a Salesman*,

James R. Spence. Photograph by Elson Alexandre of Orlando, Florida; courtesy of James R. Spence Jr.

which were quite different in purpose and result. The outdoor dramas seem to go hand-in-hand with the restoration of historical places, which goes hand-in-hand with tourism. They will probably endure into a time when they will be brought indoors, perhaps into superdomes. The remainder of his work—the stories, the novels, and the plays—in spite of fashions and speech preferences of today, has a core that is so true in its depiction of human aspirations and emotions that much of it will remain valid indefinitely.

As a boy in Harnett County I heard of that man from over the river who had picked four hundred pounds of cotton in a day, pitched baseball with either hand—and who had won the Pulitzer Prize. From that day, he was one of my heroes. My life was enriched by him, and I hope yours will be.

James R. Spence

Acknowledgments

I am sure the Southern Historical Collection (SHC), Wilson Library, University of North Carolina at Chapel Hill, is as appreciative as I am of Marilyn Younce Spence's donation of her husband's recorded interviews with Paul Green, and I would especially like to thank Mrs. Spence's brother, Charles P. Younce, and the playwright's daughter, Betsy Green Moyer, for all of their support of this project, but particularly for staying with me as their choice of editor for the book while I waited for the time to do it.

That time finally came with the help of a spring 2006 research development award from East Carolina University's (ECU) Department of English and a fall 2006 grant from the Paul Green Foundation. Additional funds for travel came from a 2005-2006 and a 2006-2007 Archie K. Davis Fellowship from the North Caroliniana Society, which paid for my research trips to the University of North Carolina at Chapel Hill to listen to the tapes donated by Mrs. Spence to the SHC and to search the Paul Green Papers; and from the Ralph Hardee Rives Chair of Southern Literature foundation account, for travel funds for my summer 2006 graduate assistant, who likewise made several trips to Chapel Hill. I also received help earlier on in this project from *North Carolina Literary Review* (*NCLR*) intern Ryan Fulcher, who scanned the typescript into a Word file and who was the first to listen to the Spence/Green tapes; Rebecca Hope Best and Jackson Taylor, undergraduate interns assigned to me by the ECU Honors Program during the last years to assist with quote-checking and documenting the excerpts from the recorded Spence interviews;

Deborah Shoop, my summer 2006 graduate assistant from the ECU English department, who also made several trips to the SHC to quote-check and properly document the Paul Green Diary excerpts and to check and document sources quoted from the Paul Green Papers; and finally, Lisa DeVries, Lorrie Coltraine Roberts, and Eugene Tinklepaugh, 2006-2007 ECU English department graduate assistants, who helped with final editing and source-checking.

I would also like to acknowledge the cheerful service of the staff of the SHC, particularly Laura Brown, and of the staff of the North Carolina Collection, Wilson Library, University of North Carolina at Chapel Hill, particularly Nicholas Graham. So many people played roles in seeing this book through to its publication; besides those already mentioned here and in the editor's preface, I want to name Lorraine Hale Robinson, senior associate editor of the *NCLR*, who read the manuscript with me when I first received it and agreed that this book was worth pursuing; Alexandra Lightfoot, director of the Paul Green Foundation; Tim West of the SHC, who oversaw the gift of the Spence collection and the recording of CDs from Spence's cassette tapes; Jeffrey J. Crow of the North Carolina Office of Archives and History (A&H); Donna Kelly of the Historical Publications Section of A&H; Melody Bentz of ECU's Office of Sponsored Programs; Michael Bassman of the ECU Honors Program; and, especially, Robert M. Topkins, the manuscript's copy editor.

Finally, thanks go to the Paul Green Foundation for permission to publish Spence's numerous quotations from materials collected in the Paul Green Papers, from the Paul Green interview transcripts collected in the Southern Oral History Program Collection, and from Paul Green's books.

Margaret D. Bauer

1: The Family

Paul Eliot Green was born March 17, 1894, in the community near Pleasant Union Church, two miles west of the hamlet of Buies Creek, North Carolina, then the home of Buies Creek Academy (now Campbell University).[1] In the summer of 1897 Paul's mother took him to visit her father, William Byrd; Paul subsequently described the experience in these words: "He was on his deathbed, a great big man with a beard. And he terrified me. I happened to reach up, and he had a Bible, and the Bible fell on the floor with a great flop, and he yelled, 'Bettie, come get this youngun. He's knocked my Bible off.' And it scared me—so horrified me that he haunted me until, oh, twenty years ago [ca. 1954], he began to disappear. [Before then,] in my dreams he was always pursuing me."[2] William Byrd haunted the dreams of Paul Green to such an extent that Green talked about it on another occasion as well:

I remember when I was a little fellow I had worms, and I had the most awful dreams. And in those dreams there was always that man with that beard, looking at me. . . . I bet he has run me a thousand times in the night down the road. There was always a road, and I was trying to run away, and the awful tiredness would get into my thighs. I couldn't run. And I'd look back and there was that man coming down the road with that great beard and gesticulating, you know, trying to catch me. And always . . . as he ran after me there would open to the side of me a big hole . . . and I knew that he was trying to catch me and put me in that hole. As I was running down the road with my tired legs, that hole stayed right with me, and he would draw nearer and he would catch me. And at the moment he caught me I'd wake up. I had that dream a thousand times, I guess.[3]

Young Paul Green had been told about God, and there was a picture in his mind of the great white-bearded man on the throne in heaven. Grandfather Byrd was likewise in heaven, and Grandfather Byrd was a white-bearded man. It was all very confusing to the young boy: "Now and then there was a wild and kind of fearful thing when the sun went down with a great fiery eye. And that [image], often, when I was a little boy, would be identified with the malevolent vengeance of God Almighty."[4] Green's sister Mary, two years older, had learned to kneel and say her prayers each night, but, she reported, "We never could get Paul to get down and pray. He was a stubborn little boy."[5] Mary apparently did not know of his fear of the man with the white beard.

John Green, Paul's paternal grandfather, was a blacksmith who lived east of the Cape Fear River. In 1837 he married Flora Catherine McLean, the daughter of a prosperous Scottish family that resided across the river. Near the place where Paul was later born, the couple began their life together in a twenty-by-thirty-foot log house that had two rooms on the first level and two attic rooms. As was the custom of the time, a separate kitchen stood thirty feet from the house. Such an arrangement reduced the fire hazard and kept cooking odors out of the dwelling. The morning after John Green's marriage he discovered that his bride could not cook breakfast and that, indeed, she had never cooked any meal in her life. The emergency was short-lived, however. Two slave girls soon arrived, sent over by the McLean family, to take on the tasks of meal preparation and housekeeping.

While he lived in the log house, John Green became a prominent man in his area, accumulating thirty slaves and two thousand acres of land. He was not as rich or as influential as the top slave owner of the county, Neill McKay, the Presbyterian minister at Summerville, who had two hundred black "servants" working his turpentine woods. But in 1855, when it was determined that a new county would be formed from portions of northern Cumberland County, John Green was one of the seven men appointed to "lay off and allot the County seat of Harnett County."[6] A little later, at the meeting that organized the county's government, he qualified as magistrate and was elected to the Committee of Finances. He was likewise instrumental in successfully promoting establishment of the first school in the area in which he lived.

When the Civil War came, John Green had just completed a new, two-story frame house. His sons Dan and John went off to fight (a third son, William Archibald Green, always called "Billy," was too young), but their father remained at home and sired a fourth son, born in 1862 and named for Robert E. Lee. John Green supported the Confederacy by investing heavily in the bonds it issued. Stories about the family's wartime experiences were part of Paul Green's upbringing. His sister Caro Mae recalls the story of their uncle Dan's return from the war. One day someone brought Dan home in a wagon, wrapped in bloody sheets but alive. According to Caro Mae's telling of the story, he had been struck by nine bullets. She reports that her father, William Archibald (Billy) Green, later told his children, "I thought my mother would die [when she saw him]."[7]

From his uncle Dan, Paul learned this story:

My daddy [Billy] was twelve or fifteen when Wheeler's cavalry came through, and following was Sherman. (Wheeler cleaned up North Carolina almost, and right behind him came the Sherman crowd that got what was left.) And my daddy was plowing in the fields. He had a little old pony. The other horses . . . and mules were hid in the juniper swamp. He heard all this jingling, and here came a group of Federal soldiers, and they hopped right over the fence, right out in the field, grabbed his pony, unhitched him and grabbed him . . . and [asked,] "Where are the rest of them?" . . . [They] stood [my father] up against a tree and said they were going to shoot him if he didn't tell [where the other stock was located]. My father never said much about it, but it was pretty clear that he thought they were going to kill him. But he wouldn't tell. They finally turned him loose and took his pony.[8]

When another party of Federal troops stopped at the Green farm, one of the soldiers was too sick to travel further. Flora Green took him in, gave him a bed upstairs, and took care of him as if he had been a member of the family. A few days later another band of enemy riders arrived, demanding money and valuables. They threatened to burn the house if they did not receive complete cooperation. It was a formidable threat, since other houses in Harnett County had already been razed by invading soldiers. But Flora Green stood up to the troop leader and told him of the sick soldier upstairs. If they burned the

Paul Green and Mary Green Johnson, 1979.

house, she told him, they would be burning one of their own because
he was too sick to be moved. Frustrated, the men left. The sick soldier
had been a cabinetmaker before the war. As he recuperated he asked
for tools and materials, and over a period of weeks he constructed two
large wardrobes for two upstairs bedrooms. According to Mary Green
Johnson, they remain where they were built; Caro Mae Green Russell
added that they are too large to have been removed from the rooms.[9]

The defeat of the Confederacy was the defeat of John Green. The
money in his pocket could not be spent, the bonds in his desk could
not be redeemed, his bank account no longer existed, and his slaves
were no longer slaves. He died shortly thereafter.[10] When his chief
asset, his land, was divided, Billy Green got his father's 174 acres. The
Green family's brief period of relative affluence thus ended.

In 1871, when Billy was nineteen, he married Elizabeth Spence.[11]
The couple had three children—Alda, John, and Will. Soon after
Will's birth, Elizabeth Spence Green died. Billy's brother Dan and his

wife, who had five girls and had always wanted a son, offered to take the baby. Unable to care for the child himself, Billy gave away his second son. For ten years thereafter Billy was a "widow man" in the community. Then, at church (about the only place in Harnett County that single adults could meet), he became acquainted with Bettie Byrd. They married in 1889 when he was thirty-seven and she was twenty-seven. By the standards of that day she was an old maid, although she had been courted for years by another man (that relationship had come to nothing).

Bettie's father, William, the man who had so frightened young Paul, had worked in the small Harnett County town of Averasboro during his youth as a farmhand for a man named Cal Avery and had married Avery's daughter. William Byrd was a fiddler, and as a young man of twenty-six he became a Baptist preacher. He taught singing schools for churches and drove his buggy about the countryside teaching music to the children of farmers. He was also considered— by neighbors, as well as family—to be eccentric. William Byrd attempted to farm his wife's inherited land, but he let the grass grow in his crop rows while he studied his books. His daughters, Bettie and Erma, seeing the work that had to be done, took to the fields like men.

On one occasion, one of Byrd's former students, then a professor in Georgia, came for a visit. At dinner the two men had such an argument over some aspect of music that the visitor left. Byrd immediately told his wife to pack his clothes, that he was going to enroll at the University of North Carolina. He actually left home and attended a summer session at the university, long enough to learn that he had been right in the argument.[12]

As he neared forty, Billy Green began his second family of children with his new wife, Bettie Byrd. Their first child together was a daughter who died at age three. Then came Mary, Paul, Hugh, Gladys, Caro Mae, and Erma. Paul Green told Rhoda Wynn, "My mother decided to dedicate her firstborn to the service of God. So she decided to name me after her favorite Bible character, St. Paul. . . . My mother, from the beginning, was interested in education for her children, so she combined the Paul name with Eliot, the president of Harvard."[13]

NOTES

1. Paul Green was born Paul Eliot Greene but later changed the spelling of his surname. Thus, although the author employs the spelling *Green* when referring to the various ancestors of the writer, those people actually spelled their names *Greene*.

2. Paul Green, interview by James R. Spence, October 24, 1974, James R. Spence audio recordings relating to Paul Green, 1974-1979 (collection #5170), Southern Historical Collection, Wilson Library, University of North Carolina at Chapel Hill (hereafter cited as Spence interview, with appropriate date).

3. Paul Green, interview by Rhoda Wynn, February 1974, tape 6, pp. 9-10, Southern Oral History Program Collection, Southern Historical Collection (hereafter cited as Wynn interview, with appropriate tape and transcript page numbers). One caveat: the entire set of Wynn interviews is labeled February 1974, but the first folder of transcripts is labeled, more specifically, February 8, 1974, and at the beginning of tape 6 Wynn comments that the date is "March the 5th, 1974." Given the length of the interviews, however, it is likely that they lasted through February and into March.

Green also talked about this recurrent dream during an interview with the author, connecting it to a frightful wartime incident he experienced on a battlefield in Belgium and to his novel *This Body the Earth* (New York: Harper, 1935). Spence interview, October 24, 1974.

4. Paul Green, interview by Billy E. Barnes, May 7, 1975, p. 55, Southern Oral History Program Collection, Southern Historical Collection.

5. Quoted from Mary Green Johnson, interview by James R. Spence, May 8, 1976, James R. Spence audio recordings relating to Paul Green, 1974-1979 (collection #5170), Southern Historical Collection (hereafter cited as Mary Green Johnson interview).

6. Malcolm Fowler, *They Passed This Way: A Personal Narrative of Harnett County History* (N.p.: Harnett County Centennial, 1955), 57.

7. The story of Dan Green's return from the war is from the author's interview with Caro Mae Green Russell, October 2, 1976, James R. Spence audio recordings relating to Paul Green, 1974-1979 (collection #5170), Southern Historical Collection (hereafter cited as Caro Mae Green Russell interview). William Archibald Green was the third son of John Green and was less than ten years old when the war commenced.

8. Spence interview, October 24, 1976.

9. The story of the convalescing soldier comes from the Mary Green Johnson and Caro Mae Green Russell interviews.

10. According to family legend, John Green, upon hearing of the Confederate defeat at Appomattox, walked out into a field and died, and his death was attributed to a broken heart. In truth, he did not die until 1867. Spence interview, October 24, 1976.

11. When the name Elizabeth Spence came up during the author's interview with Mary Green Johnson, he and Mrs. Johnson attempted to figure out if the two of them were related.

12. Spence interview, October 23, 1976. Green told the author that his aunt Emma had related to him this story about Byrd's brief stint as a student at the University of North Carolina, a story that found its way into Green's novel *This Body the Earth*.

13. Wynn interview, tape 6, p. 4.

2: Childhood

When Paul Green was a boy, his father was still clearing land:

Every winter we would get neighbors and colored people and we would cut down what they called "new ground" and get together and have what they called "log rollings." It was a community affair, somewhat like corn shucking. And I remember many times seeing these Negroes, especially, challenging each other with hand spikes. That is, you would have a spike or a lever under a log, say four under a big piece of log eight or ten feet long, big ones. And there would be one fellow at one end of the spike who would try to pull the other one down, lift more than the other. There would be lots of shouts and clamor and braggadocio, and at night these great log heaps of fire.[1]

Once a year Billy Green killed hogs on a cold winter day. The animals were slaughtered by a blow to the head with the blunt end of an ax, followed by a knife puncture of the throat. Paul saw this happen so often that he began to shudder each time he saw an ax. It never occurred to the people around him to shield him from the sight of the killings. After all, hog killing was a normal part of farm life.

A little after midnight after a hog-killing day, Billy Green would load his wagon with pork and ride off to Raleigh, where he would sell it the next day for necessary winter income. Bettie would hand him a list of all the items he was to purchase for the family—cloth, thread, needles, coffee, sugar, and a dozen or more other necessities—and he would drive off in the cold darkness. When Paul was four or five he was allowed to make the journey. Soon the boy would be freezing, and his father would use the buggy robe as a tent over the wagon seat and

Daguerreotype of William Archibald Green, Paul's father.

put his son beneath it, along with the warm lantern. The boy would lie listening to the wagon wheels cracking the thin crust of ice in the wheel ruts, the horses' hooves on the cold ground, the rubbing and snapping of the harness straps, and the creaking of the bouncing wagon.

During one of their annual trips to Raleigh, Billy Green and son arrived late and had to stay overnight, sleeping on the floor of the market house:

I'd lie over in the corner and listen to these fellows around the stove tell stories—it was just wonderful. . . . The next day we got in there, and our meat got condemned, and we had to haul it back home. We got near home—they could hear the wagon knocking in the dark—and here came the other kids running up and hopping up in the wagon. We got to the house, and my mother came out, happy. "Did you get so and so? Where's that . . . ?"—they called it "dog tallow"—chewing gum. . . . "Did you get my dog tallow?" Then the terrible news. Then we took the wagon out in the field . . . and we dug a great hole and . . . dumped [the meat] into the hole. My daddy said, "Time to go to bed, now. Tomorrow's another day."[2]

The first school Paul Green attended was held in a one-room log cabin that had been built by his father and other men in the community near Pleasant Union Church. The cabin was a mile from the Green home, and there was a creek in between. The nearby woodland was littered with pine "laps" left as waste by lumbermen. Boys in the school used an ax to cut logs from the pine tops and pulled the big pieces of wood up the middle aisle to the school's big fireplace. There were no toilets indoors or out: "On the north side in the woods was where the girls went to their—what they called bushes—go to the bushes, you know. Or go to Congress. You know that phrase? . . . Congress got in such disrepute in the eighteenth century that there was a folk phrase, 'I got to go to Congress.'" Green also recalled that "nobody had any handkerchiefs, and they [the children] wiped their noses on their sleeves, their coat sleeves. You could just see boys with coat sleeves that looked as if glazed with turpentine. . . . One cold went all over the room. Everybody got colds and coughs."[3]

Green thought all of his teachers were wonderful at the time but later realized, "We had very poor teachers. . . . One fellow kept liquor. . . . Ad Johnson had a blacksmith shop down under the hill, so every recess this [teacher] would hurry to the blacksmith shop and get on a good slug of liquor."[4]

In his first years at school the annual session lasted three months. After a few seasons the school was extended to six months. The community became dissatisfied with the log cabin and had it torn down and replaced by a frame two-room building. Better teachers were hired—teachers such as J. A. Parham, who later became managing editor of the *Charlotte Observer*.

NOTES

1. Paul Green, interview by Billy E. Barnes, March 1975, pp. 13-14, Southern Oral History Program Collection, Southern Historical Collection, Wilson Library, University of North Carolina at Chapel Hill.

2. Paul Green, interview by James R. Spence, October 24, 1974, audio recordings relating to Paul Green, 1974-1979 (collection #5170), Southern Historical Collection.

3. Ibid.

4. Ibid.

3: White Swelling

During the summer following his eighth birthday, Paul fell out of an apple tree and injured his right arm. Although it did not seem to be broken, it swelled, and at one place on the skin, pus accumulated. Neighbors called it "white swelling." He also recalled that the condition was referred to as "tuberculosis of the bone."[1] He lost weight, and his growth seemed to stop. Green recalled, "My joints got all stiff. . . . I couldn't walk down steps. I had to hop like a bird . . . from step to step. . . . My mother would wait on me." Dr. Joe McKay tried to treat him, but there was little he could do. When the physician's treatments failed, Bettie Green used folk remedies. She boiled red-oak bark and mixed the resulting tea with cornmeal to make a poultice for his arm. It did no more good than McKay's purgatives, but it was less unpleasant. Green recorded one of the neighbors as saying, "Prayer is the only thing that will save him."[2] Bettie did plenty of praying.

In the fall Paul was unable to pick cotton with the other children or to go to school. He stayed in the house mostly, helping his mother when he could, and reading anything that was available, including the stories of Edgar Allan Poe and the Bible. He got steadily worse during that year and the following year. One day, without assistance, he drove the wagon to the doctor's office at Buies Creek, using his left hand to handle the reins. Green remembered: "Dr. Joe McKay operated on my elbow, cut it open, and I'll never forget what he said before he cut me. He said, 'Look out yonder across the field, look at them crows.' And I looked—wham! He whacked my elbow open and then had that Negro to hold me, and he stuck some needles down in my arm, trying to suck out the pus. I still have scars. . . . And he finally put me back in the buggy and sent me home."[3]

The operation had been done without anesthesia, and the pain was so great that the young patient had issued awesome screams. He carried the memory of both the pain and the screams for a lifetime. The arm got no better, and Dr. McKay recommended that the child be taken to Johns Hopkins in Baltimore. At first, it seemed impossible to even think about having Paul hospitalized in such a faraway city, but upon reflection there was no real choice. It was 1904, and Billy Green was fifty-two when he made his longest journey. Father and son went

from Lillington up to Raleigh, then from Raleigh to Norfolk, and the reason we did that was we saved about three or four dollars by going from Norfolk by boat. . . . That night we traveled all night up the Chesapeake Bay, and I thought I would die [from the] terrible pain. . . . The ship was breaking ice all along. . . . When we got up to Baltimore, we got a streetcar [and] finally got to Johns Hopkins. . . . I noticed something very interesting. There were these little electric automobiles on the street. I had never seen anything like that before. . . . These things were running around there. . . .

We get to this place and go in a big hall, and my father is as overcome as I am. . . . He turned me over to these people . . . and said goodbye . . . and left me. . . . He didn't have any money to stay there. . . . [These two nurses] take me to a ward, a kind of circular place with beds all the way around. My daddy had already arranged payment—a dollar a day—that's all it cost.

Then they take me way down a hall into a room to give me a bath and to take my old Harnett County clothes and give me pajamas. I'd never worn pajamas. . . . They started unbuttoning my shirt. . . . They said, "We've got to give you a bath." . . . I said, "No, you ain't gonna undress me." And they struggled, and I had my old arm in a sling. They just finally said, "Undress yourself and take a bath the best you can." . . . I'll never forget how ashamed I was. . . . So then they took me to my bed, and then they served, and I'll never forget . . . the wonderful smell of what they called "lightbread." . . .

Two or three days later, I guess it was, they came and got me and took me to the clinic room. I was so ashamed to be in hospital clothes. . . . They put me up on a stool, and all around . . . was this . . . auditorium full of these students. A young doctor lectured. By that time they'd made X-rays of this arm, and they passed the X-rays all around. . . . They kept me there till I was just worn out. . . . Then a man came in, a little man, . . . nice face, genial,

"How's my boy?" It was Dr. Osler. . . . He was a great physician, well known, famous all over the world. He was so kind. . . .

They wired to my mother that they couldn't save my arm. They thought they would have to amputate, it was so far gone. She sent a fiery reply, "Don't you do that. . . . Operate and do what you can, and then see what will happen." I learned that later when I got home. . . . They put me in a wheelchair and rolled me into the operating room . . . and put me on a table. Then they put something like a little bugle or trumpet or a funnel over my face with cotton [soaked] with ether. I thought, oh, they think they're putting me to sleep. They can't do that. I ain't going to sleep. Next thing I knew I was in a field, a great huge field, like down in Harnett County. In the center of the field, on a stump, there was a fellow that looked like Gabriel, and he was blowing his horn. . . . I was in the field, and I was being sucked toward that horn. . . . All of a sudden I'd fly up and get in that horn and choke and choke until I'd finally go through. He'd take his lips away, and I'd pop out and fall on the ground again. I went through that all the time I was in that operation.[4]

Of his convalescence in the hospital, Green reported that after

a couple of weeks I was able to move around in a wheelchair. I got to be so adept . . . I could fly around that place. The boy with the broken leg—he and I used to run races around there until the nurses would come and stop us. . . .

Then one day here came Dr. Osler and a younger man, and they took that cast off. . . . The young man took my arm and bent it back and strapped it and, boy, did I let out some yells. Every day or so they'd come and bend it a little more and strap it. . . . Finally, . . . Dr. Osler said, "He can go through life like that," and so they stopped. . . . I was there thirty days.[5]

Green headed home with

a boxful of letters. My mother wrote me nearly every day. I cherished these letters. I rode all day with that box of letters. When I got to Raleigh . . . —Uncle Bob [Green], who lived in Raleigh, was supposed to meet me— nobody there. And I wandered around there with my box . . . looked around to see if I could find a place to sleep in the corner. I looked up and saw a handsome man—derby hat, overcoat, yellow gloves—coming, Uncle Bob, he was sort of a dandy. . . . The train from Raleigh didn't go any farther than Kipling. . . . The next day, it was only twenty-five miles, [but it] takes hours for the train to stop, load, and unload. I got to Kipling. It was already dark, cold. My father was there with the little buggy. . . . We went on by

Rory Matthew's house, . . . W. D. Matthew's . . . and finally home. And what a reunion. That night my mother says, "You got to sleep with me. I'm gonna take care of you." So I snuggled up against her breast. Talking about going back into the pre-natal. . . . Then . . . there was so much made of me. The children [would ask,] "tell us about something else."[6]

Green reported his disappointment that the numerous letters back and forth between his mother and himself (written with his left hand) were not saved: "I haven't got one scrap of my mother's letters. . . . We led such a stripped-down life, we had no place for them." Later, he would keep every letter and card from every member of his family.

NOTES

1. Paul Green, interview by Rhoda Wynn, February 1974, tape 6, p. 33, Southern Oral History Program Collection, Southern Historical Collection, Wilson Library, University of North Carolina at Chapel Hill (hereafter cited as Wynn interview, with appropriate tape and transcript page number). "White swelling," a folk term for osteomyelitis, is also the title of a section of Green's *Words and Ways: Stories and Incidents from My Cape Fear Valley Folklore Collection* (Raleigh: North Carolina Folklore Society, 1968) and of a chapter in his *Home to My Valley* (Chapel Hill: University of North Carolina Press, 1970), most of which records the story of another boy Green heard about who suffered from some bone disease. Green sets that narrative up by recalling his own experience with the mysterious ailment.

2. Paul Green, *Home to My Valley*, 35.

3. Wynn interview, February 1974, tape 6, p. 34.

4. Paul Green, interview by James R. Spence, October 23, 1976, James R. Spence audio recordings relating to Paul Green, 1974-1979 (collection #5170), Southern Historical Collection.

5. Ibid.

6. Ibid.

4: Black People

There were five thousand black people in Harnett County when Paul Green was a boy—one-third of the total population. These were people who had been slaves in Billy Green's youth and their children and grandchildren. Paul Green once met one of his grandfather's slaves:

Aunt Adelaide Green. I went up to this old wizened [woman]. . . . She said, "Come here close; see can I realize you.". . . So I went up, and she felt me and reached over and kissed me. She was an old Green slave, the last one. I said . . . "Tell me about Grandpa. Was he mean to you?" "Oh, yea." I said, "Did he whup you?" "Oh, he whupped us and he whupped us. Oh, we was mean, and we needed it. We loved old Massa, we loved him.". . . So far as I can gather from her, he was very good to them. Of course, they were his meat and bread.[1]

Green's closest boyhood friend was Rassie McLeod, son of black laborer-tenant Will McLeod, who lived on the Green farm. Rassie taught Paul a great deal: how to make bows and arrows and slingshots, how to chew tobacco, and how to chew pine needles or sassafras bark to clean your breath of the tobacco smell. Green recalled that when they were five or six, he discovered that their different races didn't make them so different after all:

One day when he [Rassie] was making a hawk caller . . . he cut his finger. . . . I looked at it and I don't know why, but I had just always thought that he was black and he must be black all the way through. So when this blood came out red, I showed my astonishment. I was very little, maybe five or six. He saw me, and he said, "What's the matter with you?" I said, "Look, look

One-hundred-year-old Aunt Fanny McDade with Paul Green, autumn 1960, Chapel Hill. On the back of the photo, McDade is quoted as saying, "I came in with Lincoln, but I didn't go out with him."

at that. Your blood is red." He said, "Yeah, what color you think it ought to be?" I said, "It's red, like mine." He said, "Of course it is."[2]

The summer the boys were ten an epidemic of typhoid fever swept through the valley. There was news of death every few days, and its threat hung over everyone. Then Rassie and his two brothers became sick. Dr. Joe McKay came, but there was little he could do. Rassie soon died. Paul went with his father to the old buggy house and got some boards that were kept there for such an emergency. Billy Green built the coffin with Paul helping as much as a small boy could. Paul's half sister Alda prepared a black cloth lining, and Paul put in some cotton on which to rest the head. They buried Rassie under a cedar tree in a hedgerow next to a field. Green reported that "later on, I remember, I went down there and tried to find his grave, but they had plowed over it. Someone had cleaned up the hedgerow, and the cedar tree under which we buried him was cut away, and the little wooden tombstone that we had put up to mark it was gone. I thought, 'Well, they are growing cotton here now, [so] let Rassie become cotton.'"[3]

In his published Rassie retellings, Green at least twice reported the doctor's disgust with the unsanitary living conditions that resulted in deaths such as Rassie's: in his 1970 *Home to My Valley* and in his *Words and Ways: Stories and Incidents from My Cape Fear Valley Folklore Collection*.[4] In *Home to My Valley*, Green's father soothed the doctor by blaming his black tenants for the condition of their home. The doctor's own racial prejudice seems to have allowed him to accept Billy Green's explanation at least temporarily (until Rassie's death, at which time he raged again). Ironically, in spite of the conditions Billy Green allowed his tenants to live in, Paul Green often heard his father say, "A nigger is like a mule. . . . You got to treat him right. You got to feed him good, so he can make a good crop."[5]

Green contrasted his father's attitude with that of his half brother John: "So, my daddy had that inheritance, had that friendship and kindness for the blacks, where my [half] brother [John] came up later, and . . . there was a . . . feeling that the blacks were getting out of control and that Ku Klux thing was reborn." At one point both of Paul's brothers were members of the Ku Klux Klan. According to Paul Green, their father disapproved of the Klan and his sons' participation in it. Paul himself said of John, "I don't condemn John; I'm just sorry, [but] that sorrow is a condemnation."[6] Paul Green also recalled an episode that reflected his half brother's attitude toward blacks:

One day I was working with John, my half brother, [and] a Negro, mulatto [named McNeill] came along with a load of lumber on his way to Buies Creek. . . . John and I were working on an old plow, trying to fix it, and we were right in the edge of the road. . . . This McNeill boy came along, and he had on some gold-rimmed specs. . . . John said, "Hey, where you going?" The fellow stopped his mules, said, "Yes, sir. I'm taking a load of lumber down to Buies Creek. . . ." John stood up and said, "Take off them specs!" The Negro looked at him and said, "Yes, sir; yes, sir"; and he reached up and took off his gold-rimmed glasses. John said, "You feel mighty proud, don't you?" "No sir, no sir." John said, "Go on, go on." Fellow started to put his specs back and then he didn't put his specs back, and he drove on with his head bowed. . . . I said, "John, what in the world?" "Oh," he says, "couldn't you see how biggity he felt as he drove by?" I said . . . "Gee, John, you hurt his feelings." He said, "You have to keep 'em in their place." I never understood.[7]

Indeed, there were often other ugly reminders of racial segregation or "keep[ing] 'em in their place." An example occurs in one of Green's recollections involving Rassie's father:

One of my relatives was plowing the field in front of our house, and Will McLeod, our black tenant, the father of the little boy Rassie that I grew up with until he died, came up to the well and drew a bucket of water, lifted the dipper from the nail [on which it hung], and drank from the dipper. This relative, plowing some distance away, stopped his mule, strode angrily across the field to the well, grabbed the dipper, the tin dipper that cost a quarter maybe . . . (a quarter was a lot of money then), threw it on the ground, and stamped it into shapelessness. When I in my instant reaction asked, "Why in the world did you do that?" . . . the relative replied, "You don't expect white folks to drink from a dipper that a nigger has drunk from, do you?" And he went back to his plow, spoke sharply to his mule, and plowed on under the burning sun, no doubt satisfied in one way with himself, but being a human being, a spiritual being, I'm sure there was some spiritual discomfort even so.[8]

Certainly Paul Green was discomfited by the racial incidents he witnessed from the time he was a boy. One such incident found its way into his sketches, and he continued to talk about it to interviewers:

I'll never forget—. . . I can still see my father's face. . . . He was chewing tobacco. I remember how his face sort of locked in—I guess suffering or sympathy or something. It happened that he and I were in the little town of Angier—had come up there in a wagon to get some fertilizer. . . . My father drove the wagon down around to where they had . . . a freight car [loaded with bags of fertilizer]. Well, it was about time for the train to come—and I've always been crazy about trains—. . . I ran right up to the . . . depot . . . and so, here pretty soon came this old round-faced . . . locomotive, a wood burner . . . coming from Dunn . . . [that] puffed and puffed and finally stopped in front of the station. . . . Several people were gathered to watch the train come in, and I remember there was an old Confederate soldier there with a heavy cane. . . . So, when the train pulled up, the train had two cars and a caboose, two passenger cars—one was for whites, of course, and one was for Negroes. . . . So there was some sort of an excursion being run in this train so that the rear car next to the caboose . . . was loaded with Negro children and a Negro teacher.

So when the old train puffed and finally got into the station and stopped, they came out of the car . . . to get some fresh air and to look around. And there were little girls and boys, all dressed out with their pigtails and ribbons and nice little suits. And the head of them was a tall yellow man, their teacher. Well, the old train in trying to come along up the curve puffed and evidently wasn't drawing too good. So when it stopped . . . the engineer got out, a white man, all greasy, and . . . crawled down under the old thing and began to pump oil from a long-necked oilcan. And the Negro, fine Negro teacher, came strolling up, a tall man, white shirtfront and big collar and tie, and he benignly gazed around the world and says, "Gentlemen, what time do the train git to Durhams?"—he pronounced it Durhams with an "s." And we didn't know, and so the old Confederate soldier pointed to the engineer who was lying down under the wheels . . . and so the Negro teacher stepped over and repeated it . . . down to the white man . . . and the engineer looked out from his incarceration. . . . "It's none of your damned business." . . . The Negro sort of swallowed and gulped and he said, "Well, Cap'n, I didn't mean no harm, no harm, sir." The very apology seemed to infuriate this engineer, and he crawled out as quick as lightning . . . grabbed the cudgel from the old Confederate soldier . . . whirled, and he hit this Negro right in the face with a tremendous blow. . . . I still remember how a sort of sinking feeling came all over me. . . . The stick was splintered, and blood was on it. That's the way I remember it. But he handed it back to the old Confederate soldier, and the Confederate soldier resumed his stance, didn't say a word.

My father had come up there and stopped and was standing there . . . and he didn't say anything. He was just staring at the Negro's bloody face. And the Negro teacher—all he said to the engineer was, "Cap'n, you done ruin't my shirt."

The children ran back and got on the train. Green concluded the story:

The Negro teacher pulled out his great snow-white handkerchief and had it dabbed against his face, and it was all stained red, and the red was spreading all over him. He turned and sort of walked blindly toward the waiting car and climbed up the steps and went in. . . . And as the last car, the Jim Crow car, passed, you could see the little children sitting straight and immobile and the schoolteacher in the front of the car with his head bowed over and his still-bloody handkerchief against his face.[9]

Another vital memory involved a man named Moody, who ran a sawmill and boarded at the Green home. One day Moody said they were not going to saw that afternoon. Green asked why:

He said that he had to go to Sanford and help lynch a nigger and so we didn't saw. . . . That night when he came back and we were eating supper, I kept looking at his hands. . . . He had nice long, sinewy hands . . . and after supper we went out on the porch and I kept wondering, I had to find out what happened. Finally I said, "Mr. Moody, what happened at Sanford?" He said, "Oh, goddammit, I got there too late. They had already lynched him, but I put three or four bullets through his damned head."[10]

Such memories were obviously troubling and indeed apparently played a vital role in Green's later social activism against, for example, the death penalty.

NOTES

1. Paul Green, interview by James R. Spence, October 24, 1976, James R. Spence audio recordings relating to Paul Green, 1974-1979 (collection #5170), Southern Historical Collection, Wilson Library, University of North Carolina at Chapel Hill (hereafter cited as Spence interview, with appropriate date).

2. Paul Green, interview by Billy E. Barnes, March 1975, pp. 40-41, Southern Oral History Program Collection, Southern Historical Collection (hereafter cited as Barnes interview, with appropriate date and transcript page number).

3. Barnes interview, March 5, 1975, pp. 45-46. The story of Rassie is one that Green liked to tell, and it was published in various printed versions as well: under the title "Rassie and the Barlow Knife" in *Home to My Valley* (Chapel Hill: University of North Carolina Press, 1970), pp. 3-16; under the title "Barlow Knife" in *Words and Ways: Stories and Incidents from My Cape Fear Valley Folklore Collection* (Raleigh: North Carolina Folklore Society, 1968), 17-20; and in the novel *This Body the Earth* (New York: Harper, 1935), 38.

4. See *Home to My Valley*, 9-11, and *Words and Ways*, 18-19.

5. Spence interview, October 24, 1976.

6. Ibid.

7. Ibid.

8. Spence interview, August 8, 1979.

9. Paul Green, interview by Rhoda Wynn, February 1974, tape 7, pp. 51-56, Southern Oral History Program Collection, Southern Historical Collection. This story is published under the title "Excursion" in *Words and Ways* (73-74), as well as in *Home to My Valley* (57-60).

10. Barnes interview, March 1975, p. 62.

5: Religion

The same summer that Rassie died, Paul finished reading the Edgar Allan Poe volumes that had been brought into the home by his grandfather John Green—and the Bible. Soon his mother was announcing to neighbors and visiting preachers that her son had read the entire Bible at only ten years old. Certainly this meant that he was going to be a minister.[1]

Much of Bettie Green's life involved the church: "My mother got a great joy out of the church because the church was to her . . . the place and Sunday was the time where the people met. It was social."[2] She played the reed organ at Pleasant Union Church, to which her husband belonged, and at Pleasant Plains Methodist Church, near Buies Creek, where she was a member. Playing at two different churches was possible because services were not held every Sunday. Most rural churches did not have full-time pastors.

Paul's father was less fervent in his religious commitment than his wife, even though he served as a deacon in his church. Paul Green explained: "I discovered pretty early that my father—he wouldn't confess it and wouldn't have to confess it—that he was more a pagan poet than he was a devout deacon in the Christian church. . . . I noticed the fervor in his voice, and his eyes would glisten when he had a good crop going. He'd look out on the cotton, and he'd go out and feel the plants and touch them affectionately."[3]

The church community likewise appears to have connected religion and farming, for church revivals were scheduled for the summer, after the crops were "hilled up" or "laid by." Green recalled a cousin's revival experience:

At the Big Meetings at Pleasant Union, you'd get a sinner like Edward Green, my cousin, . . . and [at] every Big Meeting, the revivals, they'd get after Edward. And the pretty girls, Miss Myrtle Johnson, who'd been saved, and all those that'd been saved, would get around Edward, and he'd sit there stony-faced. And they would kneel. "Edward, come and give your soul. Give up and love your Savior. Come down!" Old Edward'd sit there. . . . I think he had conviction, but he would never go to the mourner's bench.[4]

Bettie Green enjoyed having visiting ministers stay at their home during revivals. When Paul was eleven, the guest preacher for the revival was a man named Goff. One morning the man cornered Paul, perhaps at the suggestion of Bettie, and quickly got him to promise that "when I give the call this morning, you are coming down to the front to find Jesus."[5] After Green had committed himself to Goff, he was in agony because he did not want to stand up in front of the congregation and say that he had been saved. But there was no turning back. He played his role in the ritual and stood with the other converts in front of the pulpit to receive the right hand of fellowship, believing he was "a low-down hypocrite and no more saved than a snake had hips."[6]

Following the revival was a baptism ceremony in a local millpond led by a preacher named Wicker, whose sermon "The Dying Sinner" Green would always remember:

He gave a picture of this fellow dying and lying in bed. He was a sinner . . . and the people were praying, but he was a sinful man, and it won't do any good. Finally the door opened and the Devil peeps in, and he scrapes his iron hoof on the floor and he wags his tail against the door and blows smoke out of his eyes and ears. And he says, "I've come for you." He goes over to the bed, and the man's mouth is open, and he gets hold of the little white thing that flies out. It's the man's soul. He gets this soul in his claws, and he goes out, and the people around the bed, they look over—they didn't see the Devil, you see—and the man is dead. Then the preacher would let out a great whoop, you know, "Too late, and now he burns in hell in the fire that's seven times hotter than any fire on earth." And the little folks would just sit there and shiver.[7]

While Green understood the church's role in his mother's social life, he didn't like "the effect that I saw these preachers having on children, frightening these little folks with their tales of purgatory and damnation."[8]

J. A. Blaylock
Jesus Saves, Sanctifies, Fills, Heals and Keeps, Look to Him.

Cabinet card showing J. A. Blaylock, an evangelist and a distant relative of Paul Green.

NOTES

1. In the sketch titled "Age of Accountability," which appears in *Words and Ways: Stories and Incidents from My Cape Fear Valley Folklore Collection* (Raleigh: North Carolina Folklore Society, 1968), p. 10, Green wrote about having read the Bible by age ten. He also mentioned this topic to the author in the course of their conversations. He said that he may have cheated a bit and that he enjoyed being bragged about. Paul Green, interview by James R. Spence, October 23, 1976, James R. Spence audio recordings relating to Paul Green, 1974-1979 (collection #5170), Southern Historical Collection, Wilson Library, University of North Carolina at Chapel Hill (hereafter cited as Spence interview, with appropriate date).

2. Paul Green, interview by Billy E. Barnes, March 1975, p. 21, Southern Oral History Program Collection, Southern Historical Collection (hereafter cited as Barnes interview, with appropriate date and transcript page number).

3. Spence interview, October 24, 1976.

4. Spence interview, October 24, 1974.

5. Paul Green, *Words and Ways*, 11.

6. Green, *Words and Ways*, 12.

7. Barnes interview, March 1975, pp. 21-22. In the sketch "Baptizing," which appeared both in *Words and Ways*, 15-17, and *Home to My Valley* (Chapel Hill: University of North Carolina Press, 1970), 40-44, Green wrote about the Reverend Mr. Wicker.

8. Barnes interview, March 1975, p. 21.

6: Tragedy

When Paul was about ten years old he noticed a poem in the *Harnett County News* (Lillington) signed "Bettie Byrd Green": "I grabbed [the newspaper] and ran down to the back porch [where his mother] was churning. I ran up to her and said, 'Mama, Mama, did you write this?' I'll never forget it. She flushed. 'Yea, I wrote it.'" Green sighed, "I'd give anything if I had that" poem.[1] Bettie Green also sent a poem to a magazine called *Comfort*, which published it. Her daughter Erma had discovered it there more than sixty years later.[2] If Bettie had ever mentioned it, the family had forgotten.

"My mother was the most ambitious woman I ever saw," Paul Green's sister Mary said in 1976.[3] Paul himself recalled her deep concern about the look of their home:

I can remember how frantic she was to get a paling fence around the house. [She] just kept after my father. She had seen in a magazine somewhere some palings. And I don't know how long it took, but finally the palings were built around the house and the yard. . . . And she had a swinging gate that would close with a rock, and nothing would do but she must have flint rocks. Down the river somewhere there were a lot of flint rocks. So she just stayed after my father until he got Will McLeod or whoever it was with him to go down, and they'd load up the wagon with these flint rocks. And she had a walk made across the front of the house, and going down toward the gate she had flower beds on each side. . . . Well, then she got the house painted . . . and she got banisters in the front. And we have a picture of the little house—Mama standing there, and Papa, and Mary with her bicycle that our half brother John had sent her, and brother Paul and Hugh and—I think Caro Mae was a baby. But she finally got a pretty nice little house and

Bettie Byrd Green, Paul's mother. Photograph courtesy of Betsy Green Moyer and the Paul Green Foundation.

got a partition put down in the dining room and got the kitchen shut off, so we had . . . five rooms.[4]

She also had a new "garden house" built—the family euphemism for the outdoor two-hole privy that stood at the edge of the vegetable garden.

Mary Green Johnson also recalled her mother's "determination to make something out of her children."[5] Paul Green remembered, too, his mother's efforts to improve their lot by trying to convince his father to buy more land:

Joe Johnson, right next to us, had 125 acres he wanted to sell. He asked five hundred dollars for it. I never will forget that scene between my mother and father. She said, "Billy, buy it." He said, "Bettie, I can't buy it." She said, "Well, Joe will take a note for the five hundred dollars." They were talking, and I was sitting over in the corner. She was sewing away, pedaling that old sewing machine, and she started crying and begging him to buy it. And he said, "I can't." And she said, "I'll work it out. I'll sew . . . (she made clothes for the neighbors), and we'll do it. It's something for the children. We need it. Someday we've got to educate the children, and it would be something, you know, a saving." He had had such a hard time after the Civil War [that] he was frightened. He couldn't take the dare. But I was so on my mother's side. I just burned. Several scenes like that occurred, so I got an abnormal feeling for the power of women.[6]

There were other times, however, when Paul Green sympathized with his father. Perhaps Paul identified with his father's frustration over Bettie's ambitions, for Paul recalls being frustrated himself over his mother's concern about his choice of playmates—for example, a boy

working on the next farm—sort of a hired boy. . . . We'd play together. My mother called me in one day and . . . she said, "I want you to stop it [playing with this boy]." I said, "What's he done, Mama?" She said, ". . . He's a common fellow. His mother's common, and I don't want you to associate with him." Boy, I got as mad as fire. I said, "He can't help it." She said, "I thought I'd tell you. You don't want to be common. You're common if you go with common people." . . . All along she gave us the feeling that somehow, you're better.[7]

Paul Green explained his mother's drive as being linked to her father, whom Green characterized as "a frustrated man." Green believed that "somehow, from him I guess, my mother caught this unhappiness or irreconcilability to the situation. She wanted to get out of it."[8] So Bettie Green took in sewing for the neighborhood at night (including shrouds for corpses when neighbors died). All of her children remarked on how hard their mother worked. Paul Green interrupted his thoughts on the subject, recalling how his mother seemed to find strength or relief or comfort in music as she worked:

Music was such a concomitant joy to her always in her work. . . . Hymns like "Amazing Grace" or "How Sweet the Name" or "The Everlasting Arms" or "A Fountain Filled With Blood" . . . were spiritually comforting and muscle easing as she would churn away. . . . It was very early soaked into me the wonder and the comfort of music in man's daily life. And the quality of music, I didn't particularly consider. It was just the fact that there was a world of music that was brought down and yoked into the practical world.[9]

Bettie Green was anxious for her children to know music, and when Mr. George McCulloughs, the fiddle-playing man, came to Pleasant Union Church in the summer to hold a music school, she arranged for her children to be enrolled.[10]

On a Sunday afternoon Bettie might play the organ and the family might join in with singing, but for the most part her work did not let up on weekends: "On Saturday she'd be busy ironing and getting . . . everybody in the tub, getting us all cleaned up for Sunday. Sunday morning, up early." According to Green, she "was always moving, busy, just so busy. . . . She was always sweeping, sewing, . . . churning, always singing when she churned."[11] Returning to the subject of his mother trying to add to the family income, Green recalled that even as she was busy "tending to the children," she was also "cooking and sewing for the neighbors and making butter and collecting eggs and sending me down to Buies Creek to sell them."[12] Moreover, she ran a post office in their home.

In spite of her already full load of work, Bettie Green took in neighbor children on at least two different occasions when their mothers died, partly as an act of charity and partly for the compensation she earned from their families. She took in boarders from time to time even though the house was already filled with family. In the winter of 1907-1908, when Paul was nearing his fourteenth birthday, his mother, then forty-five, was pregnant for the eighth time in her eighteen years of marriage. Not allowing her condition to interfere with her routine, she was caring for three extra people in the household: their boarder, Mrs. Florence Shaw, who was a teacher at Pleasant Union School, a widow, and Bettie's personal friend; and the two Johnson boys—Preston, eight, and Clyde, six— children of neighbor Joe Johnson, whose wife had recently died.

In addition to feeding those who lived in the Green home, Bettie cooked for a black hired hand, Wesley Armstrong, who slept in a barn. Wesley ate in the kitchen while the family ate in the dining room. When he finished and said, "Could I have a little mo, please?" it was Bettie who got up from the table to get him a second helping.[13] With so many people inside on dreary winter days, it was a hectic household. The boys were playful and sometimes a bit rowdy.

On Friday, January 4, 1908, after Pleasant Union School was dismissed for the week, Billy Green took Mrs. Florence Shaw to Buies Creek and brought back his daughter Mary, who, at age fifteen, was attending Buies Creek Academy. On the following Monday he would take Mary back to the Academy and pick up Mrs. Shaw. When Billy and Mary arrived home, it was raining. Bettie was in the smokehouse hanging up sausage. The annual "hog killing" had been the day before, and there was still a lot of work to be done.

After dark Billy was reading a newspaper in the light provided by a bedroom fireplace. Caro Mae Green Russell recalled that her mother "burst into the room with a kettle of hot water." (She had been preparing to bathe the children.) She "was groaning and leaned [her head] against the mantelpiece." Caro Mae said that when Billy asked her, "'Bettie, what in the world is the matter?'" she replied, "'My head is bursting open.'"[14] Dr. McKay eventually determined that Bettie had died of "an embolism in the brain."[15] Paul Green recalled the night vividly as well:

And all of a sudden, she turned around, and her face became just blue, and she just fell right straight. So my father and I got her up on the bed, and he said, "She's gone. . . . Go get Uncle Tom, go get Uncle Tom." So, I set off up the road to Uncle Tom in the dark night, and it was sleeting, and I ran up there and told Uncle Tom that Mama had died. Aunt Chris was sitting over by the fire dipping her snuff, and she looked around and said, "Look at that boy. He's got one shoe. He's barefooted in one foot." I had run on that ice a mile and never felt it.[16]

It is not surprising that Green talked about this tragic night during various interviews. To Rhoda Wynn he added how he had rushed into his uncle's house crying,

"Mama's dead, Mama's dead.". . . Edward, the oldest son, he came in—he was about twenty-one. I'd always liked Edward, and the sight of Edward made me melt down, and I rushed up to Edward and . . . put my head in his stomach and held to him and I said, "Mama's dead, but I know she's in heaven right this minute. . . ." And, you know, I didn't believe it, what I was saying. I believed she was dead, but I didn't believe she was in heaven because I'd already become suspicious about this. . . . And Edward said, "Yes, she's in heaven. She's among the angels right now." And I didn't believe it.[17]

Mary Green Johnson, ca. 1910.

Green realized later that "When my mother died, I had a nervous breakdown, but I didn't know it. I was twelve years old, twelve or thirteen, something like that. It was a terrible time. . . . I could have easily hanged myself."[18]

Perhaps there was an element of guilt in Green's feelings about his mother's death. He did vividly recall her warning on numerous occasions: "You boys are going to kill me."[19] To a sorrowing fourteen-year-old, the memory of those words was devastating. There was also the thought that his mother's pregnancy was a cause of her death. And who was responsible for that pregnancy? His father. Thus, Bettie Green's death may have played a role in her son's problematic relationship with his father.

Paul's sister Mary dropped out of Buies Creek Academy to become surrogate mother to the children, although twice a week she returned to the academy for a music lesson.[20] She, more than anyone else, counseled Paul and helped him through his crisis. After two years, Mary took a job as a music teacher at the nearby public school at Angier, but she continued with her domestic duties at home. Soon, too, a local boy named Alton Johnson began courting her. He came to see her every Sunday until he left for the army and the war. He wrote to her faithfully while he was overseas, and he took up his persistent suit when he returned.

After Bettie's death it was not considered "proper" for Florence Shaw to remain in the Green home. She went back to Buies Creek and took tiny Caro Mae with her. One day Billy Green went to see his child, but Caro Mae sensed that he had also come to see "Miss Florence": "Children are very perceptive," she later explained, but, she added, "It didn't bother me." The possible romance between the lonely widower and the widow was not allowed to develop, however. One day Billy was dressing up, "trimming his mustache" and "combing his hair," Caro Mae recalled, when Mary demanded to know where he was going. Without waiting for an answer, Mary said, "You're going to see Miss Florence Shaw, and you're not going." He stayed at home. "His children came first," but his children did not understand then that he was lonely.[21]

Paul remembered his father coming to meals, during which the young people would chatter away but he would not say a word. Other neighborhood fathers took time to play with their sons, but Billy Green never participated in any recreation. On Sunday mornings before church he would be out early looking over his fields, and on Sunday afternoons he sat on his porch gazing out over the corn and cotton. He may have filled his own time with work, but he still did not seem to share his deceased wife's ambition. Certainly he was not as concerned about appearances as she was, for after Bettie died, "The palings sort of rotted down and were scrapped, and the flower beds disappeared. . . . We had a woodpile right at the edge of the yard, and the chips gradually oozed . . . into the road."[22]

NOTES

1. Paul Green, interview by James R. Spence, October 23, 1976, James R. Spence audio recordings relating to Paul Green, 1974-1979 (collection #5170), Southern Historical Collection, Wilson Library, University of North Carolina at Chapel Hill (hereafter cited as Spence interview, with appropriate date).

2. *Comfort* published very little poetry, although poets whose work did appear in its pages included Elizabeth Barrett Browning, Sarah Orne Jewett, Robert Burns, and Paul Laurence Dunbar—so Bettie Byrd Green was certainly in impressive company. For information about *Comfort* magazine, see Dorothy Steward Sayward, Comfort *Magazine, 1888-1942: A History and Critical Study*, University of Maine Studies, second series 75 (Orono: University of Maine, 1960), 62-63. Efforts to find Mrs. Green's poem in either *Comfort* or the *Harnett County News* were unsuccessful.

3. Quoted from Mary Green Johnson, interview by James R. Spence, May 8, 1976, James R. Spence audio recordings relating to Paul Green, 1974-1979 (collection #5170), Southern Historical Collection (hereafter cited as Mary Green Johnson interview).

4. Paul Green, interview by Rhoda Wynn, February 1974, tape 6, p. 630, Southern Oral History Program Collection, Southern Historical Collection (hereafter cited as Wynn interview, with appropriate tape and transcript page number).

5. Mary Green Johnson interview.

6. Spence interview, October 24, 1974.

7. Spence interview, October 23, 1976.

8. Paul Green, interview by Billy E. Barnes, March 1975, p. 6, Southern Oral History Program Collection, Southern Historical Collection (hereafter cited as Barnes interview, with appropriate date and transcript page number).

9. Barnes interview, March 1975, pp. 2-3.

10. Spence interview, October 24, 1974.

11. Spence interview, May 6, 1976.

12. Wynn interview, tape 6, p. 28.

13. Spence interview, May 6, 1976. Wesley Armstrong brought more music into the Green home. Paul and the other boys in the household were always getting him to play his harmonica. "He could play 'The Fox Chase' and he could play 'The Morning Train' with a choo-choo theme and then whistle." Barnes interview, March 1975, p. 7. Similarly, "He could do something called 'The Coffin Blow,' and he had a chant that would go with it . . . 'Dis is old number forty-two comin' 'round de bend,' and then he would give the long wail, and he'd say, 'Dat's de coffin blow, 'cause dat po' old woman on bo'd is dead.' . . . He was just wonderful." Spence interview, May 6, 1976. Green was inspired: "So, I got a mouth organ from Sears and Roebuck for a quarter." Spence interview, October 24, 1974.

14. This story is from the Mary Green Johnson interview. The quotations are from the author's interview with Caro Mae Green Russell, October 2, 1976, James R. Spence audio recordings relating to Paul Green, 1974-1979 (collection #5170), Southern Historical Collection, although both Mary Green Johnson and Paul Green likewise talked about their mother's death during interviews by the author.

15. Barnes interview, March 1975, p. 57.

16. Barnes interview, March 1975, p. 56. Green also talked about this incident with the author. Spence interview, May 6, 1976.

17. Wynn interview, tape 6, pp. 35-36.

18. Spence interview, October 24, 1974.

19. Spence interview, October 23, 1976.

20. Paul's half brother John, who had taken a job in Oklahoma, likewise returned home to help his father farm.

21. The story of Billy Green and Florence Shaw is from the author's interview with Caro Mae Green Russell. Later in her life Mary said that she never appreciated the depth of her father's loneliness until she lost her own husband. Mary Green Johnson interview.

22. Wynn interview, tape 6, p. 39.

7: The Youth

Paul had grown rapidly after his return from Johns Hopkins following his treatment for osteomyelitis. Soon after puberty he seemed to have caught up with his potential. He could match his strength and endurance against anyone his age, and he gloried in doing his share and more of the farm work. He not only shared his father's work ethic but also, it seems, his father's loneliness, which manifested in Green as a desire for solitude: "We had a small house, very small house, and we had an old smokehouse out in the yard. So, I would finally make me a pallet to sleep in the smokehouse, and it was hot in the summer. My dad would say, . . . 'What in the name of Mercy is wrong with you? Why can't you sleep and behave like other people?'. . . Maybe behind it was this lonely need, this need for loneliness."[1] In addition to moving out of the house in the summer, he built a tree house in the woods and used it as a sanctuary for reading, being alone with nature, and thinking.

On at least one occasion Paul was thought to be odd for doing what he considered entirely logical. His father sent him to Arch Long's mill to have a bag of corn ground. He put the bag across the mule's back and started down the road, sitting just back of the bag of corn. He was reading a book, and the sun was in his face. Since the mule knew where they were going, he turned around and rode backward as he read. Farmer Will Long, a cousin, saw the strange figure on the mule approaching and went out to the road to speak to him. To satisfy Will, Paul had to turn around, but as soon as he was out of sight he changed his position again.[2]

Paul found listening to stories as appealing as reading and remembered one storyteller who worked for his family for a time—a man named Jim Faulkner, who "looked exactly like William Faulkner" and was, in fact, a storyteller. Green remembered the man fondly and told of how "the kids would look for him in the fields" to ask him, "'Mr. Faulkner, what happened next, Mr. Faulkner?' He was always telling stories. In another world, another environment, he might have been one of the great literary people."[3] He introduced Paul to a great amount of "oral literature"—including the story of the fabulous unseen cat named Martin and the refrain "Can't do nothing till Martin comes," an anecdote that ended up in Green's play *Blue Thunder*.[4] Green said of Jim Faulkner: "He lost his wife and was down and out, and he came and sorta hired out. . . . He slept in this little shed room. . . . He worked in the fields. . . . He was full of stories. . . . He was all the time scribbling at night, and I asked him once what he was doing. He said, 'I'm writing a history of the world.' . . . He said, 'It's going to be in seven volumes.' And he measured on the wall. He said, 'It will take a space like this.'"[5]

Green went on to tell about Faulkner's fate: "In the hot summertime my sisters . . . would sleep on a pallet. And, suddenly, one day my daddy said, 'Jim Faulkner ain't gonna work here no more. . . . This morning I got up, . . . and there were the girls sleeping on the pallet, . . . and this fellow Faulkner standing there looking at them.'" Green believed Faulkner "saw beauty in these young girls," but Green's father discharged him.[6]

At some point Faulkner returned, needing work, and Billy Green "hired him back," in spite of what had happened previously. Paul Green recalled how Faulkner's misfortune continued: "The poor fellow had some nice teeth—very proud of them. . . . He was hitching a mule to a plow. The mule kicked and swung the singletree around and hit him in the mouth and knocked out all these nice teeth. And some sort of a collapse took place. He lost his interest. He wouldn't smile, . . . and [the] next year they put him in the poorhouse. . . . And he stayed in the poorhouse."[7]

After Faulkner left, it was Paul's turn to entertain the children: "Caro Mae and Erma [and I]—we used to pick cotton a lot, and the days were so long, so I got in the habit of making up stories as we picked cotton . . . all day long. And lunchtime'd come, and maybe I'd be in the middle of the story, and we'd hurry to eat and, strange to say, hurry back to pick cotton. They'd say, 'What happened next?'"[8] It was about this time that the budding author began to keep a notebook, jotting down stories and Negro songs.

When he had completed the local school at Pleasant Union, Paul Green entered Buies Creek Academy. The chief teacher there was preacher James Archibald Campbell, whom Green called "a great man."[9] At the academy, chapel was held every morning in the Kivett Building. The partition between two large rooms was then opened, and Campbell taught the entire school in whatever subject pleased him on that particular day. After prayer and Bible reading Campbell would lead in the singing and sometimes talk about words. Green recalled:

He made you feel that this is wonderful, music is wonderful, and spelling and words, and every once in a while he'd say, . . . "Last night . . . as I was finishing a letter . . . I thought of this word." I remember that morning, a great morning in my life. He said, "I ran across this word . . . *eleemosynary.* Does anyone know that word?" Boy, I stuck that hand up. "Ah," he says, "Paul." Then he calls attention to "Brother Green" over there. He says, "Spell it for the people. Stand up." So I stood up and spelled "eleemosynary." Oh, boy, folks hated my guts. Scoundrel![10]

Green returned to the subject of music: "From him [Campbell] I [also] got a corroboration and confirmation of the glory and power of music. He had a good singing voice, and he would sing and cry. He'd get so full up there that the tears would start rolling down."[11] When Green said "corroboration and confirmation," he meant that he had already made some tentative discoveries about the effects of music. He often told of a trip to Raleigh with his father, one of those trips to sell pork, and of hearing the sound of a trumpet coming from the top of a building as they approached the "fabulous city." The melody he heard was the waltz from the "Merry Widow," and the boy's hair stood up on the back of his neck. He had also seen the effect of music in the local church, when hardened sinners were reduced to tears by the old hymns. Campbell, he said, "had a theory, and I have had that theory ever since. It was that all students ought to learn to read music just the way that they learn to read words. They should be started early and just learn."[12]

As a small boy, Green wanted to be a fiddler like "old Mr. George McCulloughs," the man who came from his home north of Fuquay Springs to Pleasant Union to teach children "shaped notes." As a youth, after hearing county auditor Henry Fawcett play at a "fiddler's convention," he could not rest until he had ordered a Stradivarius-model "fiddle" from Sears, Roebuck and Company for $2.50. To learn to play his new instrument, he took a correspondence course from a firm in Baltimore and actually learned to play some from the illustrated lessons.[13] Then he got help from a country fiddler, a farmer named John Reardon, another local eccentric: "He would put a fresh shirt on on Monday . . . and Tuesday, he would put another one on and then another on Wednesday. So it went until when Saturday came, John had six shirts on. And I always looked at him and tried to find out how many shirts he had on. Well, he would come by and he would play. And he had a talking piece called 'Arkansas Traveler.' . . . Well, I learned that and 'Turkey in the Straw' and 'Old Joe Clark' and 'Cindy.'"[14] In a magazine, Paul noticed an advertisement that urged him to "sell scarf pins and earn good money."[15] Soon he was out selling the pins from house to house:

I start back up the road to go home, and I passed this Negro cabin and I heard this guitar going and Duncan McLean lived there, a tenant farmer. . . . I still was contaminated by a certain race superiority point of view. I went right up to the door, and I don't know whether I knocked or not, but I felt privileged enough to just open the door and see what was going on, and Duncan was sitting by the fire strumming this guitar. . . . We knew each other, and he said, "Come on in." I said, "That's mighty pretty. Will you play some more?" So he went on playing and then he broke into song. I remember the tune.[16]

At home, Paul picked out the notes of the song on the organ and recorded it in his notebook. The first line was "Ain't it hard to be a nigger, Oh Lord." Not surprisingly, this reflection of the racial tensions of his community left an impression on the sensitive young man, as did the racism he personally witnessed—all of which eventually found its way into his own writing.

The budding writer learned not to waste time while walking home from school at Buies Creek:

I went along by the old Sexton Mill place and made me a path. . . . I'd start out in the morning and I'd have a book of poetry or something, and my feet got to know that path. I would read and then . . . I'd memorize. I'd just memorize poetry and I'd just go along, so happy. My gosh! The woods and the birds!

One day I was going along and I heard this snickering. I looked and a fellow came out from behind a tree. It was old Mr. Johnson. . . . He always bragged that he went with his shoes untied. He said, "You know . . . Bub, since the day I got married I ain't never tied my shoes. I had 'em tied at the wedding." . . . He said, "You going to school?" I said, "Yes, sir." . . . He said, "You know any figgers?" I said, "Yes, a little bit." Then he gave me a riddle: "If two snakes got hold of each other's tails and got to swallowing each other, how would they wind up?" . . . Another thing he told me that day was, "I saw two cats a-fighting, and one climbed on one, and one climbed on another, and, you know, Bub, they went right out of sight."[17]

Many years later, a time came when Green would have use for Johnson's riddles in his writing: "I got right much education for those two miles that I walked."[18]

Given the number of poems Green memorized, it is not surprising that he attempted to write a poem of his own. When he was about sixteen,

an old lady who had lived in our house died. . . . I went to sit up with her corpse, as they did [then]. My cousin Willie Cuthson, a girl about my age, came, and we sat up all night with Miss Penny Parrish. During the night I wrote a long poem to this little lady that lay over in the corner in the bed waiting for the coffin to come from Raleigh. Then along about daybreak Mr. Joe Johnson brought the coffin and . . . Willie and I put Miss Penny in the coffin, fixed her hands, folded nice, and put some flowers on her. I was so moved—and I must say self-consciously moved—that I sat there by the firelight and wrote a poem.[19]

Recalling that incident also inspired Green to talk about a folk custom, again reflecting how his background influenced his future research and writing (Green later explored and recorded the folk culture of his region):

I've thought a lot about the custom in those days where the neighbors did the undertaking work and the place of the cooling board in the folk life of the people, where they would take the dead person and put him or her on a cooling board. . . . We kept boards for coffins. . . . Death was a thing that was made most horrible and pitiful to us as children in Harnett County because like the Greeks . . . there was a lot of to-do over the coffins and the dead people after. It was the custom to open the coffin and have all the neighbors file by.[20]

The subject of death also reflected Green's continued fascination with religion:

I told Mary [his sister], "You know, I read in a book that Lazarus wasn't really dead in the Bible, that some of his friends wanted to build Jesus up and so they got Lazarus in there and pretended he was dead. They told Jesus . . . and Jesus believed that he could do it, and he said, 'Come forth, Lazarus,' and old Lazarus came forth. He wasn't dead anyhow." Well, Mary said, "Hush your mouth." My father and I, we didn't talk about it. We didn't talk much about anything.[21]

Meeting with family resistance to his religious (which they perhaps considered "sacrilegious") explorations, Green turned to others for religious discussion. At one time, for about a year, Pleasant Union Church had a pastor, likewise named Green. Paul Green recalled:

So one night he was spending at our house, and I kept hanging around him and after everybody had gone to bed . . . I asked him, . . . "What do you really believe about the soul? Do you really believe that when you die your soul goes on and you can go to heaven or to hell?" I will never forget it. He said, "Well, Brother Paul, what I really believe is that there is a hereafter and that in the center is God. He is all glory and all beauty. And then around him is gathered all the souls that have ever been, and those that are the best souls are nearest to Him and those that are the worse souls are farther and farther away. . . . " I said, "Well then, Mr. Green, you don't really believe in hell, do you?" He said, "Well, you know, that is a kind of hell, because the farther away you are from the Divine Fire, the Divine Light, the colder you are." I never forgot that man.[22]

Many years later Paul stopped at a liquor store between Raleigh and Chapel Hill. This same preacher was working there, so Green reintroduced himself:

I said, "Do you remember the night that this boy sat up with you and we talked nearly all night about the hereafter? That was a big moment in my life." He said, "Yes, I do remember." So, he handed over the liquor and I paid him, and he felt some comment was necessary. He said, "You know, I have children that I have to educate. . . . I had to quit preaching and get a job that would pay me." I said, "God bless you." . . . He was the only preacher that I could ever talk to.[23]

Green's other source of religious discussion was writers: "I had heard somebody speak about Herbert Spencer and his lack of belief in the Deity. I'd already, through Mr. Wicker, who baptized me, and these evangelical fellows—I'd begun to be glad to get any witness against them. When I heard that Herbert Spencer was sort of an atheist, I got hold of him and read him."[24]

Green bought books from a variety of sources. The Spencer book he bought from Sears, Roebuck. He found a multivolume set of Shakespeare on the street in Raleigh and bought it for fifty cents: "I was in Raleigh once for something, and walking down Fayetteville Street just about halfway between the Capitol and the old Memorial Building at the south end there was a fellow with a pushcart . . . and he had a lot of books in his pushcart, and I stopped him."[25] He recalled reading from his new purchase:

I had, of course, heard about *Hamlet.* That's the first thing I opened up to read . . . and I came to Hamlet absolutely fresh, untampered with, knew nothing about it. I knew the name Hamlet, and I read it completely unconditioned except just as a responsive person. . . . I don't know when I ever had such an experience, and when I got to the place where little Ophelia comes in mad and singing her song—that music, you know, is what ruined me right there—I started crying just like a baby over the beauty of it.[26]

When he was about nineteen, Paul Green successfully took the Harnett County teacher's examination and thereafter worked from time to time as a substitute teacher at a local school. It was about that time that he found himself deeply in love with "the yellow-haired girl," the designation he later used to preserve anonymity. He had begun to have an interest in her when they were classmates at Pleasant Union. "I had admiration for somebody that was smart and intelligent, and this little girl was so smart. She was the same age I was, and so I fell for her early, and we used to compete in the spelling matches, and she was hard to beat."[27] Apparently Green was not bothered by the competition: "She used to laugh at me sometimes about things I would mis-do or mispronounce in school. I remember [that] once I was reading something for the teacher, and I said, 'Open see-same.' She snickered . . . and later told me 'ses-a-me.'"[28]

After he went on to the Buies Creek Academy (she did not), he began to walk her home from church. She took music lessons from his sister Mary, and Paul would dress up when he knew she was coming. One day he was plowing in his Sunday shoes because he was expecting her: "I was just crazy about her, but I never kissed her—I don't think we ever held hands or anything. But I would go to see her on Sunday and we would sit in the parlor and read poetry and talk. . . . I would write poetry to her."[29] Then one Sunday night Paul got home about eleven o'clock, and his father was waiting on the porch for him:

We never had heart-to-heart talks, and he said, "I've been waiting up for you, and I want to talk to you." . . . He said, "You've been to see this girl." I said, "Yes." He said, "Paul, she's not the girl for you to go to see." Well, I could have fought a circular saw, I was so mad right off. . . . He said, ". . . You think she's a wonderful person. . . . She's not. She's a bad girl." I will never forget the feeling, something sick just went all down, a psychological sickness. I knew deep down that he wouldn't say that if it wasn't true.[30]

His father asked him to talk to a merchant in Angier for confirmation. Paul did not sleep that night. He kept saying to himself that he believed in the girl, but he could not forget his father's face. The next morning he went to Angier and sweated while the merchant waited on a customer. Then they left the store and walked across the railroad tracks to a spot where they could talk in privacy. Paul asked him about the girl and was told she was pregnant by another man. Paul slowly walked home feeling totally betrayed and humiliated. The hurt was deeper than anything he had experienced since the death of his mother.

Well, it turned out later that this fellow . . . married her before the baby was born. Then they separated, and I heard she was in a house in Norfolk. She was a beautiful, bright girl; something just went all wrong. The last time that I saw her, she was walking along the road down at Buies Creek. I saw this great big fat woman in front of me, and I drove along and looked around, and it was this girl. She had lost her front teeth. She kind of grinned. And her face was full of some kind of sores or something.[31]

Visible in this 1887 photograph of Buies Creek Academy are Bettie Byrd (marked with arrow #1), Erma Byrd (marked with arrow #2), and J. A. Campbell (one of the men on the far left, according to markings on the photo).

Green said that he afterward often wondered: "Suppose she had really gone after me. . . . Being the way I was, we might have very easily gotten married. I would have been a tenant farmer. . . . To live as long as I have and stay out of jail and out of disgrace is a lot of luck." During that difficult time Billy Green treated his son with great understanding; Paul recalled it as "the only time we ever had any close communion."[32]

In the fall of 1913 Paul and Hugh Green entered a cotton-picking contest sponsored by the local newspaper. An ordinary teenager might pick 125 pounds in a normal workday, an adult who regularly picked 200 pounds a day was doing well, and anyone who could pick 300 pounds a day was superior. Paul and Hugh selected a choice field in which almost all of the bolls had opened. They rose early in the morning and waited until there was enough light to see the white lint. The dew was heavy, adding to the weight. They picked all day without a single rest break, and when the usual quitting time came they kept working until it was too dark to see. Exhausted and hungry, they weighed their cotton by lantern light, lifting the great tow sheets of fiber with a big lever that farmers called a "weighing horse."

The two young men had picked more than 400 pounds. The story of their accomplishment was announced in the newspaper, and thereafter they were known as the champion cotton pickers of Harnett County.[33]

During his senior year at the Academy one of Green's teachers was Hubbard F. Page, the poet. Page had been born in the Averasboro area and had graduated from Buies Creek Academy and from Wake Forest College. In 1913 he was teaching a second time at Buies Creek Academy. He had first been a faculty member there in 1902 and had then returned after earning a master's degree at Harvard. Green said of him, "I used to just follow him around and look at his great bushy hair and his striding legs and think, there goes a great genius."[34]

Green soon learned that Page loved the plays of Shakespeare and had a special interest in the British romantic poets, particularly the Scot Robert Burns and the North Carolina poet John Charles McNeill. Page's own poetry was highly influenced by McNeill, and Paul Green was soon writing similar verse. He summed up Page's infectious demeanor: "He would get so enthusiastic over his lecturing and talking about literature in a class. . . . The bell would ring to change classes, and often he would just continue talking until somebody would raise a timid hand and say, 'Professor Page, we got to go.' And he says, 'Oh you have, yes, yes.' There was something about the infatuation of this man with his work that was a great inspiration."[35] During that time, Green "used to spend Sundays in the woods . . . and write poetry. . . . It [the poetry] was so intense and [had] such a sense of the world, and the mood, and nature. I had all the feeling in the world, but I had no technique. I couldn't do it. [Of] the poetry I wrote, there's not one line in a thousand that has anything beyond sincerity."[36]

Prof. James A. Campbell had been watching Green's progress over the years and had taken a special interest in him. Once, when the Green family became delinquent in the payment of tuition, Paul became embarrassed and went to talk to Campbell about the matter. Campbell told him to return to school and not worry about the money. He prided himself in never turning away a student who could not pay.

As Paul neared graduation, Campbell called him into his office and told him that Wake Forest College had agreed to give him a partial scholarship.

I said to him, "I want to go to the university [of North Carolina], Professor Campbell." He said, "Well, I don't want you to go to the university because that is a godless place and they have especially a fellow up there named Horace Williams who is an atheist." . . . I didn't tell him that it was partly because of this godless man that I wanted to come here, but I will never forget what he did. He put his arm around my shoulder and stood in the door and pointed out to a little hillock, a little swell of ground out on the campus where the drill boys used to drill. And he said, "I'd rather see you taken out there in your coffin and buried in that ground than to go to the University of North Carolina, because you will lose your soul if you go there."[37]

Compounding his stress over this period of life-changing decisions, Paul decided that he would compete for the Declaimer's Medal, which would be awarded for the best student speech given at the all-day commencement exercises. During that last year at Buies Creek he had been a member of the debating society, walking back to the school for Friday-night meetings after his farm chores were done.

I wrote me out a speech and . . . made [it] in front of [the elocution teacher]. I had been working hard, and so when I finished, she said, "Well, that's good Paul, but, you know, I am worried about you." . . . "You look bad. You have been working too hard." Well, I had never thought about looking bad or feeling bad, and I went home and looked at myself in the mirror and said, "God, you look terrible.". . . Well, she just ruined me. I got to feeling so terrible that I couldn't sleep. So, the morning of the commencement, [the] place was jammed, and they had the brass band going. They always played "Dixie," you know. And there was an old tower there, and I went up in it and knelt down. . . . I was an unbeliever, but I prayed. I thought that this was terrible, that I was in bad shape, so if there was anything to this, I would try it. I prayed that God would stand by me. "Whoever you are up there, stand by me because I am in bad shape." So, I went out. Each speaker had to go out alone, and I went out and saw this great sea of faces. I got about halfway through, and everything blacked out, and I turned and stumbled off and got out of there. Then I had to go all day and meet other people. We had lunch on the grounds, and I think that was the most miserable day that I ever spent. But it confirmed my paganism. I didn't get any help.[38]

NOTES

1. Paul Green, interview by Billy E. Barnes, March 1975, p. 71, Southern Oral History Program Collection, Southern Historical Collection, Wilson Library, University of North Carolina at Chapel Hill (hereafter cited as Barnes interview, with appropriate date and transcript page number).

2. Paul Green, interview by Rhoda Wynn, February 1974, tape 7, pp. 12-13, Southern Oral History Program Collection, Southern Historical Collection (hereafter cited as Wynn interview, with appropriate tape and transcript page number).

3. Paul Green, interview by James R. Spence, October 23, 1976, James R. Spence audio recordings relating to Paul Green, 1974-1979 (collection #5170), Southern Historical Collection (hereafter cited as Spence interview, with appropriate date).

4. *Blue Thunder* (New York: Samuel French, 1928).

5. Spence interview, October 23, 1976. As particularly reflected in this anecdote, Faulkner became the character Blake Dewar in Green's novel *This Body the Earth* (New York: Harper, 1935).

6. Spence interview, October 23, 1976.

7. Ibid.

8. Spence interview, October 24, 1976.

9. Spence interview, October 24, 1974. Green added that he did not realize at first what a "great man" Campbell was, "because my mother did not like him. . . . I think there was some jealousy between her and Miss Nelie." "Miss Nelie" was Cornelia Pearson, a classmate of Bettie Green at Buies Creek Academy. She later became Campbell's wife. Green pondered the history of the women's relationship: "There was a contest, and she [my mother] entered the contest to make the best map of North Carolina. I've seen my mother's map, and to me it was marvelous, and Miss Nelie won the prize. I don't know whether there was any love [between Campbell and Pearson] or anything like that [yet], but my mother didn't like him." Spence interview, October 24, 1974. Green wondered, therefore, why Campbell had been selected to perform the marriage ceremony at his parents' wedding.

10. Spence interview, October 24, 1974.

11. Ibid.

12. Barnes interview, March 1975, p. 11.

13. Spence interview, October 24, 1974.

14. Barnes interview, March 1975, pp. 9-10.

15. Barnes interview, March 1975, pp. 47-48.

16. Barnes interview, March 1975, p. 48.

17. Spence interview, October 24, 1974.

18. Ibid.

19. Spence interview, August 8, 1979.

20. Ibid.

21. Barnes interview, March 5, 1975, p. 66.

22. Barnes interview, March 1975, pp. 24-25.

23. Barnes interview, March 1975, pp. 25-26.

24. Spence interview, August 9, 1979.

25. Wynn interview, tape 8, p. 20.

26. Wynn interview, tape 8, p. 21.

27. Barnes interview, March 1975, p. 67.

28. Spence interview, April 29, 1978.

29. Barnes interview, March 1975, p. 68.

30. Barnes interview, March 1975, pp. 68-69.

31. Barnes interview, March 1975, p. 70.

32. Spence interview, April 29, 1978.

33. The story of Paul and Hugh Green picking 400 pounds of cotton each was part of the folklore of Harnett County by the time I grew up in the 1930s. My father, Broughton Spence, first told it to me. One day at lunch at the Carolina Inn at Chapel Hill I asked Mr. Green about it, and he confirmed the details given here. *Editor's note*: This legend apparently intrigued Spence, inasmuch as he asked Green and his sisters about it repeatedly (see, in particular, Spence interview, February 5, 1975).

34. Wynn interview, tape 1, p. 6.

35. Wynn interview, tape 1, p. 8.

36. Spence interview, October 24, 1974.

37. Barnes interview, May 1975, pp. 1-2.

38. Barnes interview, March 1975, pp. 63-64.

8: The Teacher

Paul Green may have been skeptical about religion, but he did not reject a relationship with the local church. He continued to teach Sunday school and was promoted to teaching an adult class that met in the southwest corner of the little church. Separate rooms were not available for the classes. Sometimes portions of the church would be divided by sheets of cloth suspended on strands of wire. It was very hot in summer,

yet, I'd be there, teaching. Suffering. Teaching. One day I thought I'd sweat myself to death. The Sunday school quarterly had a section that I hadn't read too carefully. Miss Iola Upchurch read . . . the chapter, and she came across the word "womb" and read right along. And somebody snickered, and the whole thing almost went to pieces. . . . We were so puritanically . . . prurient. . . . Sex was so unhealthy in those days. . . . I'll never forget that day, that word, I couldn't use it then. . . . Even then I didn't quite believe this whole system of salvation. I read Herbert Spencer back then and got acquainted with Darwin a little bit.[1]

In spite of his discomfort with both the heat and the hypocrisy (of teaching that which he didn't completely believe), teaching held an appeal to the hard-working farm boy, for it seemed to Paul and his brother Hugh that there was no end to farm work. Green recalled their father always saying, "'You boys go and do that and then do that.' I hated it, and then one year he gave us a little patch of ground for my brother and me to plant cotton. And, gosh, we would go out there after we had plowed all day. We would get in there and work just as long as we could see. And that taught me a lot—that if something belongs to you, you can really love it."[2]

The year Paul graduated from Buies Creek Academy, he decided to try growing tobacco. No one in his area was planting tobacco at the time, and he knew nothing of the intricate steps necessary to produce a quality leaf, but he had heard of the good money that was being made with the crop by a few farmers in western Harnett County and in adjoining Wake County. He got so excited that he was able to talk his father into building a curing barn. The barn was heated by a brick furnace that used wood for fuel. Since the wood burned rapidly, it had to be replaced every two hours or so, day and night. Paul did the curing, which for the whole crop took five days a week for six weeks. During the long, boring waits between stoking the furnace, he read Latin. His Latin teacher at Buies Creek had once chastised him for not being prepared in the subject that day. She said, "If you'll get out and work at it, you'll like it."[3] As she had predicted, the more he read, the more fascinated he became. After that it was one of his favorite subjects.

In the fall he took his tobacco

to Fuquay Springs and sold it for nineteen dollars, that's all I got. And right down at the hill in front of the spring was a store, and I saw some books and I went in there and found some poetry books [and] Milton's *Paradise Lost. . . .* I got home and I had fifty cents left. But then I worked in the summer in a sawmill, and I carried that Milton, and at noon hour I would sit and eat my lunch and read that. It's not that I enjoyed it so much, but I knew that that was the kind of thing you ought to do. I would also hear these boys telling their stories. I was always collecting stories.[4]

As the season for cotton picking neared its close, the local schools in Harnett County opened. Paul had agreed to take the position of principal of the four-teacher school at Olive Branch, near the Kipling community. The school was seven miles from his home, and he made arrangements for room and board with his uncle Dan Green's daughter Ella for ten dollars a month. He bought a bicycle for transportation.

I taught there for fifty dollars a month. I paid ten dollars for room and board in a nearby house. I had a four-teacher school—a music teacher, an elementary teacher, and a primary teacher, and the teacher under me, the next one, got forty dollars a month. The primary teacher got twenty-five a month, and the music teacher got twenty-seven. I insisted on having some music, and we finally looked around and got a teacher. There were no funds in the county appropriation for a music teacher, but we got enough citizens to have their children take music at a little fee, so she averaged about twenty-seven dollars a month.[5]

Twenty-year-old Paul found that his reputation as a champion cotton picker had preceded him, but it took more than that to establish control of the situation. Some of the boys in the school were as old as he was and just as big. One burly young man was very disruptive, and Paul expelled him. The boy refused to be expelled, however: "'The one way you can make me leave school is you got to whup me,'" challenged the young man.[6] Paul told him that if he stayed he would have to behave. The fight took place before the whole student body and proceeded with severe blows and on-the-ground scuffling until the student finally said, "All right, that's enough. You whupped me. . . . I'll behave." And he did. Paul then had to go to his cousin Ella's and change clothes.[7]

It was not unique in Harnett County for discipline to be established by combat between principal and student. Principals had to establish dominance by available means. School boards and courts seldom became involved in such matters. Green reported of teaching at this school: "I loved it. It was a tough, tough thing." But Green is remembered fondly by his students. Dwight M. Spence, who later became a Methodist minister, was a student at Olive Branch during the two years Green taught there. Spence reported that Green let him move ahead with his math and that the teacher played baseball with the boys. Green recalled his student: "Dwight was better at math than I was—really, he was a keen boy, very keen."[8]

During the time he was teaching at Olive Branch, Green read some of the great writers:

I was an idol follower. I would hear about some big fellow, and because he was big I ought to get acquainted with him. That was the kind of philosophy my mother had, you see. Get out there and learn. So, when I'd read about Plato, I got to learn about Plato. Not that I gave so much of a hoot about Plato, but the fact that he was big, I want to find out who he is, you know. . . .

I ordered me a set of Plato from Sears, Roebuck. I'd read him, and all I remember from my early reading is that Plato, in one of his dialogues, said that darkness and lightness are twins . . . that only out of death can life be, and only out of life can death be. . . . I liked him. Then I read some Aristotle and liked him.[9]

While teaching at Olive Branch, Green also maintained contact with Hubbard F. Page:

I remember one Saturday I made a date to go with him to his house there below Buies Creek, and he would read me his poetry and I would read him mine. So I get down there to his house and knock on his door, and he opens it, his hair flaring in the wind, and [he] said, "Come on in," so we go into a room there. Kind of a Sears, Roebuck old iron-and-brass-knob bed, and sitting up on top of the bed frame at the head of the frame was an old hen roosting there. And this hen bothered me, for every once in awhile she would cluck, and he said that she liked to roost there, so he let her roost there. And he started reading his poetry—he had it all over the place—and he had a wonderful way of talking, and his bluish eyes would stare off and look as if he was in a trance—and I guess he was. . . . The noon hour came and my belly started growling, but no letup from Professor Page. All the time, my poetry was itching in my pocket. I wanted to get my poetry out and read it, but he kept on. It must have been four o'clock in the afternoon when he woke up and he said, "What time is it?" . . . and that old hen sitting up there on the bedpost . . . was still there. And so he never did ask about my poetry. So I said goodbye and left.[10]

Green wanted to be a poet like Professor Page. And he loved playing baseball—and played for pay with a local semiprofessional team when he could.[11] But his great ambition was to enter the University of North Carolina: "At the end of the year, I hadn't saved much. So, they offered me a second year, and then in the summer I was pitching baseball around to pick up a few dollars, not much. I was so broke, I had to go another year [teaching]. They raised my salary to fifty-five a month, a great increase. Well, at the end of that [year] I had three hundred dollars saved up."[12] He was offered the opportunity of teaching a third year with another raise, and his father advised him to take it, but he decided the time had come to make the great leap to college if he was ever going to.

NOTES

1. Paul Green, interview by James R. Spence, October 23, 1976, James R. Spence audio recordings relating to Paul Green, 1974-1979 (collection #5170), Southern Historical Collection, Wilson Library, University of North Carolina at Chapel Hill (hereafter cited as Spence interview, with appropriate date).

2. Paul Green, interview by Billy E. Barnes, March 1975, pp. 66-67, Southern Oral History Program Collection, Southern Historical Collection, University of North Carolina Library, Chapel Hill (hereafter cited as Barnes interview, with appropriate date and transcript page number).

3. Paul Green, interview by Rhoda Wynn, February 1974, tape 7, p. 14, Southern Oral History Program Collection, Southern Historical Collection (hereafter cited as Wynn interview, with appropriate tape and transcript page number).

4. Barnes interview, March 1975, p. 61.

5. Barnes interview, May 1975, pp. 2-3.

6. Wynn interview, tape 8, p. 52.

7. Wynn interview, tape 8, p. 53.

8. Spence interview, October 24, 1974.

9. Spence interview, October 23, 1976.

10. Wynn interview, tape 1, p. 7.

11. As a boy, Paul Green had not been "all work and no play," particularly once baseball came into his life. Because of the problem he had suffered with his right arm (now fully healed), he could throw a baseball with either hand: "With my left hand I developed a tremendous crooked ball. I could throw the darndest curves." Green noted that while plowing in the summer, sometimes he'd read poetry, holding a book in one hand, but when "We had a ballgame coming up Saturday . . . I would think about that game and figure out how I was going to throw this ball—hour after hour, so sweet and wonderful to think about. . . . I was just crazy about it. Talk about mad about something, I was about baseball." Wynn interview, tape 6, pp. 55-56.

12. Barnes interview, May 1975, p. 3.

9: The University

In September Paul dressed in his best clothes, put on his flat-top straw hat, said goodbye to his sisters and brothers, and rode a two-horse wagon driven by his father to the railway station at Angier. He had to change trains both at Durham and at a place called University Station, finally arriving at Carrboro, the nearest depot to Chapel Hill. The trip, not more than sixty miles by crow-fly, took all day.[1] Green and another arriving student arranged for a black man with a wagon for hire to take them and their trunks to their dormitory at the university. Green soon moved out of the dorm, however, because of a snoring roommate, and took a little outbuilding in the yard of a Mrs. T. J. Wilson, the university registrar, across from the campus.[2] The diminutive building "had been an office for her husband, a doctor, right there on Cameron Avenue. . . . It was a wonderful place to work. It had nothing but cold water and no bathroom. I would have to go to the university to go to the bathroom, but I somehow stood it and it didn't bother me."[3]

Green enrolled in Latin, Greek, and English and was granted special permission to take an advanced course in English literature. He immediately realized that he was far ahead of most of the other freshmen—including sixteen-year-old Thomas Wolfe.[4] "I had read so much poetry and read so much English literature, that when I got here I applied for a chance to take advanced work. So, they let me have an examination and I got into the junior class in English . . . and in Romantic literature under Dr. [Holly] Hanford, a great teacher, and under Norman Foerster, also a great teacher."[5] Green was certainly an enthusiastic student:

I [had] finally got here, and to me it was such a great place. . . . It came hard, and I was thankful for every bit of it. I know that, for instance, in the fall of '16 when we were playing Virginia in football, that was the great day. They had a special train running to Charlottesville, and I thought to myself, "Oh, I wouldn't think of going. This will be a good day." So when the campus got pretty well deserted . . . I went to my room and pulled the blinds down or put a quilt over the window . . . and I sat in there all day full of superiority, reading *De Senectute* in Latin, getting ready, you know."[6]

Not surprisingly, Green began to distinguish himself. In November two of his poems were published in the *Carolina Magazine*, the campus periodical—one called "To a Lady," the other "James Whitcomb Riley."[7] At the end of the semester his grades were near the top of his class, which apparently drew the attention of his professors: "One day, when I was a freshman, Dr. [James Finch] Royster [head of the English department] came in and said, 'We're short a . . . teacher to teach freshman English. Would you be interested in teaching English?' And I'd just come in here, and it scared me, but he said, 'We've got five hundred dollars.' Well, that suited me. So I taught some English here while I was studying."[8]

During that first year of study, another of Green's professors, Dr. Foerster, approached him about a contest sponsored by the Omega Delta fraternity that "offered a five-dollar prize for the best original play," which would then be presented at the Community Spring Festival at Battle Park.[9] Green responded, "'I've never seen a play!' But I had done pretty good in their courses, and they had sort of picked me out. Well, anyway, I wrote a play . . . called *Surrender to the Enemy*."[10] Green may have never seen a play—the schools at Pleasant Union and Buies Creek had never put on plays—but he was apparently interested in trying his hand. He read Kemp Plummer Battle's two-volume history of the university and decided to base his play on an incident that had shocked Chapel Hill soon after the Civil War. The president of the university had been David L. Swain, former governor of North Carolina. There had been some fear that riotous Federal soldiers might burn the university, and young Brig. Gen. Smith B. Atkins of the United States Army was sent to take charge of occupying troops. Swain's daughter Eleanor and Atkins fell in love and married.

One day after class Foerster told Green that he had won the prize. Green later suggested modestly, "I won the contest, but I mighta been the only guy that turned in a script."[11] The play was performed on May 3 on the hillside on which the Forest Theatre was later built. Green sat through the performance with all the excitement of any new playwright, a little bewildered that his written lines were being acted out before him. As he left the play that night, he heard people pointing him out as the author: "'There he goes!' And then the awful giggles and titters that smote upon my tingling ears! I aged considerably before I reached the dark peace of my little old room," he said later, continuing, "That experience was what could be called exquisite anguish."[12]

Green's freshman year brought other achievements. The March issue of the university's *Carolina Magazine* published his poem "Sienkiewicz," and three of his pieces appeared in the May issue: a poem, "Under a Window at Dawn"; a three-page "verse sketch," "Of Course"; and a prose sketch, "Evening on the Farm."[13] In the latter, he wrote of the sounds of a harmonica coming from a Negro cabin, whippoorwills, and zig-zagging bats. He also won a poetry contest that yielded a prize of two tickets to the opera *Martha*, which was performed in Durham. It was, of course, the first opera he had ever seen. Finally, he won the freshman English prize. And then he began summer school—a part of his plan to get through the university in three years.

NOTES

1. Paul Green, interview by James R. Spence, October 23, 1976, James R. Spence audio recordings relating to Paul Green, 1974-1979 (collection #5170), Southern Historical Collection, Wilson Library, University of North Carolina at Chapel Hill (hereafter cited as Spence interview, with appropriate date). See Richard Walser, "Paul Green Undergraduate," *Pembroke Magazine* 10 (1978): 29-38, from which many details of this chapter are taken.

2. Spence interview, October 23, 1976.

3. Paul Green, interview by Billy E. Barnes, May 1975, p. 8, Southern Oral History Program Collection, Southern Historical Collection, Wilson Library, University of North Carolina at Chapel Hill (hereafter cited as Barnes interview, with appropriate date and transcript page number).

4. Spence interview, May 6, 1976.

5. Barnes interview, May 1975, p. 3.

6. Barnes interview, May 1975, p. 7.

7. *Carolina Magazine* [old series] 47 [new series 34] (November 1916): 25, 39.

8. Spence interview, October 24, 1974.

9. Walser, "Paul Green Undergraduate," 31.

10. Spence interview, October 24, 1974. Unfortunately, Green told the author, "The script is all gone. I don't know where it is." Green writes about this, his first play, in "Symphonic Outdoor Drama: A Search for New Theatre Forms," the first essay in his collection *Drama and the Weather: Some Notes and Papers on Life and the Theatre* (New York: Samuel French, 1958).

11. Spence interview, October 24, 1974.

12. Barrett H. Clark, *Paul Green* (New York: R. M. McBride and Company, 1928). Richard Walser, likewise purporting to quote Green, offers another version of Green's reaction: "It has been said that the neophyte dramatist, on hearing for the first time his own words coming from actors, leaped from the audience with consternation and fled into the night. But no, he sat there, looking with pleasure upon the scene below him, sensing the audience's favorable reaction, and thinking, 'This is fine and good.'" (Walser, "Paul Green Undergraduate," 31.)

13. *Carolina Magazine* [old series] 47 [new series 34] (May 1917): 321, 342-344, 334-335.

10: The Army

The United States declared war on Germany on April 6, 1917. In his fictional account of that time in *Look Homeward, Angel*, Thomas Wolfe said, "Before the month was out, all the young men at Pulpit Hill who were eligible—those who were twenty-one—were going into service."[1] Green witnessed the same thing: peer pressure was at work, but he resisted. It had taken him a long time to get to the university, and he was not about to leave for less than compelling reasons.

There were some valid arguments for joining up, however. He wanted to write, and he believed the experience of war would make him a better writer—and he was out of money. Several times he had appeared at the office of J. A. Warren, who handled loan funds for the university. He dreaded each visit because Warren was a tough lender who required that every note have a co-signer. Sometimes it was someone at the university; sometimes it was his father. "One day I showed up there trying to borrow a little, and he said, 'Oh, you are back again.' I said, 'Yes,' and he said, 'A free horse rides easy, don't he?' It really crucified me."[2]

What really inspired Green to actually enlist, however, were the words of Woodrow Wilson: "The catapulting thing was Woodrow Wilson's speech. . . . I felt it was Wilson's dream. . . . I was walking across the campus [with] a copy of Wilson's speech—[I had] bought the paper and read it: 'This is the war to end war. The war to make the world safe for democracy.'"[3] Green enlisted on July 16, 1917, in Company B of the North Carolina Engineers. The recruiting officer assured him that he would be at the front in three weeks.

He went home to see his family and then left on July 24 with Lloyd Johnson, another young man from his home community. They joined their unit in Goldsboro the same day, and Green began keeping a diary, a practice that he continued, except for brief periods, for the rest of his life.

We all lined up and got our mess, and after supper the sun was sinking. I go back to my tent, and a great big guy comes up. He was a blacksmith. . . . So then several fellows joined this big guy . . . and they had a blanket. . . . These guys were old army fellows, and they had come up from the border. . . . They had been sent down there to chase [Pancho] Villa, and they were tough. . . . And so they said, "We will initiate you." So they spread out the blanket. . . . They said, "Well, we are going to throw you up in the air a little bit. Come on, bud." . . . All of a sudden I knew that I wasn't going to allow it. I wasn't a cussing fellow in those days, but I stood in the tent door and I said, "Well, you and me maybe." And they were so surprised. . . . It was just plain stubborn, but I was going to fight and claw and beat somebody up or I'd get beat to death. Well, it just happened that an officer came along and said, "What's going on?" They said, "Nothing, nothing, sir." I didn't say anything either. Well, somehow that broke the spell, I guess. . . . The old blacksmith and I became great friends after that.[4]

As with many young men, the army was a shock to Green. He was surprised, for example, that almost all of the men smoked. He slept little the first night because of "the hard cots, gibes of the rough soldiers, mosquitoes, [and] a feeling of loneliness."[5] By the following night he was writing, "My whole soul revolts at this kind of living. The want of honor among many of the soldiers, their ceaseless vulgarity and profanity are hateful in the greatest degree. What pleasure can there be in such a life. I'm glad I learned those words of [Robert] Browning—in more ways than one—'A brute I might have been but would not sink in the scale.'"[6] The company took a train to Charlotte, where it was set up in temporary camp. Green recorded that "the Captain has given orders that we are to have absolutely nothing in our tents but necessaries," but he secretly kept *The Rubaiyat of Omar Khayyam*, *The Iliad*, the plays of Sophocles and Aeschylus, and "three French books."[7]

In spite of being reared as a Harnett County, North Carolina, segregationist, Green was already sensitive to matters of racial injustice.

He recorded two incidents that caught his attention while he was in Charlotte: "The boys of our company caught a little negro and pretended they were going to shoot him. He was placed against a tree and told to say his prayers. All the while he sobbed as if his heart would break. I pitied him from the bottom of my heart but I knew I could help him none."[8] "At dinner several of the fellows caught a 17 year old negro boy and tossed him up in a blanket. During the performance one fellow dropped his corner of the blanket. Consequently the colored lad fell to the ground and severely sprained his back. Shame on such an outrage."[9]

On a Sunday night Green attended a service at a Baptist church but came away saying, "They told the same old foolish and futile story of seeking salvation. I wonder when the world will realize that each man must seek out his own salvation and in his own peculiar way!"[10] One night he watched as his old quartet friend "Rass Matthews entertained the crowd [of soldiers] with a negro sermon and a vocal solo."[11]

In October the company was moved to Camp Sevier, near Greenville, South Carolina. There Green had a reunion with his brother Hugh, who was a new recruit. A few days later their sister Mary came down and brought a trunk of food. They gathered ten men from Harnett County and had a feast. Another weekend, hearing that part of his flock was located at Sevier, the Reverend Lee Johnson, pastor at Pleasant Union, came down to visit and minister. Johnson, a slender, one-armed man, was the type who believed in a literal interpretation of the Bible, but he was a likable man with a genuine interest in the young men who were going off to fight. When he insisted on holding religious services for the Harnett group, they went along, but they could hear the soldiers snickering outside their tent and were embarrassed.[12]

While at the South Carolina camp, Green paid a printer seventy dollars to produce thirty copies of a small leather-bound volume of his poems. He called it *Trifles of Thought*.[13] He was afraid he would die in the war and that his work would be lost. Men were dying all around him from outbreaks of measles and meningitis—as many as six men in a single night. There were rumors in the camp that the death rate at Sevier was higher than among frontline soldiers in Flanders. A strict

Paul Green, 1917 or 1918.

quarantine was enforced and proved effective.[14] Ninety days passed, and there seemed to be no indication that Green was to be sent overseas. With patriotism overflowing, he wrote: "Every drop of red American blood within me cries out for action. Will the order to move for France never come?"[15]

Because of his education, maturity, and obvious qualities of leadership, Green was promoted to sergeant in November, skipping over the ranks of private first class and corporal. He was moved into the sergeant's tent but did not appreciate the privilege, calling his new tentmates "a crowd of roughs . . . [who] ease their feelings by cursing one another and exchanging dirty jokes."[16] A First Sergeant Huff made a particular impression on Green when he explained his two missing fingers: "A goddamned nigger bit 'em off. . . . I used to be a deputy sheriff, and I went to arrest this son of a bitch one day, and he scuffled with me and somehow he got my hand in his mouth, and he bit these two fingers off. You know what happened to him? . . . I drilled him with cold steel."[17]

Then Green was assigned to be in charge of the sixty-four men of
the Fourth Platoon:

My platoon, when we started out, was a gang of jailbirds and drunks, and I
was put in charge of 'em. . . . I guess they thought if the hard guys can't do
anything, let's put this Sunday school fella in charge. I didn't know what
they thought I'd do. I sat down with this whole crowd all around. . . . And I
just talked to 'em; I said, "Fellas I can't do a thing without you. Here I am in
charge of you—supposed to be—but you're in charge of me." And they
laughed. And the old blacksmith finally said, "Let's give the feller a chance.
Let's help the sarge out." Well, in three months we won a prize as the
best-drilled platoon in the regiment. . . . That taught me a real lesson of real,
real democracy. If that big ole rough blacksmith hadn't sorta taken pity on
me . . . —and then they got interested in excellence.[18]

The unit was moved out of Camp Sevier on May 18, 1918. Their train
traveled north through North Carolina, with Green thinking of his
family only a few miles away. There was no way to visit them, and he
wondered if he would ever see them again.

The train stopped at Camp Mills in Long Island, and, in the few
hours available, amateur playwright Green rushed to the center of
New York to see Broadway. It was dark and silent. The platoon
subsequently arrived at Montreal and boarded a transport vessel
named the *Talthybius*, a Canadian ship that had formerly been a cattle
boat. "I looked it [the name] up, and he was the messenger of the gods.
. . . [The ship] was packed. By that time I'd got to be a first sergeant, so
I rated a room . . . with another sergeant. Down in the hold it was
horrible."[19] Green was surprised to learn that a great portion of the
ship's crew was Chinese.

The vessel headed quickly down the St. Lawrence River, past
Quebec and the island of Anticosti. It was May 30. There was snow
visible on Newfoundland, and the temperature on the ship's deck was
38 degrees. The ship reached Halifax, Nova Scotia, the following day,
where it joined seven other transports loaded with troops. Within
twenty-four hours the eight ships were at sea, headed for Liverpool.[20]
On their third day out, the men were upset by a false submarine
sighting.[21] On the sixth day they received news that thirteen ships off
the American coast had been sunk by German submarines. By then

they were halfway to Ireland and would soon be entering a danger zone of the Atlantic.[22]

On the tenth day of the voyage a soldier was buried at sea, but no guns were fired because of the danger from submarines. That night sub-chasers joined them, and the men felt safer. On the following day a German submarine attacked the convoy off the coast of Ireland, and one ship was damaged. The sub was destroyed on its second appearance above the water by "depth bombs," but tension aboard the troop ship was very high. That night on the Irish Sea the vessel navigated in total darkness. No exterior lights of any kind were allowed. The men reached Liverpool on June 12. They immediately boarded a train and rode through the night at sixty-five miles per hour. To Green, still thinking in terms of his all-day rail trip from Angier to Chapel Hill, this was a remarkable speed.[23]

They passed through London, the "town dark and mysterious,"[24] blacked out for protection against air raids. At dawn they reached Dover and marched a mile with heavy packs to Dover Castle, a great structure that had been taken over from its owner, Lord Salisbury. Green reported, "We just followed the course of others. All on the walls marks of Irish troops and everybody else."[25] They looked out across the English Channel and wondered what it was like on the other side.

Before he had enlisted, Green had taken quite seriously the rumors he had heard about German atrocities in Belgium. At Dover he decided to find out the truth: "I had a day or two there and I got right busy. Went out in town to see the people. I asked about all the refugees coming across. We had read about women coming in open boats from Belgium with their breasts all cut off. When I asked about it, they would look at me—'Are you crazy?' They never heard of such a thing."[26] Green, however, would see enough atrocities for himself to confirm the horror of war.

NOTES

1. Thomas Wolfe, *Look Homeward, Angel: A Story of the Buried Life* (New York: Scribner's, 1929; reprint, New York: C. Scribner, 1957), 349-350.

2. Paul Green, interview by Billy E. Barnes, May 1975, pp. 6-7, Southern Oral History Program Collection, Southern Historical Collection, Wilson Library, University of North Carolina at Chapel Hill (hereafter cited as Barnes interview, with appropriate date and transcript page number).

3. Paul Green, interview by James R. Spence, May 6, 1976, James R. Spence audio recordings relating to Paul Green, 1974-1979 (collection #5170), Southern Historical Collection (hereafter cited as Spence interview, with appropriate date).

4. Barnes interview, May 1975, pp. 23, 25.

5. The material in much of this and the following two chapters is from the diary Green kept during World War I. The Paul Green Papers (collection #3693) in the Southern Historical Collection include numerous volumes of Green's diaries, referred to as the Paul Green Diary. Eight volumes of typed transcripts are likewise available in the North Carolina Collection, Wilson Library, at the university. The entry quoted above is dated July 24, 1917.

6. Paul Green Diary, July 25, 1917, Paul Green Papers (collection #3693), Southern Historical Collection (hereafter cited as Diary, with entry date).

7. Diary, July 30, 1917.

8. Diary, August 2, 1917.

9. Diary, August 15, 1917.

10. Diary, August 19, 1917.

11. Diary, August 20, 1917. Green sang in a quartet with Ernest Spence, Rass Matthews, and Gordon Long.

12. Spence interview, October 23, 1976.

13. *Trifles of Thought by P.E.G.* (Greenville, S.C., 1917).

14. Spence interview, October 23, 1976.

15. Diary, November 7, 1917.

16. Diary, December 8, 1917.

17. Barnes interview, May 1975, pp. 26-27.

18. Spence interview, May 6, 1976.

19. Ibid.

20. Ibid.

21. Diary, June 3, 1918.

22. Diary, June 6, 1918.

23. Diary, June 9-13, 1918.

24. Diary, June 13, 1918.

25. Spence interview, May 6, 1976.

26. Ibid.

11: The War

In Dover, Green marched his men two miles to a wharf, where they were packed aboard small ships with other units and quickly transported across the English Channel to Calais. There they saw a hospital train just arriving from the front with hundreds of wounded soldiers aboard. Then they marched three miles to an encampment outside of town.[1] The following day they marched back to equip themselves with Enfield rifles, then another six miles to the Ordnance Depot to get helmets, gas masks, and ammunition. Green's farmer eye noticed how the country along the canals was well cultivated and that crops were excellent, but that the peasants seemed very poor. "Oh, the black robes I saw today," he wrote. "Women do not smile ever."[2]

Green and his men took a short train ride inland, then marched a dozen or so miles to a place called Alendon. The men carried full packs, and the weather had turned hot. There had been little opportunity to keep up their physical endurance since they had left South Carolina. After a little while, some of the men began to collapse along the way. Green recalled: "We'd just straggle along. The fellows were out of step, so we got the idea of singing, marching in time. We found out we were just half as tired. We'd fall out for ten minutes every hour, march fifty minutes, and fall out for ten. We'd get back and start up a song—'A Long Way to Tipperary' or whatever. I learned a lesson about the power of music, about a concerted rhythm where all are together as one."[3]

When they were within hearing range of the battle guns in the direction of Boulogne, Green wrote, "Hell there. But I like this.

The beautiful lanes of France, the birds singing in hawthorn hedges, the peasants working in the fields contrasts with our aims. Madness!"[4] Reports reached them that several 30th Division officers had been killed at the front and that a major from that division had died of poison gas. Their unit was now attached to the 105th Engineers of the division. None of the reports deterred Green. He wrote, "One officer and our 1st sgt. went to firing line tonight. Platoon Sgts. go next. Anxious to go."[5] At night Green and his men tried to sleep through the sounds of heavy bombardment. During the day there were gas mask drills lasting two hours. Some of the men would get sick, vomit, and have to remove their masks. Here on the very edge of the battle there was still a civilian population. One night, peasant women came and served Green and his men wine for dinner.

The regiment marched with full packs twelve or so miles to a place called Mesand. They pitched their pup tents and shivered through the night under the one blanket each man carried. The ground shook from the bombardment. The next day they marched again, to Arques. There was a big moon that night, and German and Allied planes were in the air. Searchlights swung back and forth, and a German plane caught fire and crashed. They marched again until they reached an encampment of three French divisions just east of Cassel. Green and his friend Sgt. Harry Coulter walked around the area. At a little churchyard they saw seventy freshly dug graves of soldiers. The British artillery passed during the night on the way to the front.

On July 2 Green drilled his platoon and conducted maneuvers in trenches. After supper he walked down to Ville St. Sylvester and found the town deserted and partially destroyed, with a large shell hole through its church. When he returned to his encampment, another air battle was taking place nearby, and another German plane went down in flames. The whole area was covered with a network of trenches, and ammunition was piled high all around. Fields of unharvested grain had been mutilated by German shells. Green and his men built barbed-wire entanglements in front of "reserve trenches." During the day, observation balloons were sent up, and the Germans fired at them, but they were out of range. One night a bombardment began on a three-mile front. Shells flying over their mark came close to Green's platoon, and the ground trembled. There were more air battles.

The war at that point was not one of direct clashes of soldiers. Positions were being maintained, and the damage was being done by shelling. For those who were out of range of the main shellfire, there was a routine: "Fired on target range today. Used gas mask part of [the] time."[6] "Drilled platoon in a meadow nearby. Practiced the British formations for assault approach, etc."[7] (Apparently Green was already aware that he would be working with the British.)

After practice that same evening, Green "took a stroll after supper to town of Lumbres—a small ville. Met pretty French girl."[8] The following day he and his men received orders to move. On the road to Ypres, they marched four miles beyond Watou, Belgium. Some of their regiment had been there several days, and they were glad to see each other. They received their pay, which called for a mild celebration. A few got drunk. Green and Sergeant Coulter walked up to the town of Proven, which they found full of soldiers—"Hindus, Negroes, French, British, Belgian, and American."[9]

Green's diary reveals contrasts. One day there were the hardships of war: "Men grumble more and more about short rations. Several under guard now. Something must be done."[10] On the following day "British held steeple chase race in honor of France's Day," but, on that same day, "Went to town in afternoon. . . . Spent short while with Belgian maid. Told me of German cruelty. Brother killed, sister ruined and a prisoner of the Germans. At dusk the heavy artillery fire began."[11] On Bastille Day he recorded: "Late this afternoon German prisoners began to go by on the road. Mostly all of them mere boys. Shame! Lots of drunkenness among our soldiers. Many in stockade."[12] Green remembered First Sergeant Huff (mentioned in the previous chapter) as "a top sergeant" and added this story about him:

When we got to France, [then] up there in Belgium . . . he showed up drunk, and of all things I was given the job of punishing him. . . . Captain Bosch from Durham . . . a wonderful officer . . . said, "You take Top Sergeant Huff out and drill him with double-pack." This was the prescription for punishing because Huff had shown up drunk. So there I was, and I felt so apologetic, but his eyes were red and he got the pack, double-packed, and put it on, and we went out on the field in Belgium in a sort of a place behind the lines five or six miles. So there I was in the hot July weather, "Forward, double-time." And there was this man—he was about fifty years old—big fellow, a powerful-looking man with his heavy jowls and red complexion and fiery eyes, and so he would do double-time.[13]

One July evening Lt. Col. Joseph Hyde Pratt, commander of Company Three, prepared his men for the night's encampment. Green wrote:

I was associated closely with [Pratt]. Had charge of all the messages that went out. He and I (whatever office we had, we had together . . . we had horses. . . . we had some tents) started putting up the tents out in this pasture. There was a big hedge of trees fifty or sixty feet through. Since I'd gotten close to the colonel by that time . . . I raised the question, "Why do we have all these men out in these pup tents in the open? Maybe we should snuggle 'em back in among the briars." Well, they put the horses among the trees. I was with a boy named Harry Coulter. We slept on the ground. Col. Pratt slept down in a ravine somewhere nearby.

Along in the night I heard this buzzing. . . . [A plane] kept buzzing. I said [to Harry], "There's something funny here. . . . I believe that's a German plane, and I believe he's spotted us." He said, "That would be a hell of a mess." All of a sudden the whole world illuminated. They had dropped what they called a Very Light, a little old thing in a little parachute, and it came down and lighted us up, and it sank down and just illuminated the whole landscape. We both dived right down on the ground, and then this thing came down—a bomb. . . . Just one. It was one of these things that hits the ground and bounces and explodes. . . . It hit just the other side of the field kitchen. . . . You never heard such pandemonium. Horses neighing, men screaming, and no lights.[14]

The bomb blew Supply Sergeant John Huffman of Hickory, North Carolina, to pieces and killed six horses. In the morning the men buried Huffman with the band playing Chopin's "Dead March." That afternoon they practiced on a rifle range just east of Proven and prepared to move out.

The platoon marched to Poperinghe, a Belgian town that was wrecked and deserted. A shell had struck a house and blown its contents in every direction. Green saw a Madonna statue lying in the street, with the tiny feet of the baby Jesus broken off. He picked it up and kept it. They rode a train for an hour and marched three and a half hours. In the moonlit night they could see that not a tree was standing anywhere. The destruction was total.

As they approached Ypres at two o'clock A.M., the German and Allied bombardment at nearby Kemmel Hill was deafening, and shells were dropping on either side of them. The night was lighted with flares. Green recalled, "It got worse and worse. Pretty soon the whole land was gutted. . . . Then we'd lie around and hide the best we could in the daytime. . . . Had a fellow named Green. He was an old man, thirty-two years old. He [suffered] shell shock before we even got to the front. He dived in a ditch and tried to go in the ground like a mole."[15] The platoon spent the remainder of the night in dugouts on the bank of a canal. Cooties and rats bothered them, but Paul Green was more concerned about the fact that his head was beginning to pulse from shellfire.

They were at the point at which the British and French lines came together. Both had sustained so many casualties that it was necessary to send American platoons to fill in the gaps. Green's men had received very little infantry training because they were in an engineering unit, but they were needed at the front and so were assigned to the British 33rd Division. The platoon stayed out of sight, flooring dugouts and building cots. Feeding themselves was suddenly a problem. They had bags of meal, flour, and beans, along with some canned food and a cooking pot. When darkness came they saw a little train moving along on a narrow gauge railroad. Its flatcars were loaded with the bodies of soldiers, stacked like cordwood. Green and his men slipped out into the night to dig more trenches. The country was low and ill-smelling. There were rats and mosquitoes in the marsh grass. Green later recalled:

We were crawling through the grass toward the German lines, creeping through the grass, and I came on these big patches of grass, higher, and in the first one, I crawled in and there was a uniform, and I looked and couldn't see much. . . . Then I realized we were right where the first Canadian boys were gassed in 1915. First use of gas was against these Canadian troops. . . . It was the queerest thing. Rather than being particularly horrified, I said [to myself], "By damn, they took it. I can take it. They died. I can die." I think I learned that the suction of death, making buddies of the living in such situations, helps them pull through.[16]

While they worked, snipers continually shot at them. A British soldier in their group was shot through the heart. After they returned and went to bed, the night lighted up again with the bombardment at Kemmel Hill, and the earth trembled.

Late one afternoon Green took thirteen of his men on a patrol headed by a Canadian lieutenant. "Visited all demolition posts in and around Ypres. . . . Destruction appalling. Not a building. Famous 'Cloth Hall' a pitiful picture. Saw ruined paintings in some buildings. Great asylum in ruins." He learned that an entire battalion of British troops was buried under the ruins of "Cloth Hall," trapped there in a sudden bombardment of Ypres. At dark, he was out again with a patrol "digging trenches, resetting, a-framing, etc."[17] They found the remains of more long-dead soldiers, some buried in shallow graves now exposed by the rains.

Green also recalled "dawn patrol": "Every morning before dawn . . . my group would go into no-man's-land between us and Lorraine and the Germans to be sure that none of them were creeping over to get at us. And to be sure, there was one fellow, a sniper somewhere, that kept shooting at us. I used it in [the play] *Johnny Johnson*, the sniper. One night we were ordered to get that sniper."[18] They went out with a young swagger-stick-carrying English lieutenant who would bend over a little while going through the tall grass but would never get down and crawl like Sergeant Green. They made their way forward as the Germans dropped Very Lights over them. One man was shot in the leg, but they never got their sniper. Somehow the proud lieutenant came out unharmed. They returned before dawn, had tea with the British, and lay down in their bunks.

Each night there were German shells (eighteen-pound "whizz-bangs") that screamed in around them. At Kemmel Hill the Allied guns seemed stronger, the German guns weaker. The sound of the shells caused another case of shell shock. A young man named Stockton in Green's unit would "sit and moan. . . . 'Oh, can't you hear 'em falling? Can't you hear 'em falling? Mama, Mama, Mama!'" Green would "never forget the look on [the] faces" of soldiers like this man.[19] He was more than casually sympathetic. The sounds of the shell explosions were throbbing in his own head as well. Already there were explosions in his mind when no shell had exploded.

On the night of July 22 Green, along with two North Carolina friends, slipped up to the most forward of the frontline trenches. He was surprised to find it sparsely manned, one soldier about each fifteen yards. While he was there a shell exhumed the bodies of dead horses and men. The stench was terrible. The platoon received orders to pull out, apparently to be replaced by infantry. Night came, and they said goodbye to their British friends. It was raining, and shells were bursting nearby. They marched three miles through the wet darkness to a rail siding, thinking that soon they would be back where birds were singing and trees growing. There they waited in the rain, but no transportation ever came. They marched over to British headquarters, where Green learned that the orders had been canceled. They were to go back to the trenches at the front. A German attack was expected.[20]

In the darkness and rain Green told his men they would have to go back to the line. A six-foot-three corporal named Lowe said, "Goddamn, we ain't going. We ain't going back."[21] There was "a chorus" of agreement from the platoon. Green gave them a lecture about the rules of war and why they had to obey their orders, but the corporal stepped out of his rank and said, "I ain't going."

I said, "Listen; these are my orders, and if you don't get back in line I'm gonna kill you. I'm going to shoot you." I pulled my pistol. I didn't intend to shoot him at all. Then all of a sudden I knew I would. It was a strange thing. The way I spoke to him, he knew it. . . . You learn a lot of things about yourself you didn't know. . . . I never intended to kill a man, and then all of a sudden I did. There's a beast in all of us.[22]

Like the student young principal Green had had to fight to discipline, the corporal stepped back in line and then began marching through the steady downpour to their former station.

The Germans attacked with a heavy bombardment before Green's platoon could get there. By the time they arrived, the guns were silent. The very dugouts they had occupied the day before had been blown up. A British captain and four British lieutenants had been killed. Green's friend, the lieutenant who wouldn't crawl through the grass, was wounded and had to be evacuated. A delegation of British soldiers asked Green to be their lieutenant, replacing their leader who had been killed. Of course, he could not become a lieutenant in the

British army, but he was flattered. He said, "I'll be here till your lieutenant arrives."[23]

Green's agreement was short-lived, however. His platoon was immediately moved eight miles back, to Perel. There he recorded, "Saw several peasants moving their belongings out on wheelbarrows. Pitiful! Pitiful. At nearly every house there are refugees. Mothers who know not where their children are. Children who have no parents."[24] He also saw the sad, hopeless looks of the Belgian peasants as soldiers trampled through their ripening grain, building more barbed-wire fences.

Green marched his men to Proven for a Saturday visit to the bathhouse, but when they arrived the water was exhausted. Three-fourths of his men had lice, but there was nowhere they could go to get cleaned up. On Sunday the great Christian armies stopped killing one another for a day, and the men rested. They had never appreciated the Sabbath so much. Somehow Hugh Green learned where his brother was located and came over from Kemmel Hill. It was the first time they had seen each other since Greenville, South Carolina. Hugh's company had been caught in a barrage during the week and had lost twenty-two men. At the end of the afternoon the brothers parted to return to the weekday business of war.

Word came that the Germans were preparing a breakthrough. Green was supposed to get as much barbed wire put up as was possible in a short time. He took thirty men and went to work. After more than five hours they had surpassed all of their previous records, having constructed seven hundred yards of fence. He was standing by a hedge surveying the construction when "I looked around, and all of a sudden there was a hole about thirty feet across—a great deep hole in the earth—went right down. I looked at that hole and said, 'Where the hell did that hole come from?' I went over to look down in it, and there was no hole. . . . Then I realized what was happening. I was going crazy. I was getting shell shock. We had several by this time who were shell-shocked."[25] Green knew that the manifestation of his shell shock went all the way back to Harnett County; the hole in his mirage was

a great big one, much bigger than ever before. . . . The boys were working in the dark in the field. So I got behind a hedge and started running. I just ran

During his wartime service in France and Belgium, Paul Green served as a platoon sergeant. In a diary, he recorded many of his experiences and in particular noted a number of atrocities committed by German troops. Here German soldiers congregate behind a trench. The tall officer in the left center is the Crown Prince William, oldest son of Kaiser Wilhelm II.

up and down, up and down, trying to beat this thing off. . . . I was just pouring with sweat. Gradually, the thing disappeared. My granddaddy had haunted me . . . by trying to put me in a hole, and here was the hole. Suppose I had gone over. The shrieking and hollering, and they'd had to come and take me away. How would you ever get cured? [Some] boys never did recover.[26]

Recounting this incident at another time, he added, "Now I don't know why, but I knew that if I didn't make this body take charge of this mental thing . . . this brooding would destroy [me]."[27] Fortunately,

It never did come back, except it changed its nature. . . . It turned into a queer thing, a great hairy hand that was always reaching, would grab me back here [pointing to the back of his neck]. When a whizz-bang would explode, my head would explode. . . . I knew that these shells that kept falling around were unrhythmical. They didn't fall in a sequence. . . . It got so [that] even when there were no shells, I would still hear the explosions. I got so that objects began to take on strange–. . . I would look at an object, and it would suddenly explode. . . . Yet behind all this was a consciousness that this is silly. . . . I wouldn't let myself think about this hairy hand, but every once in a while I'd turn around to be sure there was nothing back there.[28]

The following day he had his men in the fields again. They were out of lumber but found a supply of poles used for scaffolding hop vines. But when they started using them, a peasant came out of his cavelike home built in the side of a hill and attacked them. They had to hold him while they worked. Then a young woman came out of the same hole:

I could talk in French some. . . . She said, "What do you think you're doing?" I said, "We're trying to stop this weak place here from a German attack." She laughed, "German attack? What of it? Suppose they do attack? Why do you object?" Then I let loose one of my Woodrow Wilson . . . speeches, how we'd come to save [her]. . . . This girl laughed and laughed and let loose a little statement about "how crazy you people are. There's nothing you can do for us. Nothing."[29]

She went back in the hole. Green recorded: "The old man raised such a ruckus that soon a crowd of refugees were clamoring with him. We had to evacuate."[30]

The same day, he received orders to take full equipment and report to regimental headquarters for special duty. He said goodbye to his men "with a feeling of sadness mingled with one of relief."[31] When he arrived at the headquarters at Proven, he was informed that he had been promoted to regimental sergeant major. There he would have a desk job, but the facilities were not plush. The rainy season had begun, and mud and water came into the tents. At night German planes dropped a few bombs. Some nights a few shells reached the area. In spite of the tedium of working on files and the confinement of the tent, however, he could still see beauty. While noting that sandbags were being placed around the tents, he observed, "Sunset beautiful this evening. A rosy tint, a dog barking in farmyard, gaunt windmills silent—a Flanders sunset!"[32]

In Proven, too, Green received a half-dozen letters from home, which raised his spirits. One was from a female acquaintance with a rose from the arboretum at Chapel Hill. Then he became depressed by processing the reports of casualties. "Ah, what thoughts must be with those at home! The gray old man, the wrinkled mother receive the yellow slip of woe every day. God preserve them. Oh, who began this hell on earth?"[33]

One day King George V came for a visit and shook hands with several of the soldiers. Three shells from a German battery burst a few hundred yards from him. On a day that the Germans shelled Proven, killing twelve townspeople, the peasants carried on with their harvest. A woman who had already lost her husband had two children blown to pieces in that attack. Over and over she kept saying, "I have nothing to live for. Somebody kill me."[34]

Green was moved to a point called F22 Central. In late August he wrote, "Everything is going well except my health. For three weeks I have been a fit subject for hospital . . . and the everlasting bombardments have put my head into a sort of shell-shock condition. Nervous! Nervous!"[35] This is the first mention in his diary of his personal encounter with shell shock. The three-week period he mentions dates back to the incident involving the hole that turned out to be a mirage. His self-concern prodded him to record on different days: "Finding time to write out some of the thoughts that trouble me so." "Wrote bits of verse. Felt better today." "Wrote a great deal today. Health wretched."[36]

On September 4 he went up to see his brother Hugh, who had been blistered by gas, and heard more accounts of what Hugh had been through. Paul's fortunes were about to change, however. He was moved to Ostreville, near St. Pol, where he took a room at a peasant's house and had fried eggs, a delicacy: "Tonight I sleep in a real bed and in the best room in the house, although my nearest neighbors are two cows that persist in raising a racket sighing, etc." Two days later he reported, "I can sleep at night."[37]

Soon his unit was moving again, and he had the duty of supervising the transfer of the records: "I got two old lorries with solid rubber tires. . . . We couldn't travel in the daytime, so we had to do it at night. . . . The whole valley had not a tree standing. Shell holes were everywhere. We'd get stuck, get out and push. Sometime in the night we came to a ruined town, Albert."[38] In his diary he wrote:

Never shall I forget Albert, a city frozen in terror. God, what a sight! A great brute of destruction has passed over it. Death here, death there. A blade of grass ashamed to show its head. In the edge of the town is the cemetery, the

Paul Green (*right*) and his brother Hugh. Photograph courtesy of Betsy Green Moyer and the Paul Green Foundation.

last stronghold of the Germans. Tombs burst open, once umbrageous trees shot from their stumps. A thousand years of thunderbolts concentrated upon this spot could not have wrought the destruction visible here. Man! Man! Man! What a mistake is thy creation.[39]

By moonlight he could see in the destroyed cemetery "a statue of Jesus Christ, twelve or fifteen feet high, apparently untouched."[40] At noon on September 23 he located Division Headquarters in Buire Woods, now set up in quarters built by the Germans, with German signs still on the doors. German graves were in the woods nearby, marked by rifles and helmets of the dead. "The stench was awful. . . . A lot of the German soldiers were half-buried. Their feet would be sticking out of the ground."[41]

Green and his brother Hugh met up again: "I was walking in the woods . . . to check on something, and I saw a black man sitting under a tree. . . . He had a machine gun, a Lewis gun. I went over to him. I looked, and I said, 'My Lord, Hugh!' He looked up, eyes all bloodshot and said, 'I've seen things I never want to see again.' He'd been in the battle." Four Germans had run out of hiding and offered to surrender to Hugh. He had been warned that three of them would divert his attention and the fourth would shoot him. He killed all of them, as he had been instructed to do. The gentle farm boy was now a hardened veteran, but the incident would haunt him for the rest of his life.[42] Standing only a few yards from a dead German, the two brothers planned to get together that night, but Hugh's regiment moved out. Paul recorded: "Told him goodbye with many a misgiving. We make the big drive here. I may never see him again. But he told me to cheerio, he was no better to be knocked off than anyone else. Righto he is, but—the father back home."[43]

The next day Paul Green watched the preparations for battle, which included carpenters building crosses for graves and the readying of rolls of burlap in which to bury the dead. He also witnessed attack strategy meetings:

I had the opportunity of being at the meetings where they planned attacks. I was standing at the back of the room, listening. Then they'd issue an order and stamp it and hand it to me, and I'd go outside where we had these couriers. We had one boy, a very fine fellow, named Jake Callum from Greensboro. He was able to ride a motorcycle in the dark. I remember they gave me one order. . . . I said, "Jake, it's a bad night, Jake." He said, "Oh, I'll be all right." He went off with this thing and got killed.[44]

Green did not have a high opinion of these strategy meetings:

Another thing I learned standing there listening to these generals plan battles: one would say, "If we send a regiment down here, how many men do you think we'll lose?" "My God, we might lose five hundred.". . . I realized, great guns, these guys really don't know [what they're doing]. That was another great awakening: that men of authority, big men with stars on, they knew everything. And then I realized that they didn't know and that they were . . . diabolically ignorant, therefore more diabolically cruel.[45]

Rumors were rampant about the nature of the Hindenburg Line. There were even tales that in the underground passages there were vats used for boiling enemy bodies and making soap. The Allied attack on the line began on September 28, and it was the greatest bombardment he had seen. Troops moved forward, and messages were sent here and there. Green sat in his tent and fretted one night, "Perhaps I'm worth more doing the job I am than I would be firing a rifle. Anyway I will do anything that is asked of me for this the supreme cause. These days of horror and unthinkable happenings strike one mute."[46] Within three days the Hindenburg Line was broken. The engineers had lost 108 men—10 killed and 98 wounded.

Almost as if the war was over, an order came appointing Green as an officer candidate. Again, someone considered him a leader and put him in charge of a group of fellow officer-candidates from his regiment. On October 3 Green set out for the engineers school at Langres. It had been just four and a half months since he had left Camp Sevier. It seemed like years.

NOTES

1. Paul Green, interview by James R. Spence, May 6, 1976, James R. Spence audio recordings relating to Paul Green, 1974-1979 (collection #5170), Southern Historical Collection, Wilson Library, University of North Carolina at Chapel Hill (hereafter cited as Spence interview, with appropriate date).

2. Paul Green Diary, June 16, 1918, Paul Green Papers (collection #3693), Southern Historical Collection (hereafter cited as Diary, with entry date).

3. Spence interview, May 6, 1976.

4. Diary, June 19, 1918.

5. Diary, June 21, 1918.

6. Diary, July 8, 1918.

7. Diary, July 9, 1918.

8. Diary, July 19, 1918.

9. Diary, July 11, 1918.

10. Diary, July 12, 1918.

11. Diary, July 13, 1918.

12. Diary, July 14, 1918.

13. Paul Green, interview by Billy E. Barnes, May 1975, pp. 26-27, Southern Oral History Program Collection, Southern Historical Collection (hereafter cited as Barnes interview, with appropriate date and transcript page number).

14. Spence interview, May 6, 1976.

15. Ibid.

16. Spence interview, May 6, 1976.

17. Diary, July 18, 1918.

18. Spence interview, May 6, 1976.

19. Paul Green, interview by Rhoda Wynn, February 1974, tape 6, p. 20, Southern Oral History Program Collection, Southern Historical Collection (hereafter cited as Wynn interview, with appropriate tape and transcript page number).

20. Spence interview, May 6, 1976.

21. Ibid.

22. Ibid.

23. Green also spoke of this offer by the British on another occasion, remarking that he was "flattered." Spence interview, October 23, 1976.

24. Diary, July 25, 1918.

25. Spence interview, May 6, 1976.

26. Ibid.

27. Wynn interview, tape 6, p. 20.

28. Spence interview, May 6, 1976.

29. Ibid.

30. Diary, July 30, 1918.

31. Ibid.

32. Diary, August 3, 1918.

33. Diary, August 5, 1918.

34. Diary, August 13, 1918.

35. Diary, August 22, 1918.

36. Diary, August 22, 23, 25, 1918.

37. Diary, September 8, 10, 1918.

38. Spence interview, May 6, 1976.

39. Diary, September 22, 1918.

40. Spence interview, May 6, 1976.

41. Ibid.

42. Ibid.

43. Diary, September 24, 1918.

44. Spence interview, May 6, 1976. One of Green's couriers during this period was his friend Rass Matthews.

45. Spence interview, May 6, 1976.

46. Diary, September 27, 1918.

12: Love in Paris

When Green and his group reached Langres, a lieutenant met them at the station and showed them their billets. Green recorded, "Was told to sleep in billets with negroes." He may have been liberal for his day, but he was still a southerner and apparently not *that* liberal. Consequently, the diary entry continued: "Didn't 'company'. Slept on the ground."[1] He later told of another incident that occurred about the same time: "I took a walk out to the edge of town. . . . I came around a curve and here came a black—just as black as the ace of spades, looked extra black to me—American soldier with two French girls. He had an arm around each one of them, and they were laughing and so on, and I didn't like it. . . . I just didn't like it. So I still had it," he concluded, disturbed upon recollection by his own apparent prejudice.[2]

Green and his group celebrated the end of the war on November 11:

One of the most embarrassing moments of my life was to come in during officer training at Langres to find a number of my companions having a merry time with a lot of . . . sheets of paper between them and reading and passing one to the other. They had found my diary under my bunk . . . and were reading aloud . . . and having a lot of fun. I was more embarrassed than I was mad, but after a while they evidently felt a little ashamed, and they helped me gather up the sheets and put them together, but some I never recovered.[3]

Shortly afterward, Green was designated acting lieutenant and placed in charge of his group to go back to their unit. "They were nice," he later recalled. "They didn't seem to object for me to be their boss."[4]

Green remarked facetiously, "Unfortunately, our way lay through Paris. . . . We went to Paris and stopped to wait for the train the next morning that would take us up toward the front. . . . Then, when we got near the front, we would have to get out and walk. . . . We got out; it was dark. And as we got out of that train, we were swarmed with girls." Green's men scattered everywhere. "Three or four girls got hold of me, and oh, I wanted to go with one of them so bad . . . but I kept remembering things."[5] His mind was distracted by his war experiences.

He went to the Hotel Pavillion. The man at the desk asked him if he was a deserter. There were "thousands of American" deserters in Paris at the time. There was no room, but he was given a cot in a hallway. He later recalled what transpired a few hours after midnight:

About three o'clock in the morning all of a sudden there's a light shining in my face. It was an officer, with a pistol. . . . I said, "What in the world's happening?" He said, "You'll find out.". . . I was marched downstairs, and there were three or four of my buddies. All had been arrested as deserters. I said, "No, no. Something's wrong. I've got the papers.". . . I'd put the signed document in one pocket and an unsigned copy in the other. . . . I got out this copy. Fellow looked at it and said, "Okay, out you go." I thought he had [the right document]. He marched us all out. He had a lorry out there . . . like a van. He piled us in there—must have been forty or fifty of us. . . . [It was] cold. . . . Some of them said they were just having a time with some girls.[6]

In the confusion, Green had handed the officer an unsigned copy. After spending the night in an unheated jail, he and his men were brought before a provost marshal and given an opportunity to present correct credentials. They were released and took a train for Le Mans.

Back at his company headquarters, Green learned that Rass Matthews had been killed prior to the Armistice, a blow indeed.[7] His spirits were lifted at one point by Woodrow Wilson's appearance in France. Wilson

stayed at the hotel there in Paris. . . . I got a leave of absence to come to Paris to be there when he first arrived. . . . From the Arc de Triomphe way up as far as you could see, the Champs Elysees, I reckon 350 feet wide, was packed with millions of people. . . . As he rode down . . . people all knelt in front of him. You've seen broom straw fall as the fire burned it. . . . He was the champion of democracy. . . . People all around . . . were crying. . . . He was their savior.[8]

Green, too, idolized Wilson. He felt that he was a moral leader who was going to change the world.

On January 17, 1919, Green was sent to Paris to work with a group charged with the duty of disposing of captured war goods. He was given quarters at the Clignaucourt, a group of high-rise stone barracks. He found himself in close proximity to Alton Johnson, his sister Mary's suitor, who had become inspector of two candy factories. There was a regular, almost civilian-like work schedule, and Green could go down to the YMCA library at noon to read works such as George Bernard Shaw's *Arms and the Man*.[9] But he was still trying to shake off the psychological effects of battle, recording, "My health is very bad. Ah, where can I find relief."[10]

On Sunday, February 9, Green went to a Red Cross recreation establishment and there met "a Miss Cummings from Omaha, Nebraska," a woman four or five years his senior. He wrote that "she was kind; that was enough." After dinner, "she, taking pity on my loneliness, agreed to go to the Palais de Place with me for the evening. We had a wonderful time—at least I did." The next day he was back at the Red Cross but learned that she was taking a two-day rest. The following night he confidently wrote, "Tomorrow I shall see Miss Cummings, the interesting 'agnostic.'"[11]

He saw her briefly upon her return and made a date for Thursday. She was not able to keep the engagement, however, because of the death of a friend. On Friday, which was Valentine's Day, he called on her at 14 Rue G-Lussac and recorded, "She is such a good and charming woman." The following day he learned that she had left work "weeping, sick, worn out." He rushed to her side. "Poor woman, far away from home, sick, few friends."[12] During their acquaintance, Green helped this woman with her attempts (on behalf of a friend back home) to locate the remains of a soldier who had been killed.

He spent Sunday afternoon with her and recorded, "How shall I describe this afternoon, little book! It is beyond description." He wrote to her the next day and received a reply that prompted "what a letter!"[13] He received a second letter from her and promptly paid her a visit, during which the two went walking in the Luxembourg Gardens.

On another occasion "we strolled out towards the Bois de Boulogne and back again in the twilight, stopped at every other lighted window to gaze at the shopkeepers' fancies."[14] The next day he called on her at her hotel: "Again we strolled around for hours. Later in the evening we stood in the dimness of the Arch of Triumph. And gazing at that quickening group representing the soul of the Marseillaise we both sang 'Allons Enfants de la Patrie,' etc. Then we leaned against one of the many cannons and talked and talked."[15]

There were more meetings with his friend—and more letters: "a Frenchman brought me a wonderful letter from Miss C.— wonderful— wonderful." On the following day he met her again at the Arch, after which he wrote: "O world! O life! O time! And I am the biggest fool there is. But I shall never forget these hours we've spent in the violet colored evenings."[16] For unexplained reasons, the romance cooled quickly after that. Perhaps she had not intended to become so deeply involved in comforting a shell-shocked soldier. She returned his letters, and he made the entry: "Oh, woman, ye are birds of strange voices and come from far countries."[17]

Green next turned his attention to other charms of Paris. Along with a North Carolinian named Joe Blythe, an engineer from Charlotte with whom he shared a room, he applied to the Sorbonne but was disappointed again:

I was rabid to go to the Sorbonne; so many of the boys were allowed to go. So Joe and I applied for entrance in the Sorbonne, and he was accepted and I was turned down. I never understood it. . . . Joe would get up in the morning to go to the Sorbonne, and he'd go and check in, and then he was on the town the rest of the day. I had to get up and go work with the brigadier general who was in charge of that particular section, and then I found out later that he opposed my going to the Sorbonne because he wanted to keep me . . . helping him in his office.[18]

Green reread *Hamlet*; he read E. V. Lucas's *A Wanderer in Paris*. He spent an evening rereading Ecclesiastes: "this and the book of Job are to my mind the best of all." He arranged to have a young Frenchwoman who was about to get her doctorate take him through the Louvre: "She showered me with her learning."[19] He read Henry James. He went to the opera. He read Henrik Ibsen's *Peer Gynt* and O. Henry's *The Four Million*. He tried to get into a Sarah Bernhardt performance but was kept away by an overflow crowd that had turned into an angry mob. He went for a tour of Versailles. He and Alton Johnson visited Musée de Cluny and the Pantheon. He got to Hugo's house. He went to art exhibitions. He bought a violin and began to practice playing it.

In spite of work and study, there was time for his old passion—baseball. By then Alton Johnson had come over to live at Clignaucourt, and there are frequent entries such as "Played ball with Sgt. Pellett and Alton." He noted that the French people were only used to softballs and wouldn't believe the baseball was dangerous until it hit them. There were opportunities for team play: "Capt. Glessner wishes me to play with them and of course I must. Nothing I like better."[20]

General John J. Pershing came for a visit. There had been talk of the general running for president. Green wrote what he was not free to express openly:

he is very unpopular with the men. Bah! President. He wouldn't get a smell. His ideas concerning an army are purely anti-democratic. Yes, we've been trying hard to crush the militarism of Germany while we are growing the same thing in our midst. . . . The system of military discipline used in our army is wrong. It crushes the individuality and freedom of men. I know. I've experienced it. . . . O that I might step out from the whole thing. This having to bow down to men because they are in authority hurts me.[21]

In spite of Green's feelings about the military, however, he was happy and proud when he finally received his commission as a second lieutenant. His new status allowed him to move out of Clignaucourt—"with your everlasting passes and discipline"—to private quarters in the home of a Madame Cassard. One Sunday he "saw Miss C. [Cummings] with her everlastingly pale face" at a restaurant. That day's diary entry also included a more flattering reference to another woman: "Met a visitor here, Mlle. Renee Bourseillier. Very attractive. She speaks English well. Works uptown, so I learned. Her people once had money but now her father dead, money gone, and mother an invalid, she has to work. Why do the fool French people look down on one who has to work."[22] Mademoiselle Bourseillier was completely different from Miss Cummings. The latter was somewhat plain, midwestern, motherly; Bourseillier was younger than Green, a beauty, and sophisticated.

Green's new acquaintance began showing up regularly in his record: "Tonight Mlle. Renee and I walked in the Bois and talked, talked, talked. She sang for me . . . her voice is remarkably sweet"; "After supper Mlle. Renee and I walked to the Bois . . . where she said her brother-in-law had proposed to her sister"; "At night Mlle. and I read <u>Les Bouffons</u> by Miguel [Z]amacois." The next day he "bought two copies of the <u>Rubaiyat</u> for Mlle. R.," from which they read that night.[23] On the following evening they read from a leather-bound edition of Francis Turner Palgrave's *Golden Treasury of English Songs and Lyrics*, which he had purchased that day. Then, on Sunday, "Early in the morning Mlle. R. [and I] took lunch and went far into the woods beyond St. Cloud. Finding a pretty secluded spot with running ivy making a thick carpet we made our home. Read and talked all day, took pictures of each other, and came home in the evening. Took dinner with her and her mother." On Monday there was a small party at Madam Cassard's, "Mlle. R. being among them. We sat in the garden a long time talking—and—oh, les baises d'amour!" On subsequent days Green mentions borrowing violin music from "Mlle. R."[24] and walking with her on several occasions. He had dinner again at her mother's house, but when his brother Hugh visited him twice, he did not bother to bring around his French friend for introductions.

Otherwise, he regularly spent time with her: "As usual went to see Mlle. R. last night. Today I felt tough. Could not work, so after getting dinner on Rue Washington, I took the train home and went to bed. At 8:20 went to see Mlle. R. Had a pleasant evening of course. She gave me a few drops of an opium mixture in order to make me sleep."[25] The following day he didn't awaken until one o'clock in the afternoon. When he went to meet his friend, she had been waiting a long time, uneasy that she might have given him too much opium.

One might conclude that Green had seen enough of destruction, but one weekend he went alone to Reims and rode out to the battlefields, taking pictures of the shell-torn German tanks and the scenes of recent horror. Then he traveled to Lille, Albert, and Donai. Apparently he again turned to his new woman friend for comfort: when he returned from his travels, he went straight "to Mlle. R.

She was crazy with joy, me too. Mutual tears and kisses. Stayed late, of course."[26] On the following night they went to the opera.

Green received a letter from Miss Cummings asking him to come to see her, and he called on her at the Hotel Famille. They walked in the Luxembourg Gardens for the last time and said their final good-byes. He immediately went back to his French friend. Their time together was growing short. On Monday night, June 30, he stayed with her "late, very, very late." Tuesday, "Went to office: with Mlle. R. We both all in tears. Told all friends in office goodbye. At 11:30 met Mlle. R. at Hotel Crillon. Had Dejeuner at Duval's. Walked around a while. Got a room at Hotel Louvais, for 40 frcs. for night. Mlle. and I went back to Boulogne. Packed my remaining luggage, told them all goodbye; caught #16 train to Madeline. Taxi from there to Hotel."[27]

Green then went to Janeville to see Hugh but found that Hugh had gone to see him. He waited, and his brother returned. They "played ball" awhile, and then the idea struck them that they should find the grave of Rass Matthews before they left Europe. Late in the afternoon they took a train for Busigny, arriving very hungry at 10:30 P.M. They walked through the town until they found a restaurant, where they ate and shared a quart of wine. "Hugh was a sight to behold. Another glass and he would have been drunk."[28] It was raining, but it was warm summertime, and in their condition they decided that the weather should not keep them from their mission. They wandered out into the night and sloshed in the mud through Vaux Audigny, Moloin, and other small towns. Worn out, they reached Abie de Guise, where they slept in a peasant's barn.

The next morning, although their feet were sore and blistered, they hiked on to Mazingheim. They searched the fields and cemeteries all around, looking for the graves of English and American soldiers, but nowhere did they find familiar names. After a time they met a cross-eyed boy who claimed to know the burial place of some Americans. They walked a mile to a peasant's house, and the man took them through his empty barnyard to his orchard. There, among a few other burial sites, they found the grave of Rass Matthews. Other friends were buried within a two-mile radius, and they spent four hours trudging through the fields. Then they returned to the house, where they were given ale and bread and jam. They gave the peasant 150 francs, and "he promised us to plant flowers around Rass' grave, to tend it jealously."[29]

Paul sailed for home aboard the ocean liner *Kaiserin Augusta Victoria* on July 9. Just before leaving, he ran into Bryce Little of the 30th Division, whom he had known at Chapel Hill. They talked of "Carolina" and of expecting to see each other there in September. During the voyage Green recorded an incident reflecting his continued notice of racial segregation. Someone was playing the piano, and hundreds of men were singing. There was a large contingent of black soldiers aboard who were smiling and enjoying the music but who did not join in.

They left all that pleasure to the white soldiers and sailors. And as I looked down on them from a deck I seemed to see the negro in his forlorn condition. Here were hundreds of black soldiers who came to do their bit, soldiers every one of them. But, in all this enjoyment they did not forget, could not forget, they were black. And, therefore, they let their white brothers sing and shout and be happy while they stood silent. And again it is shown by the isolated condition of the negro officers. There are several aboard. They always walk together, a people of another race. Is it right? O Lord![30]

When the ship reached New York, he was so anxious to get home that he took the first train south. In Raleigh he boarded another train, the slow little one that was supposed to go to Lillington, but it broke down after a few miles. He got off and started walking and came to the home of George McCulloughs, the fiddle-playing man who had taught him music at Pleasant Union Church. In the yard stood the convenient well at which Billy Green had stopped to water his mules in the middle of the night on those long wagon trips to Raleigh. Mr. McCulloughs was glad to see Paul, and, ignoring protests, the old man hitched up his buggy and drove Green to Pleasant Union along the still unpaved roads of Harnett County, where little had been changed by the Great War in Europe. Finally home, Paul was reunited with his whole family, Hugh included: "Man, what a reunion we had. My brother Hugh was back."[31]

NOTES

1. Paul Green Diary, October 4, 1918, Paul Green Papers (collection #3693), Southern Historical Collection, Wilson Library, University of North Carolina at Chapel Hill (hereafter cited as Diary, with entry date).

2. Paul Green, interview by James R. Spence, October 24, 1976, James R. Spence audio recordings relating to Paul Green, 1974-1979 (collection #5170), Southern Historical Collection (hereafter cited as Spence interview, with appropriate date).

3. Spence interview, August 9, 1979.

4. Ibid.

5. Spence interview, May 6, 1976.

6. Ibid.

7. Diary, December 17, 1918.

8. Spence interview, May 6, 1976.

9. Ibid.

10. Diary, February 7, 1919.

11. Diary, February 9, 11, 1919.

12. Diary, February 14, 15, 1919.

13. Diary, February 16, 19, 1919.

14. Diary, February 28, 1919.

15. Diary, March 1, 1919.

16. Diary, March 10, 11, 1919.

17. Diary, March 20, 1919.

18. Paul Green, interview by Rhoda Wynn, February 1974, tape 2, p. 8, Southern Oral History Program Collection, Southern Historical Collection. Green also discussed this matter with the author. Spence interview, May 6, 1976.

19. Diary, March 14, 23, 1919.

20. Diary, March 31, May 14, 1919.

21. Diary, April 2, 1919.

22. Diary, May 22, 26, 1919.

23. Diary, May 29, 30, June 5, 6, 1919.

24. Diary, June 8, 9, 12, 1919.

25. Diary, June 24, 1919.

26. Diary, June 27, 1919.

27. Diary, June 30, 1919, July 1, 1919.

28. Diary, July 2, 1919.

29. Diary, July 3, 1919.

30. Diary, July 11, 1919.

31. Spence interview, May 6, 1976.

13: Return to Chapel Hill

Sixty days after his return from France, Paul Green was back at the university. A new class of sixteen-year-olds was arriving on campus, along with returning veterans. Enrollment soared to a record 1,350 students. Green was still suffering from the psychological effects of the war. The hairy hand at the back of his neck had gone away, but there were other hallucinations: "I was often wary of picking up a telephone. I'd look at the telephone, and all of a sudden it would explode. You knew it didn't explode. Yet at the same time there was the sensation of this thing. Then there was a sensation of your head exploding."[1] Occasionally, too, he would still have the old dream about the man with the white beard trying to put him in a hole. Years later he wrote of this period in his life: "Meanwhile I had grown more and more interested in religion and philosophy. Only in these could I find some sort of answer to the troubles that tortured me—the meaning of my life and what I was here for, and what others like me were here for."[2]

He corresponded with Renée Bourseiller in Paris, sending her a poem that indicates something about his state of mind:

I shall knock at her door someday
when the violets bloom
coming up the old sweet path
in the evening gloom:

And her flowers will still be blooming
in the scented air
and a warm close sense of her nearness
will enfold me there.

I shall wonder if she had suffered,
spent many a sigh
known the hurt of tears and heartache
in the years gone by.

And a stranger will come to meet me
in the lamplight's glow,
and will say to my quick question
"She died long, long ago."

The grave is there in the garden
where she used to sit
with a lilac tree and a rosebush
bending over it:

I shall knock at her door someday
when the violets bloom
coming up the old sweet path
in the evening bloom.[3]

Green and Mademoiselle Bourseiller continued to write to each other for more than two years after he left France.

In spite of the trauma of war and the searching, the time away from school had allowed Green to plan his career: "I had my career pretty much fleshed out. I wanted to be a professor, I wanted to teach philosophy, and I wanted to become the president of a college or university." That included the possibility of becoming president of the University of North Carolina. But these ambitions he kept hidden away: "I was a very discreet fellow."[4] He went back to Mrs. T. J. Wilson's cottage to live but took in a roommate, veteran Bryce Little. He no longer had the overwhelming need for privacy that had been so significant in his life before the war.

Green had been well acquainted with young Thomas Wolfe before the war and had perceived Wolfe as "shy and sensitive."[5] Now Green received an invitation signed by Wolfe to join the literary society Sigma Upsilon. While Green had been away, "shy and sensitive" Wolfe had blossomed. He had become a star student in Prof. Horace Williams's philosophy class and in Prof. Frederick Koch's playwriting class. He was editor of the school newspaper, *The Tar Heel*, and there were those who felt that he was practically running the campus.

Green was happy to join Sigma Upsilon and quickly accepted, but he soon learned there was more to it—an initiation that the combat veteran thought too juvenile to participate in. Nineteen-year-old Wolfe was offended when Green didn't show up for the initiation and thought Green should not be admitted to membership. Wolfe, of course, had no way of knowing that he was dealing with a man who had resisted military hazing and thus wasn't likely to put up with it in college.[6] Ultimately, though, when given another chance, Green decided to accept the humiliation, be a good sport, and participate in the initiation. He showed up at the designated spot, where "Wolfe and several other members jumped [out] and began beating him, Wolfe pounding away hardest in revenge for the [previous] defection." Green responded calmly to this violent hazing, saying, "Tom, don't hit me any more. I want to be in Sigma Upsilon but don't hit me any more." Wolfe responded by hitting him even harder. "For a while I hated Tom Wolfe," Green said when recounting this incident.[7]

Green had not been allowed to take a course under Horace Williams while he was a freshman. In the fall of 1919 he greedily took two. Williams, at that time sixty-one years old, was the entire philosophy department. He was also well known throughout North Carolina. People like James Archibald Campbell thought he was an infidel. Thomas Wolfe later wrote that when students went up to Williams's house to talk, it "was never about sex—About rather a union with God."[8]

On the first day of class, Williams assigned reading from texts and other sources and hardly referred to them again. The rest of the semester was spent in pursuing his Socratic method. He might ask, "What is the most important part of an oxcart?" A student would say, "The wheels." Williams would say, "No, it's the concept of a cart, the blueprint. After the blueprint has been made, any jackleg can do the rest. . . . Science changes; the concept never changes."[9] Thomas Wolfe has a scene in *Look Homeward, Angel* in which a fictional Williams holds up a stick and asks, "What is a stick?" After many students attempt to answer, Eugene Gant (the fictional Wolfe), who has caught on to the method, says, "A stick . . . is not only wood but the negation of wood. It is the meeting in Space of Wood and No-wood. A stick is finite and unextended wood, a fact determined by its denial."[10] Green noted, "Tom was so young—about sixteen or seventeen—and he had that quick mind, and he caught on to Horace's manner and he would adopt it in a way. He would ask questions that would be a little startling. . . . Tom stuttered pretty bad. Sometimes I thought he deliberately stuttered for attention . . . that stuttering— everybody would listen."[11]

It was in this esoteric atmosphere that Williams kept the class most of the time. He had studied under Harvard's Charles Carroll Everett, used the textbook that Everett had written in 1869, and used Everett's classroom methods. His main philosophy was from the German Georg Wilhelm Friedrich Hegel.[12] Wolfe suggested in *Look Homeward, Angel* that "Socrates begat Plato" and then traced a line of begats down to Kant, then Hegel.[13] So if Hegel then begat Williams, who would Williams beget? For a while it looked as if it might be Wolfe. When someone got an "A" in one of Williams's classes, it was an event. Toward the end Wolfe got two "A's," and there is no doubt that Williams was enchanted with this student's "brilliant flights." But Wolfe was going off to Harvard to study playwriting under George Pierce Baker, and Williams began to turn to Paul Green.

In philosophy class Green noticed a pretty young woman named Elizabeth Lay:

Elizabeth always sat on the front row, and she had this tremendous flood of red hair with a slight yellowish streak in the front. I used to wonder, "I wonder if that is false hair." . . . I remember one day, I felt real sorry for her. Maybe that's when I first started noticing her. . . . Horace Williams was asking us if we believed in the Deity. He didn't say "God" but "Do you believe in the Deity?" And people were sort of silent. They were scared of this old fellow. He would trick you, you know, and that was part of his charm. So, he looked down at Miss Lay, you know, knowing that she was a minister's daughter, I guess. And he said, "Do you believe in the Deity, Miss Lay?" And she came back quite bright, "Oh, yes, I do, Dr. Williams, I do. I believe in God." He said, "Do you believe he is all-powerful?" "Oh, yes, he is all-powerful. He is God." Then he looked out the window. He had a way of looking out before he would throw this hand grenade at you. He said, "Well, do you believe that the Deity could cook breakfast with a snowball?" A little silence and then some snickers here and there and finally laughter. She was very much embarrassed, and I felt sorry for her. Then, later, we got to discussing that as we walked out. I said, "Well, what do you believe?" She said, "That was so unfair of him."[14]

Horace Williams, ca. 1920.

Green soon learned more about Elizabeth Lay. She had spent her childhood in Concord, New Hampshire, where her father, the Reverend George Lay, had taught Greek at St. Paul's School. When he became rector of St. Mary's School in Raleigh, she matriculated there, graduated, then taught a year in a rural school in Northampton County, North Carolina. She had enrolled at the University of North Carolina at a time when women were not accepted for freshman or sophomore work, and there were no dormitories for them.

Elizabeth had been a member of Frederick Koch's first playwriting class, which was all female except for one person, Thomas Wolfe. When Koch arrived at the class the first morning, Wolfe spoke up, Koch later recalled, and said, "I don't want you to think this Ladies Aid Society represents Carolina. We have a lot of he-men seriously interested in writing here, but they are all disguised in army uniforms now. I tried to get one myself but they didn't have one long enough for me."[15]

Elizabeth wrote *When Witches Ride*, the first play that Koch's group produced.[16] She worked on sets for plays, was a reporter for *The Tar Heel*, wrote poems and sketches for the university magazine, participated in student government activities, and sang in the choir of the Chapel of the Cross. She was the first female student to act the female lead in a campus play. Paul Green

wrote a play called "White Dresses" about [a] sort of . . . love affair, the tragedy of white and black, and read it in this small group. Well, Professor Koch finally said, "Would you like to read it to the senior group?" I said, "Yes, sir." So, then I came to the senior group with it one day, and Elizabeth was in that and I was very conscious that she was watching. . . . So then pretty soon Mr. Koch asked the class if, "Well, would you welcome Mr. Green into the senior class?" "Oh, yes, yes," they said, "let's have him in our group." I got into that group and got more acquainted [with Elizabeth], and we used to work together and paint scenery together, way up in the loft of the old Alumni Building, way up there where they had the bust of Napoleon and all kinds of stuff that had been laid aside. We used to paint scenery and court, and so it went.[17]

Folk drama had come to North Carolina by a circuitous route. In Ireland, William Butler Yeats, Lady Augusta Gregory, and others founded the Abbey Theatre and encouraged the writing of and production of "folk plays." George Pierce Baker of Harvard was enthusiastic about the movement and passed it on to his student Frederick Koch. Koch brought it to Chapel Hill in the fall of 1918. He had been born in Kentucky and brought up in Illinois. After earning a master's degree at Harvard, he returned to Grand Forks, North Dakota, where he had already done some teaching. In 1914 eighteen of his students wrote the historical *Pageant of the Northwest*, and in 1916 twenty students wrote *Shakespeare the Playmaker*. At the same time, individual students were writing plays about local historical subjects.

Koch was a force in establishing in Grand Forks the outdoor Bankside Theatre, where students wrote and performed "prairie plays." He sent a playbill to his former student Maxwell Anderson. Anderson wrote back: "What! Native folk plays of Dakota—like the Irish? If I thought that, I would walk all the way back to Dakota, to put my foot on the old sod!"[18] He learned a short time later that his former teacher had indeed caused Dakota folk plays to be created and produced, like the Irish.

Edwin Greenlaw, then head of the English department at the University of North Carolina, was

a very broad-minded man. He had an appraisal of the state. The English people made a lot of the mountain traditional music that we carried on. The old English ballads and folk songs in the mountains here. In fact, some British scholars came over and . . . edited a lot of the mountain material, showing how it went back to English ballads. And he [Greenlaw] got the idea that with all the storehouse of folklore in this state, we ought to be able to do some things similar to what the Abbey Theatre was doing in Dublin. . . . Greenlaw looked around . . . and found that Koch was carrying on this sort of thing. . . . So, he invites Koch here.[19]

Koch was forty-one when he came to the University of North Carolina. He immediately became known for his tweed Norfolk jacket and Windsor tie, and soon the students were calling him "Proff," which when written had two "f"s. Green was charmed by him: "Professor Koch believed that good teaching is the forming and guidance of students into the realization of their best latent possibilities. . . . More than once I heard him say, 'The longer I live the surer I am that what people need is not criticism but encouragement.'"[20]

At Koch's urging, Green was soon studying the "Irish upsurge," the Abbey Theatre, and particularly the plays of John Millington Synge. In spite of Green's enthusiasm for Koch and his methods, however, he continued to believe that his writing future was in poems and short stories. He searched through his war experience, wanting to write about it, but little emerged. There were a few poems that appeared in the university magazine. One, which begins, "Over the top! Over the top! / Like hell with yer bayonets rushing!"[21] and another, "Song of the Dead":

We are the dead who speak
After long nights of woe
Hearing the wild shells shriek,
The hurrying to and fro
Of armies upon the hill,
And dead men under the plain
Broken and lying still
Are cold in the falling rain.[22]

Both poems reflect his view of war as odious. Green wanted to communicate what he had experienced at Ypres and Buire Woods, but most of it was locked up inside.

Green's story "Other Judases," with a mountain setting, was entered in another five-dollar prize competition sponsored by Sigma Upsilon. He won and was awarded the prize, "five dollars in gold," at a meeting of the society. The story was then published in the university magazine.[23] In spite of such successes, university life seemed meaningless to Green. So much of it was like the Sigma Upsilon initiation—sophomoric. Latin no longer seemed important, and at the end of the winter quarter he dropped it. He returned to a study of the English Romantics but no longer found them exciting. In March, without taking examinations for the quarter, he dropped out and went home to Harnett County. There he visited his sister Mary and his war buddy (and Mary's new husband) Alton Johnson, but he was unable to explain to them exactly why he was home. He stayed at his father's place and plowed his father's fields with a mule, enjoying the smell of the turned sod, the sounds of the birds in the nearby woods, and the physical fatigue at the end of the day.

After two or three weeks, he was plowing one day when the thought came to him "like a voice," asking, "What the devil are you doing here in the field, sixty miles from Chapel Hill?" He decided to go back, believing that somehow he would get enough money to keep going. He brought the mule to the barn in mid-afternoon and told his surprised father of his decision. His father said, "Son, I wish I could help you, but I can't."[24]

It was not a simple thing to return to the university. Paul had to make another trip to see Mr. Warren at the loan fund, and another note had to be endorsed. Since he had missed examinations, he had to go around to each teacher and ask for his help and indulgence. All of them ultimately allowed him to make up his work. Professor Williams, for example, believed in "The Wilderness Experience," in which a person went off alone and wrestled with his soul. He seemed to understand what Green had been through, and made this statement to his class:

Mr. Green has been in the middle of the ocean. He is sensitive, and he is an industrious student. He left school last semester without taking the examination, and he came up to me in a humble sort of way when he came back. I said to him that he was out on the ocean and when he dropped anchor he did not touch anything. He agreed, and I told him that it was all right and that he should come ashore when he could. It was his trip, and I would be there waiting for him when he came. He has got to make the voyage or else drown philosophically. Is that a wise procedure or not? It would have been easy for me to become furious when he failed to take the examination, for I want him to go to Europe next year to study philosophy. But I knew his state of mind exactly. I have been in it myself. For about five years the bottom was out of everything for me. I would fight anything, especially orthodoxy. But there are plenty of good people who would have negated him completely. That is an expression of power, and it is not intelligent, not spiritual.[25]

Williams must have had in mind some kind of scholarship that would take Green to Europe, but nothing ever came of it.

During that spring quarter Koch started the rehearsals for a production of *White Dresses*, with author Paul Green playing the part of the black suitor. The play was about two generations of interracial love and its effects on the black women involved. One day UNC mathematics professor Archibald Henderson showed up where they were rehearsing. He sat and watched a little and afterward took Koch and Green aside and said they could not do the play. "I would have fought it," Green said. Yet he was impressed with Dr. Henderson. Koch, who was not a propagandist, was not about to wreck his program and the future of the Carolina Playmakers Repertory Company by colliding with North Carolina's racists.[26] He withdrew *White Dresses* and substituted another of Green's plays, *The Last of the Lowries*.[27] Elizabeth Lay designed the set for the play's original production.

This early Green play, about the Croatan outlaw Henry Berry Lowrie and his escape in 1874, used the plot of John Millington Synge's *Riders to the Sea.* Just as Leonard Bernstein would later use *Romeo and Juliet* as the basis for *West Side Story*, Green used Synge's play to create an entirely new work of art. *The Last of the Lowries* was so popular that it was performed again at commencement. Several years later it became a standard in the repertory of the Playmakers as they toured the state.

In the fall of 1920 Frederick Koch's pageant-drama, *Raleigh, The Shepherd of the Ocean*, was performed at the North Carolina State Fair at Raleigh. It had a cast and chorus of five hundred, drawn from colleges, churches, and the community. Six thousand people attended, and it received favorable reviews in *Theatre Magazine* and the *Christian Science Monitor*.[28] Although it did not have the depth of story, poetry, and music of later outdoor dramas, there were certain other aspects—the spectacle, the chorus, and the participation of local people—that must have made an impression on Green.

At Christmastime in 1920, as Elizabeth Lay was preparing to visit her parents, who then lived in Beaufort, North Carolina, Green brought her a present to the little house on the corner of Franklin and Hillsborough streets, where she roomed with Mary Thornton. She unwrapped the package carefully, thinking it was perhaps a hairbrush. Instead it was a Madonna, the one he had found blown from a house when his platoon had marched through Poperinghe in France. She did not fully understand the object's significance, but she knew that it was beautiful (although it was only plaster of Paris) and that it was important to the giver. She had viewed him as something of an unpolished country boy, but the gift changed that: "I think that was a real revelation of Paul's character and a real reprimand to me for any criticism that I might have had of his taste or any expectation that he didn't have the finest sensibilities of anybody I'd ever known."[29]

Green became more and more fascinated with Horace Williams and philosophy: "'Those of us who sat under him in the classroom, who followed him with all his vagaries, his dreamings, his ponderings, his punches and plumbings, his challenges of life's circumstances—we knew it was wonderful.'"[30] In the winter quarter, after Green received an "A" in philosophy, Williams summoned him for a talk.

Williams said he was looking for someone to be his assistant who could take over the department when he retired. He thought Green was the man, if he would continue his studies. Green later remembered another encounter with Williams that occurred around that time:

Then one day I decided I would try to smoke a cigarette. . . . I got a cigarette and I lighted up in my little house and was puffing away, and there was a shuffle of feet outside and I looked out and Horace Williams was out there with an umbrella. There was a little bit of rain falling, and there he was. Well, I hid this cigarette as fast as I possibly could and came out, and I knew that he could smell me, and so he stood around and finally said, "I walked out [to see Green]," . . . and that's a long way from Horace Williams's house, way out there. . . . So, he said, "I thought that I would come out and tell you the good news. We have awarded you the Philosophy Prize for the year."[31]

Green was also continuing his writing. One of his poems was published in the *Carolina Magazine*, and he presented his play *The Old Man of Edenton* at an author's reading in December. In February the Playmakers produced his play *The Miser, a Farm Tragedy*.[32] They took it on tour in May, along with Elizabeth Lay's *When Witches Ride*. The home folks may have been impressed, but young Jonathan Daniels, son of Josephus Daniels, publisher of the influential Raleigh *News and Observer*, was not. He was in the senior class and was a reviewer for *The Tar Heel*. He found *The Miser* to be a rather "'overdrawn, gruesome tragedy'" and said that in *The Old Man of Edenton* "'the element of horror is carried to such an extreme as to be almost nauseous.'" In spite of Daniels's bad review, the campus yearbook honored Green by devoting a full page to each of his plays that had been produced—but in the humor section ran a mock announcement: "Death to You and All Concerned, a Tragedy, by Paul Green."[33]

At the end of the quarter Green was elected to Phi Beta Kappa and named Class Poet, an award that had gone to Thomas Wolfe the year before. Green was far from satisfied with the university, however. He had read H. L. Mencken's famous essay "The Sahara of the Bozart," in which the South was depicted as a cultural desert. He felt that more should be done to make Chapel Hill an oasis in that desert. In a radical mood, he prepared a long, critical, poem-like diatribe against university teaching to be delivered at Class Day as a part of his duties as Class Poet. At the last minute, however, he lost his nerve and composed a lyrical "Hail to Alma Mater." Before his graduation he sent his play *Granny Boling* to the magazine *Drama* in Chicago. It was about the conflict and lack of understanding between a black grandmother and her grandchildren. He was soon notified that it would be published in the magazine's August-September 1921 issue.[34]

NOTES

1. Paul Green, interview by James R. Spence, October 23, 1976, James R. Spence audio recordings relating to Paul Green, 1974-1979 (collection #5170), Southern Historical Collection, Wilson Library, University of North Carolina at Chapel Hill (hereafter cited as Spence interview, with appropriate date).

2. Paul Green, *Drama and the Weather: Some Notes and Papers on Life and the Theatre* (New York: Samuel French, 1958), 5.

3. During the author's interview with Paul Green on May 6, 1976, Green walked into another room of his house, away from the library in which the interview was transpiring, got the poem, and gave the author a copy. To the author's knowledge, it had not been published, and it is not listed among the poems cited in the extensive bibliography found at the end of Lynn Veach Sadler, ed., *Paul Green's Celebration of Man, with a Bibliography* (Sanford, N.C.: Human Technology Interface, Ink, 1994).

4. Spence interview, October 23, 1976.

5. Spence interview, May 6, 1976.

6. In a later recollection of military hazing, Green remarked, "There is something cruel in people, just cruel." Paul Green, interview by Billy E. Barnes, May 1975, p. 26, Southern Oral History Program Collection, Southern Historical Collection (hereafter cited as Barnes interview, with appropriate date and transcript page number).

7. The hazing incident is recounted from Richard Walser, *Thomas Wolfe Undergraduate* (Durham: Duke University Press, 1977), 102. Walser draws the quotations from his own interview with Green, conducted on July 18, 1968.

8. Quoted in Walser, *Thomas Wolfe Undergraduate*, 126.

9. Quoted in Walser, *Thomas Wolfe Undergraduate*, 126-127.

10. Thomas Wolfe, *Look Homeward, Angel: A Story of the Buried Life* (New York: Scribner's, 1929; reprint, New York: C. Scribner, 1957), 495.

11. Spence interview, August 9, 1979.

12. Walser, *Thomas Wolfe Undergraduate*, 131.

13. Wolfe, *Look Homeward, Angel*, 497.

14. Barnes interview, May 1975, pp. 10-11.

15. Quoted in Samuel Selden, with Mary Tom Sphangos, *Frederick Henry Koch, Pioneer Playmaker: A Brief Biography*, University of North Carolina Library Extension Publications, vol 19, No. 4 (Chapel Hill: University of North Carolina Library, July 1954), 13.

16. This play appears in Frederick H. Koch's first volume of *Carolina Folk-Plays* (New York: H. Holt and Company, 1922).

17. Barnes interview, May 1975, pp. 12-13. Paul Green distinguished himself to his future wife in another way as well. In her volume *The Paul Green I Know* (Chapel Hill: North Caroliniana Society, 1978), Elizabeth Lay Green wrote of how he attracted her attention with his neat appearance: "Many of the returning veterans were agitating for the government

to pay them a bonus. In their protests they wore bib overalls and various outlandish costumes to class. Green took no part in such antics, always wearing a tie with a shirt and collar" (p. 3).

18. Quoted in Archibald Henderson's foreword to *American Folk Plays*, ed. Frederick H. Koch (New York: D. Appleton-Century, 1939), xli.

19. Spence interview, October 23, 1976.

20. Paul Green, *Drama and the Weather*, 162-163.

21. Richard Walser, "Paul Green Undergraduate," *Pembroke Magazine* 10 (1978): 34.

22. Poem quoted from Agatha Boyd Adams, *Paul Green of Chapel Hill*, University of North Carolina Library Extension Publications, vol. 16, No. 2 (Chapel Hill: University of North Carolina Library, January 1951), 15.

23. Walser, "Paul Green Undergraduate," 34.

24. Paul Green, interview by Rhoda Wynn, February 1974, tape 11, pp. 41-42, Southern Oral History Program Collection, Southern Historical Collection.

25. Quoted in Walser, "Paul Green Undergraduate," 34-35.

26. Spence interview, October 23, 1976.

27. *White Dresses* is collected in Paul Green's *Lonesome Road: Six Plays for the Negro Theatre* (New York: R. M. McBride and Company, 1926), and *Last of the Lowries* is included in his *The Lord's Will and Other Plays* (New York: H. Holt and Company, 1925).

28. Quoted in Samuel Selden, *Frederick Henry Koch, Pioneer Playmaker*, 21-22.

29. Elizabeth Lay Green, *The Paul Green I Know*, 4.

30. Walser, "Paul Green Undergraduate," 33.

31. Barnes interview, May 1975, p. 9.

32. Both of these Green plays are collected in *The Lord's Will and Other Plays*, previously cited.

33. Walser, "Paul Green Undergraduate," 36.

34. Walser, "Paul Green Undergraduate," 36-37.

14: The Postgraduate

After graduating in 1921, Green made plans for the summer with his classmate Hubert Heffner, who later chaired the drama department at Stanford University. Green recalled that Heffner

> got the idea that he wanted to go to sea. . . . I had read Eugene O'Neill's stuff, and I wanted to write, and so we both decided that if we could go to sea and have a lot of experiences. . . . So, he and I enlisted to go on a freighter and went to Norfolk to go on it. Before I went up there I pitched a game for Lillington—just a hired pitcher, against Sanford, and we won easy. I just happened to be good that day. Just as I was going aboard the freighter with Hubert, a fellow came through calling my name and said that they had a telegram. So I go over there, and there is a telegram from the Lillington group, some businessmen, offering to pay me some money and board and room and all if I would come back and pitch for the summer. So, I had a struggle right there over this money. So I told Hubert goodbye and came back to Lillington.[1]

Mrs. Neil Matthews had a room with two double beds for four baseball players. Green, experiencing a need for privacy again, soon moved to the Caviness Hotel on Front Street in Lillington, an old frame structure with porches upstairs and downstairs running around three sides of the building. He was on the "hot-stove third floor," and the bedbugs made his nights miserable. One night the chairman of the local school board came to see him about becoming principal at Lillington. The school had a new two-story brick building with big white columns out front and dormitories for both boys and girls. (It would be two years before buses came into operation.) It was a tempting offer for a man who liked teaching, but, having other goals in mind, he declined.

In spite of the bedbugs and the heat, Green did some writing in the Caviness Hotel. It was there that he set down the first draft of a story he called "The Devil's Instrument," about a local fiddler who got religion and decided it was sinful to play such music. The man could not bear to destroy his fiddle, however, and carefully wrapped it and buried it. When he later "fell from grace" he dug it up and began playing again. It is a delightful piece about local farm and church life and human resolve that fades quickly.[2]

One way that Green earned money during this period foreshadowed the folklore work he would later do with his wife. He worked in the courthouse with a "fellow named D. P. McDonald. He was a local historian. He and I were supposed to work on the tax books, and every time we'd get a chance we'd be off traveling the old grave yards. . . . We just talked history all the time."[3]

On July 22, 1920, the *Harnett County News* (Lillington) carried a front-page story headlined "Paul Green, Playwright": "In the July 16 number of Summer School News," the article said, "appears an illustration from the play by Paul Green, 'The Last of the Lowries,' . . . to be presented by the Carolina Players in their program of original folk-plays on July 22 and 23." People around the courthouse began to point him out as the fellow that pitches baseball with either hand and writes plays.

As if playing baseball and working at the courthouse were not enough, Green became involved in several other activities. A social worker who had an office in the courthouse was promoting activities for young people. In talking with this Miss Camp, Green got the idea that they could organize the whole county and have singers and musicians from each precinct come to Lillington for a big "sing." The town council of Lillington cooperated, and the event took place in a tobacco warehouse on a hot summer day, with thousands of people in attendance. Green had formed another quartet, this time with his cousin Ernest Spence and Leslie and Carlyle Campbell, and the group performed in the competition. In addition to the banjo pickers, fiddlers, and other music makers, there was a speech by the commanding general of Fort Bragg. Perhaps because the warehouse burned down soon afterward, or perhaps because of the long, militaristic speech by the general in the steaming weather, the event was never held again. Some of the singing groups lasted for years, however, and Green tried to encourage a revival of the project from afar.[4]

One day during Green's project with Miss Camp, a Lillington woman said, "I hear you and Miss Camp are getting married." He was astonished. There had been no romance between the two. In fact, once back in Chapel Hill to begin his graduate work, Green met Elizabeth Lay again. She had graduated but continued to work with the Carolina Playmakers in her capacity as field agent for the Bureau of Community Drama of the Extension Division of the university. The two Koch students collaborated on the play *Blackbeard, Pirate of the Carolina Coast*.[5] Green recalled:

I decided when I was about twenty-five or twenty-six that I would never get married because I wanted to have my work, you know, and write poetry and not be bothered. . . . Then I met up with Elizabeth and something happened. It was too much for that resolution, and I said, "I've got no business getting married. I haven't got a dime." . . . Elizabeth didn't have anything [either], but she had a trust of the future. . . . I don't think that there was ever any (or not much) doubt that . . . Elizabeth wanted to . . . get married. With me, it was one day this and one day that. . . . I would go to see her every night. . . . I would stay late and go away and say, now I'm not going tomorrow night. I want to be studying, stick to my books. And the next night I would be back there. . . . I ought to have had more manhood or something.[6]

Elizabeth later said she had "decided he was the one I wanted, and I pursued him!"[7]

When the Playmakers went on tour in January, they took Elizabeth's play *Trista* and Paul's play *The Miser, a Farm Tragedy*. At Chapel Hill in March, their co-written play *Blackbeard* was produced, along with Green's *The Lord's Will*.[8] Green had seen the poor people of Harnett County go to work in the cotton mill in Erwin and come out debilitated with lung problems. A part of *The Lord's Will* dealt with that problem. One day after the tour, Green received a call from the office of Harry Woodburn Chase, president of the university, asking him to come in. Chase showed him a letter he had received

Elizabeth Lay Green on her wedding day, July 6, 1922.

from W. A. Erwin, president of Erwin Cotton Mills, that complained about Green's play. Although Chase assured Green that he was not going to do anything about the letter, Green could not help considering the fact that two of his plays had already ruffled the establishment. It was a little frightening, but exhilarating.

At the same time, Horace Williams was still pulling him toward philosophy:

One day [Horace Williams] announced to the philosophy class that he had good news, that Mrs. Graham Kenan of the Kenan family—you know, the stadium and all, the Kenan professorships— . . . had sent him a check for

$25,000 to establish the Kenan Fellowship in Philosophy. . . . So, when the spring came on and the graduation . . . he called me into the classroom after the others had gone, and he said, "I want you to have the first Kenan Fellowship in Philosophy. It pays $1,500." Gosh, what an amount of money, $1,500. So I rushed to tell Elizabeth the good news, and I don't know whether I proposed to her or she did, but we could get married on that.[9]

Williams wanted Green to go to Cornell University for a doctorate in philosophy. A few days after hearing about the Kenan Fellowship money,

James Finch Royster, the dean of the graduate school and the head of the English department for a while, came to me and offered me a fellowship in English. He wanted me to become a professor in the English department. I told him that Dr. Williams had offered me this Kenan Fellowship—$1,500. He looked at me—he was a high-tempered man—and he said, "You know, Green, some day I'm going to lose my temper, I reckon, and I'm going to take a chair and go in . . . and knock Horace Williams's head off." . . . He said, "He's the worst influence we've got in this university for scholarship."[10]

Green enjoyed recalling how he was courted by both departments. And his courtship with Elizabeth was progressing as well. The young couple went down to Beaufort, North Carolina, to have her father, who was rector of the Episcopal church there, perform the marriage ceremony. They were married on July 6, after which they took a train for Ithaca, New York. Green explained, "At that time Cornell had the best philosophy department in the country. That's why I went there. They had three head men: Omby, Creighton, Hammond. They were terrific. And they had the *Philosophical Review*."[11]

Green had three classes a day and a seminar once a week and kept on writing—"in a hot room with a little old Corona typewriter"—which resulted in "something like ten or eleven one-act plays in three weeks."[12] Proud and naïve, Green took some of his stories and plays to the philosophy professor under whom he was working for his doctorate. After reading the material and making favorable comments, the professor asked, "How are you getting along with your philosophy?" Green told his teacher that he was getting along well and that he wanted to write as well as study philosophy. The man seemed to understand and said, "You'll find your way."[13]

Green described his writing routine: "many a night I hammered my typewriter through the long hours and joyfully saw the sun come up—writing about the Negroes and poor whites of my boyhood remembering in Eastern North Carolina, and pouring out on page after page my indignation at their piteous and doleful lot."[14] During that year he sent to the Raleigh *News and Observer* two of his poems and three "Carolina Sketches," which were published.[15]

Green had also published some one-act "Negro" plays in the literary magazine *Poet Lore*. Noting this accomplishment, Prof. Martin Sampson, whose playwriting class Green audited, berated the other students in the class for not having published their plays. And he would harshly critique what they did write: "By the time Dr. Sampson was through with [a] script, the boy . . . had no enthusiasm." Green resolved that he "would never teach like that";[16] rather, in his own teaching he would follow the examples of Frederick Koch and Hubbard F. Page. In his writing, Green was influenced by a literary discovery: "I finished reading the tragic story of *Jude the Obscure*, and from then on Thomas Hardy its author was my man. I didn't change that opinion with the reading of his other novels and his poems. Rather my admiration for him increased, even right on through to the last wrung grudging bit of optimism in *The Dynasts*."[17]

On one occasion when the Greens were at Cornell University in Ithaca, they were able to go to New York City. Green described the journey: "We sat up all night [on the train] in order to save a little money so that we could use the money to buy tickets to the theater. There we saw [Max] Reinhardt's wonderful *Miracle*. And also a play that really got next to us was Somerset Maugham's *Rain*, with Jeanne Eagles. . . . It was sort of a *Thaïs* story such as Anatole France had written."[18]

During the second summer the Greens were at Cornell, Paul received a letter from Horace Williams telling him "that the philosophy department had grown so that they needed a teacher, and could I come back and teach philosophy, although I didn't finish my degree and that later I could maybe go back in another summer . . . and finish. He said, 'We are able to offer you twenty-five hundred dollars a year.' . . . We had gotten down to where we were pawning off our stuff to keep going. So we came back."[19]

NOTES

1. Paul Green, interview by Billy E. Barnes, March 1975, pp. 74-75, Southern Oral History Program Collection, Southern Historical Collection, Wilson Library, University of North Carolina at Chapel Hill (hereafter cited as Barnes interview, with appropriate date and transcript page number).

2. Paul Green, interview by James R. Spence, October 23, 1976, James R. Spence audio recordings relating to Paul Green, 1974-1979 (collection #5170), Southern Historical Collection (hereafter cited as Spence interview, with appropriate date).

3. Ibid.

4. Green told the author that he wrote a rough script of a play about these music groups and set it in the mountains. Spence interview, October 24, 1976.

5. Agatha Boyd Adams, *Paul Green of Chapel Hill*, University of North Carolina Library Extension Publications, vol. 16, No. 2 (Chapel Hill: University of North Carolina Library, January 1951), 20.

6. Barnes interview, May 1975, pp. 71-72.

7. Quoted in Richard Walser, "Paul Green Undergraduate," *Pembroke Magazine* 10 (1978): 33.

8. Elizabeth Lay's *Trista* is in Koch's *Carolina Folk-Plays*, second series (New York: H. Holt and Company, 1924). In addition to *The Miser* (as mentioned previously), Green's *The Lord's Will* and his and Lay's *Blackbeard* are collected in his *The Lord's Will and Other Plays* (New York: H. Holt and Company, 1925).

9. Barnes interview, May 1975, p. 12.

10. Spence interview, August 9, 1979.

11. Ibid.

12. Barnes interview, May 1975, p. 14.

13. Spence interview, August 9, 1979.

14. Paul Green, *Drama and the Weather: Some Notes and Papers on Life and the Theatre* (New York: Samuel French, 1958), 5-6.

15. Adams, *Paul Green of Chapel Hill*, 23.

16. Paul Green, interview by Rhoda Wynn, February 1974, tape 12, p. 2, Southern Oral History Program Collection, Southern Historical Collection.

17. Green, *Drama and the Weather*, 185.

18. Spence interview, August 9, 1979.

19. Barnes interview, May 1975, pp. 14-15.

15: Connecting with New York

Green became an assistant professor. With his modest income, he and Elizabeth decided to rent a rather large house at 51 Davie Circle in Chapel Hill and to begin assisting their sisters with their education. Their landlord, Bob Strowd, reserved a room for himself and one for a roomer and leased the remainder of his big house to the Greens. One of the bedrooms upstairs was soon occupied by Elizabeth's sister Lucy and Paul's sisters Erma and Caro Mae. From time to time over succeeding years Elizabeth's sisters Virginia and Ellen lived with the Greens while studying at the university. Green's sister Caro Mae later called life in that home "one great joyride."[1] The sisters were enjoying their freedom as living-off-campus co-eds in a community of more young men than they had ever seen. And the Greens were always having interesting people as guests.

Green enjoyed being a true faculty member at last but felt "sort of divided. It was unfair to Professor Williams. He ought to have had him a fulltime, enthusiastic philosophy teacher, who never thought of anything else. But there I was, and he was very patient with me. He still wanted me to head the thing . . . after he retired. And I began more and more to know deep down that I wasn't going to do it."[2]

The Greens' first child, Paul Eliot Jr., was born January 14, 1924. Soon afterward Green was approached by Dr. Joseph Hyde Pratt (who had been his commanding officer during the war) about buying some land for a house. Pratt owned a beautiful hillside between Franklin Street and Battle Park on the east side of town. The tract, which was situated in a glen, was difficult to get to, with access by a single lane at a very steep angle, and not easy to build on, but there

Erma Green at Paul and Elizabeth Green's wedding, July 6, 1922.

was an unusually pretty, mountain-like view from it. Green recalled his response to Pratt's offer to sell him the land: "I said, 'Col. Pratt, I don't have a cent of money. . . .' He said, 'That's all right. You can just give me some notes. . . . ' Well, I couldn't say no. He sort of insisted. So I signed these several $500 notes. . . . Then Dr. Lay said he would lend us $3,500 to build a little house, so we borrowed from him. . . . One of these lots I sold to him [when] he retired."[3] For that sum they were able to construct a home with three rooms downstairs and two upstairs, equipped with an Arcola hot-water heating system.

One winter, while the Greens were visiting with Paul's family in Harnett County, the temperature dropped to freezing. Leaving his wife and child, Paul rushed back to Chapel Hill to check on his heating system. It had already burst and had flooded the downstairs.

Caro Mae Green at Paul and Elizabeth Green's wedding, July 6, 1922.

During the next few days he got plumbers to begin repairs, and while they worked so did he: "I went upstairs and sat at the typewriter just to try to forget it, and I wrote two days and nights solid on a play. . . . About the second night, about three o'clock in the morning, I heard bees in the house. I said, 'Where in the world did these bees come from?' I searched all around and I couldn't find any bees, and then all of a sudden I realized they were in my head. . . . I nearly fainted. It was that war stuff."[4] Green telephoned a physician friend at that very inconvenient hour. The man asked him what he had been doing. When he described the past few days, the doctor told him he needed to get some rest.

In early 1924 the *Atlantic Monthly* accepted Green's story "The Devil's Instrument," the one he had written while playing baseball at

Lillington. The magazine sent him a check for $125, the equivalent of about two bales of cotton.[5] In March *Poet Lore* published his plays *The End of the Row* and *The Hot Iron*. In April the magazine *The Reviewer* of Richmond published his play *In Aunt Mahaly's Cabin*. In June *Poet Lore* published the play *The Prayer Meeting*.[6] Later, Barrett H. Clark called *The Prayer Meeting* "the first successful attempt to introduce into our theatre the full-blooded negro, the healthy animal, neither a downright villain nor a dreamy Uncle Tom's Cabin sort of sentimentalist."[7] Such a statement was not considered patronizing in that day.

Green sent *The No 'Count Boy* to *Theatre Arts Monthly*. Edith Isaacs, the editor, wrote him an encouraging letter, saying she would like to publish it but that the Negro dialect was so terrible they could hardly read it. He clarified it a little by putting in some final *g*'s and *t*'s, and it appeared in the November 1924 issue.[8] Soon it was produced by an amateur group in Chicago known as the Studio Players. In writing this play, Green had remembered Wesley Armstrong, the harmonica-playing boy who had worked on the family farm, and he made the male lead a happy-go-lucky young man who wanted the girl to run away with him. A part of the young man's charm was his harmonica and the songs Green remembered from Wesley.[9]

That year Erma Green, Paul's sister, was taking playwriting under Frederick Koch. She asked Paul if he could suggest some subject matter for her. He gave her a long poem he had written while at Cornell about a farmer who loved land and his wife who loved "fixin's." She wrote her play, but a typed copy had to be ready by a certain deadline. Then she was hospitalized and asked Paul to type it for her. In the process of copying it, he could not resist using his creative skills. The finished product was substantially changed, emerging as *Fixin's, the Tragedy of a Tenant Farm Woman*. Koch accepted it as the joint work of Erma and Paul Green and published it in his second volume of *Carolina Folk-Plays*.[10]

The Carolina Playmakers took *Fixin's* on a tour of North Carolina and to Atlanta. A review published in the *Atlanta Constitution* said:

Never, it would seem, has any stage given us a more perfect gem than *Fixin's*. It gripped the onlooker until the walls of the theater melted into mist and we lived in the bare shack the Carolina tenant farmer called his home, and we felt our hearts wrung with the tragedy of the life. . . . True folk plays of America, holding, in addition to their present delight, the promise of marvelous things to come. . . . Can't somebody start something like this in Georgia?[11]

The play has been widely produced and has frequently been referred to as a Paul Green play with no credit to Erma. She later contended that she was no playwright and made no effort in that field after leaving Koch's class.[12] Her sister Caro Mae, likewise enrolled in the class, wrote a play called *Jumping the Broom*, which Samuel French published as part of a collection in 1929.[13]

In 1924 Emily Clark wrote to Green from Richmond, saying that she wanted to give up publishing *The Reviewer*, which she had founded four years earlier. (She had recently married, and this may have had something to do with her decision.) She asked if Green would be interested in bringing the magazine to Chapel Hill and editing it.[14] *The Reviewer* was an interesting project. In her first issue, Clark had cited H. L. Mencken's essay "Sahara of the Bozart" and admitted that the South was something of a cultural desert. Mencken was delighted and began to refer writers such as Gerald W. Johnson, Ellen Glasgow, and Frances Newman to her. Soon he wrote another piece, "Violets in the Sahara," and when he came to Richmond and met Emily Clark, it was the beginning of a lasting friendship.

Green was excited about possibilities for *The Reviewer*. He had been interested in "watering the Sahara" for a long time.[15] He mentioned the matter to a friend, Robert Pickens, a man of some financial means, and, at Pickens's suggestion, they drove to Richmond to confer with Emily Clark. Pickens agreed to back the project financially, and the arrangements were made to move the publication to Chapel Hill.

The first issue was published under Green's editing in January 1925, with high expectations. In an article titled "A Plain Statement about Southern Literature," Green wrote: "I am not declaring for a complete renunciation of the past in Southern letters, but rather for truer and fresher interpretation of our environment and our relations to that environment; for a rejuvenation of our spiritual instincts so long dead to curiosity and wonder; for a food to feed upon different from the sweetened wind and other cotton-candy stuff dished out by our party leaders and preachers and windy gullibles."[16] These were brave words in a year when the university had had to fight off the anti-evolution forces in the legislature in Raleigh to keep its academic freedom.

After three issues had been published, Pickens was no longer able to continue his support. Green got the University of North Carolina Press to underwrite the project by paying off the accumulated debts and publishing the October issue. Soon, however, it was decided that the press was not equipped to handle a publication of that character. Arrangements were made to merge the magazine with the *Southwest Review* in Texas.[17]

At about the same time, Paul and Elizabeth Green were contributing to "The Literary Lantern," which billed itself as "a weekly column of notes on literature in the South, appearing in leading Southern newspapers." The column had been created by others, but it soon became "a Green family enterprise." Elizabeth was editor for several years, then turned it over to Prof. Phillips Russell, Caro Mae Green's husband. Later Caro Mae herself edited the column until 1945.[18]

In the spring of 1925 the Dallas Little Theatre entered Green's *The No 'Count Boy* in a New York competition for the Belasco Cup and won. Green wrote in *Drama and the Weather* that "a few days later I had a wire from Henry Holt offering me a contract for a book of one-act pieces, with a sizable financial advance. And the birds sang to me from every bush on the campus as I walked home in the evening. I had had a play done on Broadway. True, a short play but still done on Broadway."[19]

Green rushed down to see Koch and tell him the good news about the book offer. Green recalled that Koch "looked at me and said, 'Well, that's nice, Paul, but of course you can't do it.' I said, 'Why not, Proff?' He said, 'Because they don't belong to you. They belong to the Playmakers. . . . In fact,' he said, 'I have in mind getting out some volumes myself.'"[20] Koch had required participants in the Playmakers project to assign their writings to the organization. The same Henry Holt had published two volumes of *Carolina Folk-Plays* for Koch. In response to Koch's remarks, Green almost exploded. I went home and told Elizabeth he was the damned most selfish man I'd ever seen in my life. . . . The next morning I came up there and I said, "Proff." [He said,] "How're you doing, boy?" I said, "I'm going to publish these plays." He said, "You can't do that." I said, "The heck I can't. I'm going to do it. . . . " He looked at me and [he was] so hurt. I said, "Proff, you're wonderful at inspiring young people. Here you have a chance to inspire me, but you want to put the clamps on me. I want to publish my volume, *by me*, and you know that's right. It's not right for you to own these plays." He looked at me, said, "I wouldn't have thought it." I said, "Too bad," and out I went—slammed the door. And next morning I came up and passed Proff, and he turned and said, "Hi, Paul." I said, "Hi, Proff," He said, "Put 'er there boy." Says, "You're right. You're right. Go to it." Slapped me on the back. I could've hugged him. Maybe I did.[21]

The volume was published in the fall of 1925 as *The Lord's Will and Other Carolina Plays*, with a foreword by Koch. (In 1928 another book of Green's plays, *In the Valley and Other Carolina Plays*, was dedicated to Koch.) Barrett H. Clark, literary editor for the publisher/agent Samuel French, "was always looking for plays, and we had some kind of a drama meeting down here and he came along with [drama critic J.] Brooks Atkinson and others. So Barrett got interested and he asked if I didn't have other one-act plays. So, I turned some over to him and he wrote me one day and said he had a publisher for this first volume."[22]

Some of Green's work was also produced in groups of one-act plays at the off-Broadway Cherry Lane Theatre in New York City, but the critics said, in effect, "'Well, this fellow Green, he's a folk playwright and he can only write one-act plays.' So, I decided to try my hand on a long play and see if I could do it."[23] He rewrote two of his one-act plays and connected them with a new section. The result was *In Abraham's Bosom*.[24] Green explained the title:

I always liked that phrase in the Bible where Lazarus ate at the rich man's table and later the rich man was condemned to hell and Lazarus was "in Abraham's bosom." He was safe, and the old rich man down in hell, he looked and called for a drop of water and Lazarus wouldn't give him any, [for] at the rich man's table Lazarus had eaten the crumbs with the dogs. You know the Bible story. That Bible, you know, it'll ruin you; it was vengeful, the Old Testament. So I loved the phrase and then I named the fellow Abraham and suggested that his trouble was in his own bosom and that's true, I guess, because he had a high temper in the play. . . . [Also,] his ambitions outran his possibilities.[25]

—That is, the possibilities allowed him in a white-supremacist society. Near the same time, Green completed another full-length play, *The Field God*. He sent both to Barrett Clark, and Clark sent them "to every producer who might conceivably have been able to use them."[26]

On February 25, 1926, the Greens' second child was due. After the prospective father left for classes, Elizabeth's labor pains began. Her sister-in-law Caro Mae called Dr. Eric Abernathy at the college infirmary. Dr. Abernathy said he would drive over and pick them up. Since the tiny road down to the house in the glen was very muddy, the two women decided to walk to the top of the hill and meet the physician. Dr. Abernathy arrived, and they got in his car. A mile down the road the baby was born. Child and mother were quickly transferred from the automobile to the porch of one James Turrentine. Caro Mae told the woman of the house, "'A lady is having a baby out on your porch,'" whereupon "Mrs. Turrentine went and got a clean sheet in which [the doctor] wrapped the baby." In the meantime, Green had taught his classes and gone by to visit Horace Williams. Someone finally found him and said, "The whole town is out looking for you." They named the new baby Nancy Byrd.[27]

In May 1926, the plays Barrett Clark had taken to New York were published as *Lonesome Road: Six Plays for the Negro Theatre*. The volume included an introduction written by Clark, who said:

I feel that [Green's] greatest gifts are his instinctive talent for seizing upon a dramatic situation, his poetic imagination, and his intuitive knowledge of character. I believe that poetic imagination is what our theatre stands most in need of. We have skilled technicians a-plenty, and in O'Neill a great artist of many aspects. But as yet we have no genuine folk dramatist besides Paul Green. If he were at this moment to cease writing he would be entitled to a place of honor in the development of the American drama.[28]

Clark told of sending Green's plays to producers and said, "It was to be expected that such poignant and heart-breaking tragedies as . . . *In Abraham's Bosom* should frighten the average producer; and, after all, it does take time for any original dramatist to reach Broadway. But this is a detail, and sooner or later Mr. Green's plays will be produced professionally."[29] It was the beginning of a long friendship between

Clark and Green, the first close friendship Green had had with a Jew. Green called Clark "the greatest friend I ever had."[30]

The publisher had offered to bring out the volume of plays if Green would also give them "a volume of fiction. Well, I wanted to get them published, so I said, that's fine. I'll write some stories. Later on I sent them a volume of . . . stories. I got a letter that said, 'We like the stories and are willing to publish them. We can get them published in Europe, but we won't expect to make anything out of stories—they don't sell much. . . . Give us a novel.'"[31] It was as a result of this exchange that Green first began to consider writing a long work of fiction.

NOTES

1. Quoted from the author's interview with Caro Mae Green Russell, October 2, 1976, James R. Spence audio recordings relating to Paul Green, 1974-1979 (collection #5170), Southern Historical Collection,Wilson Library, University of North Carolina at Chapel Hill.

2. Paul Green, interview by Billy E. Barnes, May 1975, p. 15, Southern Oral History Program Collection, Southern Historical Collection (hereafter cited as Barnes interview, with appropriate date and transcript page number).

3. Paul Green, interview by James R. Spence, August 9, 1979, James R. Spence audio recordings relating to Paul Green, 1974-1979 (collection #5170), Southern Historical Collection (hereafter cited as Spence interview, with appropriate date).

4. Ibid.

5. Paul Green, "The Devil's Instrument," *Atlantic Monthly* 134 (July 1924): 81-92. Green later included this story in his short story collections *Wide Fields* (New York: R. M. McBride and Company, 1928) and *"Salvation on a String" and Other Tales of the South* (New York: Harper, 1946).

6. *End of the Row, The Hot Iron,* and *The Prayer Meeting,* the latter a revision of *Granny Boling* (previously mentioned in chapter 13), are all collected in Green's *Lonesome Road: Six Plays for the Negro Theatre* (New York: R. M. McBride and Company, 1926), and *Aunt Mahaly's Cabin* (without *In* in the title) appears in his *In the Valley and Other Carolina Plays* (New York: Samuel French, 1928).

7. Barrett H. Clark, *Paul Green* (New York: R. M. McBride and Company, 1928), 12.

8. Green later included this play in his collection *The Lord's Will and Other Carolina Plays* (New York: H. Holt and Company, 1925).

9. Spence interview, August 9, 1979.

10. New York: H. Holt, 1924. Thomas Wolfe's play *The Return of Buck Gavin* likewise appeared in this volume.

11. Quoted in Samuel Selden, with Mary Tom Sphangos, *Frederick Henry Koch, Pioneer Playmaker: A Brief Biography,* University of North Carolina Library Extension Publications, vol. 19, No. 4 (Chapel Hill: University of North Carolina Library, July 1954), 18.

12. Erma Green Gold, interview by James R. Spence, October 2, 1976.

13. *One-Act Plays for Stage and Study,* fifth series (New York: Samuel French, 1929).

14. Green talked about his involvement with *The Reviewer* during his August 9, 1979, interview with the author. See also Agatha Boyd Adams, *Paul Green of Chapel Hill*, University of North Carolina Library Extension Publications, vol. 16, No. 2 (Chapel Hill: University of North Carolina Library, January 1951), 25-28.

15. Spence and Green were talking about Green's work on *The Reviewer* when Spence used the phrase "watering the Sahara" to describe Green's promotion of southern writers. Spence interview, August 9, 1979. The phrase came up again when Green talked about the southern writers conference he was involved in planning (discussed in chapter 18).

16. Quoted in Adams, *Paul Green of Chapel Hill*, 27.

17. Louis R. Wilson, *The University of North Carolina, 1900-1930: The Making of a Modern University* (Chapel Hill: University of North Carolina Press, 1957), 492.

18. Adams, *Paul Green of Chapel Hill*, 26.

19. Paul Green, *Drama and the Weather: Some Notes and Papers on Life and the Theatre* (New York: Samuel French, 1958), 6.

20. Spence interview, October 23, 1976.

21. Ibid.

22. Barnes interview, May 1975, p. 17.

23. Barnes interview, May 1975, p. 18.

24. The original one-act version of this play is collected in Green's *Lonesome Road: Six Plays for the Negro Theatre* (New York: R. M. McBride and Company, 1926).

25. Barnes interview, May 1975, p. 19.

26. Clark, *Paul Green*, 18.

27. Elizabeth Lay Green, *The Paul Green I Know* (Chapel Hill: North Caroliniana Society, 1978), 14.

28. Barrett H. Clark, introduction to *Lonesome Road*, xviii.

29. Clark, introduction to *Lonesome Road*, viii.

30. Spence interview, October 23, 1976.

31. Ibid.

16: The Pulitzer Prize

Paul Green was awarded a fellowship for the summer of 1926 to go to the MacDowell Colony for writers and composers in Peterborough, New Hampshire, where all ate breakfast in a common dining hall and then went out to isolated individual cabins to work. There was a lot of talent around during Green's tenure there, including Thornton Wilder, Frances Newman, Irita Van Doren, and Edwin Arlington Robinson. DuBose and Dorothy Heyward were there writing the script that later became the folk opera *Porgy*. Green pitched baseball with composer Roy Harris. He was not comfortable with the overall situation, however: "I found it very difficult to write, too. I would go to this cabin there in the woods all alone. I had been used to noise. . . . It seemed to me a sort of a pose. Why in the heck should a fellow trying to write . . . be off set up in a special kind of a thing like this? . . . Then, along about the noon hour, you would hear a little truck or something and a fellow would quietly put your lunch out. I thought, 'Oh, hell. I ought to be out there waiting on that guy rather than him on me.'"[1]

The opportunity to write free of such daily chores as preparing one's own lunch ended when Green received word that his father had died. He rushed home for the funeral. On the way home, he reviewed in his mind his relationship with his father: "When he died, the county papers had wonderful things to say about him. And people loved him. He was a great man, but you know how boys often are. I didn't know it until he was gone."[2] Green felt that he had been so "full of my own self" that he had never understood or enjoyed his father as he should have. He remembered that once when Billy Green had come to Chapel Hill to visit, his son had been so busy with his own affairs he had not been anxious to see his father. "I didn't want to see him. . . . Isn't that funny? . . . It was just terrible. Now it would be all different. . . . I was so full of my own self then."[3]

In turn, Paul Green recalled that when he was a youth, his father "never played with us. . . . I was just crazy about baseball. We'd come out of the field and I'd try to get Hugh during the noon hour and say, 'Let's catch some.' My father would say, 'What's the matter with you? Why can't you rest?'" Similarly, Paul and Hugh would want to participate in a neighborhood baseball game on Saturday afternoon, and their "father would say, 'Well, you boys can get off if you'll pick 200 pounds of cotton before you go.' We'd get up before day and go down there and pick cotton, wet as rats. Then get off to play."[4] Green added that his father's lack of interest in education left him "closer" to his mother.[5] In later years Green expressed his "wish that I had done a little more to establish communion with my father and brothers than I did, but youth sets patterns of selfishness. . . . A difference was felt on both sides . . . the more that I went away."[6]

The funeral service for Billy Green was held on the porch of the Green farmhouse, with James Archibald Campbell, president of Buies Creek Academy, officiating.[7] When Campbell finished speaking, Paul raised a hand and asked for a few moments. His sister Caro Mae later remembered the moment and her embarrassment. She said that Paul was highly emotional, "but then, we all were," she added.[8] Paul recalled that he "was very nervous and excited. Mr. Campbell made it all seem so un-tragic. So I burst out. Later on I thought, 'Now why did I do that?'"[9] There is no record of exactly what he said. Some remembered that he spoke of his father as a man who liked to plant and then watch things grow. Perhaps he was trying to articulate the idea that his father had his own form of art. Caro Mae remembered that he said his father was one of the greatest men he had ever known.[10] Some of Paul's remarks struck some of the listeners as heretical, however, and word spread through the community that the listener could tell that Paul didn't believe in the hereafter.

The death of his father marked a turning point in Paul Green's life. The big commercial producers of Broadway still ignored the young playwright's work, but Barrett Clark had acquaintances connected with the Provincetown Playhouse, an organization that operated in Greenwich Village. It had moved from Massachusetts in 1917 and had made its place in the world of theater by setting high standards and refusing to bow to commercial tastes. It had already introduced Eugene O'Neill, Helen Hayes, and Katherine Cornell. It would soon give experience to young Bette Davis. In 1926 it was operated by the joint management of Robert Edmond Jones, Kenneth Macgowan, and Eugene O'Neill.[11]

At Clark's prodding, the group agreed to produce *In Abraham's Bosom*. Clark also found an unknown producer, Edgar Wolf, who was willing to put on *The Field God*. Green believed that Wolf may have just "wanted to star his [Wolf's] wife," but he was not complaining, since "both the plays were produced that season in New York." In conversation with Green, the producer learned that the playwright had in mind a set very much like his homeplace in Harnett County. So Wolf decided to go down and look at the farmhouse, with Green as his guide. As they drove back after the visit, Wolf was silent for a while and then said, "You love that land, don't you?" Green said that he did, and Wolf responded, "To me it was the most desolate, godforsaken part of the earth I've ever seen."[12]

When Green learned that the Provincetown Players were going to perform *In Abraham's Bosom*, "I said, 'I want one man to play the lead, Paul Robeson.' . . . We got Paul Robeson to come down to the theater, and we had a reading. . . . I'd never seen him before. . . . He listened, and he got up and walked out. He said, 'I think you have a good play from some points of view, but I could never act in it. . . . You have a scene in there where Abraham is beaten by a white man. . . . I could never play that part.'"[13]

In Abraham's Bosom is a play about racial injustice. Its title character is a black man who wants to raise himself and others of his race by becoming literate and setting up a school for black children. He is held down by whites who want to "keep him in his place," until he explodes in violence. In writing his play, Green was thinking of, among others, the black schoolteacher he had seen as a boy at the railway station in Angier, struck in the face but unable to strike back. His genuine indignation from that experience came through in the play.

The play opened December 30, 1926. At first the reviews were unenthusiastic, and many major reviewers did not bother to leave

Broadway to go down to Greenwich Village to see it. On January 11,
1927, Barrett Clark wrote Green that *Abraham* seemed to be doing
"nicely" and that Green's play *The Field God* was going into
production. A few days later he wrote again that Sidney Howard,
author of the screenplay of *Gone with the Wind*, wanted to meet Green.
On February 2 DuBose Heyward wrote to Green on hotel stationery:
"We are in New York for the first time since your play opened, and
have just seen it. I cannot refrain from writing you at once, and telling
you what a big thing we think you have done. We were simply bowled
over by it. You have created a tremendous and deeply moving
character in Abraham and my hat is off to you for your bravery as well
as your art."[14] Heyward clearly recognized Green's courage in writing
such a drama.

After six weeks *Abraham* was moved uptown to the Garrick
Theatre,[15] and *New York Times* reviewer Brooks Atkinson went to see
it. In a long review on the front page of the Sunday Drama-Music
section of the paper, he mentioned that "Negro plays are in the wind

A production of Paul Green's *In Abraham's Bosom*, staged at the Café Theatre of the Allens
Lane Art Center, Mt. Airy, Pennsylvania, in 1984.

just now" but that "[n]one of the other negro dramas speaks with the authority of *In Abraham's Bosom*. It comes not from a theatrical workshop but from the heart of the author." Atkinson said that Green's play "glows with the purging white flame of authentic tragic character study."[16]

Almost a half-century later Brooks Atkinson and Albert Hirschfeld wrote again about the play in their book *The Lively Years, 1920-1973*: "*In Abraham's Bosom* was the first play written by a white man who understood the intricacies of the life of the black people in the South. . . . The play had no predecessors."[17] Only a handful of writers, chiefly H. L. Mencken and Sinclair Lewis, were true critics of American society at that time. Most authors seemed quite happy with the country and its prosperity. Green, by building the character Abraham as the personification of all black Americans and showing the injustice inflicted upon him, was joining that small band of social critics.

The Field God began a trial run in Brooklyn during April, opened at the Greenwich Village Theatre, and was soon moved to the Cort Theatre.[18] It was also produced at the Gate Theatre in London during the 1927-1928 season. This play is a study of a man in conflict with the local narrow religion. He is the natural man who is tested, Job-like, against the "unnatural" religion. It was one of Green's favorite subjects. *The Field God* had a short run in Greenwich Village, but it was important to Green. Reviewer Joseph Wood Krutch, writing in *The Nation*, indicated that he had not cared for *Abraham* but that the second play served "definitely to raise [Green] out of the ranks of promising beginner and to make him a man to be watched."[19]

During rehearsals for the two plays, Green had been able to become better acquainted with the professional New York Theatre. He liked O'Neill's *The Emperor Jones* and the Jewish folk drama *The Dybbuk* but was "disappointed" in the other productions he saw. He explained: "Perhaps I was expecting too much from Broadway. I met a lot of theatre people and shared in a number of high-cackling cocktail parties, and I grew more and more unhappy. . . . I learned about the star system, unions, and contracts, and rents, and guilds, and agents' commissions. These I realized were necessary, but the lack seemed to me to be in the dramas themselves. Something I wanted wasn't there."[20]

Perhaps Green was filling that gap himself, for his own reputation was about to rise closer to the level of Eugene O'Neill's: on the first of May "I went over to the post office to get my mail, and . . . there was a letter from Columbia University" telling him he had been awarded the Pulitzer Prize in drama for *In Abraham's Bosom*.[21] The judges had selected Green's play over such other entries that year as Sidney Howard's *The Silver Cord*, Maxwell Anderson's *Saturday's Children*, and George Kelly's *Daisy Mayme*. Green's win was news. In North Carolina, a state that had never before produced a Pulitzer Prize winner, he took on a special status that he never lost. He remained one of the state's leading literary figures as long as he lived. Green's achievement also put the spotlight of publicity on Frederick Koch and the work he had been doing in building the Carolina Playmakers. Soon there were people in New York and other centers of culture who began to speak of the University of North Carolina as the most progressive state school in the South.

As for Green's criticism of North Carolina racial attitudes in *In Abraham's Bosom*, there were no significant repercussions. Citizens were apparently willing to accept (or overlook) words couched in art, spoken indirectly, that would have ended the career of any politician speaking them directly. As a follow-up to the Pulitzer Prize, drama critic Walter Prichard Eaton, writing in the *New York Times*, had high praise for Green, writing, "His plays may well become weapons for the liberalizing of the lives of his people."[22] The fact that Green escaped the wrath of the home folks did not mean they liked his theme, however. *In Abraham's Bosom* may be the only Pulitzer Prize play that has, to date, never been produced in any southern state, including the playwright's home state of North Carolina.

Green believed that he had received the award not for one play but for both his plays. Curiously, he did not go to New York for the ceremony. He explained, "I was sort of afraid of the occasion or something. . . . I guess that I felt that there was some sort of show-off about this thing. . . . It was some sort of a lack of pleasure in display."[23] Green responded similarly to the producers' wish to revive the play after it received the Pulitzer Prize, sending a telegram to Clark saying:

I wish to protest against it absolutely. Have thought of arguments against my attitude but still I feel that this capitalizing on a windfall is illegitimate and vulgar. Let Abraham rest with some dignity in his grave; there is a damnable cheapness about this sudden bestirring over the Pulitzer soup (the publicity, that is, not the prize itself). I will have nothing to do with it and wish you would do what you can to stop the movement.[24]

But Green's artistic rebellion against crass commercialization had not taken into account the other people involved. There were actors and stagehands who could have had a few more weeks of work. The Provincetown Players, by producing *The Emperor Jones* and *In Abraham's Bosom*, had opened up jobs on the serious stage for black artists. It was important that these opportunities not be closed. It was also important that the Provincetown Playhouse get all the revenue it could out of the play in order to recover its losses. It re-opened the play in Greenwich Village, ran it for six weeks, closed it, then opened it a third time at that location in the fall. The last run was very brief, but then the playhouse took it on two road tours.

The Pulitzer Prize brought new patrons of Green's work as well. For example, one day he received a check for $1,500 from Otto Kahn of New York with a note saying, "I have been following your work, and I would like to just send you a little something. Use it any way you please."[25] Kahn, Green learned, was head of the Wall Street firm of Kahn and Loeb and was a great patron of the arts. Financier then invited writer to visit him, and Green later recorded their meeting:

He had asked me to have lunch with him down at his palatial Wall Street office. And there while he ate his milk and mush, and I ate ham and eggs, he had talked encouragingly to me about the theatre. He was a fine sympathetic man and was always ready to help beginners in the arts, whatever the field. "Get out of North Carolina," he said, "get out and broaden yourself. Find new subject matter to write about. Folk things are all right, maybe, to begin with. But they're too narrow, too provincial. If you're going to be a real playwright, you must write about things that count."[26]

Green listened with interest and respect. Then Kahn took him on a tour of the New York Stock Exchange. Pointing to the frantic trading floor, Kahn said, "Mad. We're mad in America, and some day we are going to pay for it."[27]

In the spring of 1928 Robert M. McBride and Company published Green's book of short stories *Wide Fields*. The volume was based on material from Harnett County, which Green called fictionally the

"Little Bethel Community." There was Tim Messer, the fiddler, wrestling with the question of the morality of his dancing music, burying and then digging up "The Devil's Instrument" (the story he'd written in the Caviness Hotel while playing baseball in Lillington and later published in the *Atlantic Monthly*). In "Cornshucking" there was the yellow-haired girl (the one he had loved until she became pregnant by another man). There was black Arth Loring in "The Lost Ford," saving his money until he could buy a car and then having it stolen while he was at church (never to be recovered). And, of course, there were dozens of other characters, all familiar, all close to the land. Green considered the book the beginning of an epic about the people of his home area. A short time later, Samuel French published *In the Valley and Other Carolina Plays*, a collection of Green's one-act plays.

Green's Pulitzer may have opened doors for other writers. Brooks Atkinson has noted that during the fall following Green's award, *Porgy and Bess*, a folk opera by George Gershwin based on DuBose and Dorothy Heyward's *Porgy*, appeared on Broadway.[28] Not surprisingly, given their similar subjects for art, when the Heywards went to Chapel Hill for DuBose to receive an honorary doctorate at commencement that spring, it was arranged for them to meet the Greens one night at the home of a mutual friend. Green read some of his Little Bethel sketches for the assembled group, and Heyward read some of his poetry. The co-creator of *Porgy* gave an account of the Charleston goat driver who was the model for his character. While Heyward was tracing the man, an old woman told him that "Porgy" had shot his wife for the third time, the last time because she stole his wristwatch, and that he had died while in jail. Green wrote of Heyward, "Lack of humanity and warmth, something conscious and over-comradely about him. Still he's an artist and I fear I'm not."[29]

While the graduation ceremonies were going on the following day, Green worked in his office and set down some of his thoughts:

During the last few months I've thought of nothing but teaching. . . . How exciting it has all been. Nerve exacting for me. Sometimes in class after a sleepless night I have been frightened at the eager inspiring faces before me and have had to turn and look away through the window to get a grip on myself. For how could I answer them? What peace does it do then to tell them that the existence of God can be either proved or disproved. . . . What intellectual prayer meetings we have held in my office. And my helplessness. . . . And yet something I hope to have waked. Maybe a zest for life, a sharper appreciation, sensitiveness, bravery to play the play out.[30]

He explored some of his own ideas about religion:

When I would go to get the beauty of the music and ritual in the church, to give myself up to the sonorous adumbrations of the mighty and shadowy past and the fitful destiny of man, the loud-mouthed illogicality of the preacher mars all, mars all until after a conscious struggle and tension I draw away as it were and view him also as a piece in a play, even a puppet. But so often this puppet plays his part so badly . . . outraging every decency of honest intelligence. I must come away with the total effect of this show sprayed out, scattered. Thus the Eastern church of high ritualism which throws away logic and accepts a convention du theatre at the start is the essential Church. Give me either Boehme, St. Francis, or the philosophical religions of Confucius and Buddha. These present sects of Baptists, Presbyterians, Methodists which straddle two diverging roads, carrying along a cafeteria and swimming pool . . . seem to me not in the most heavenly way.[31]

Green knew there was no single answer, however: "But even as I write I remember the holy ecstatic face of my Aunt Nannie Spence at a Methodist revival, and the revival is part of the Methodist institution and that miraculous certainty and peace of Aunt Nannie a part of that."[32]

The day after commencement Green went to Raleigh to attend the state Democratic convention "and made some notes on a very live theatrical presentation of examplized [sic] popular government." The windy oratory was not to his taste, but the humanity of the situation appealed to his instincts as a writer: "Reporters at table writing it all down and smiling at it. Uproar and turmoil. Drunken fellow at right with a sweet-faced wife calling attention of those around him, 'Look here boys, ain't I got a sweet wife'—Heat, sweat. . . . 3000 fans winking back and forth. Judge F. D. W. walking about on the rostrum drunk and trying to testify unto Democracy. Cries of 'Set down, set down, you old fool!' Entrance of carnation-holed Senator Overman, with his, as always, empty dignity."[33]

Green also seems to have been inspired to work on his folklore project, for after the convention he took a trip down the Cape Fear valley all the way to Southport, stopping to talk with people, poking around old houses looking for abandoned papers, visiting old plantations, and listening to the banter of Negroes on the waterfront.[34] Back in Chapel Hill, though, he let Elizabeth work on assembling folk material while he struggled with a new play, *The House of Connelly*: "Can't get it to come right. Patsy should die at end—error in judgment and in deed aesthetically demands it." The next day he recorded: "Same—and no sleep. Fool!"[35]

In the latter part of June, Green finished the preface to an anthology of one-act plays that was to be published by Samuel French that fall—"for which comes a good $100. High price at that."[36] In the preface he vented some of his frustrations about the theater: "My theatre for the present is the published play. Five or six years ago I could think of nothing more alluring than the chance to have one's fill of seeing plays."[37] But he was disappointed. He found "the New York stage" to be

an industry and not an art . . . a business run to the pattern of supply and demand, with its standards of excellence derived from the general want of the buyers. He had been "behind the scenes," he said, where he "saw fights and quarrellings of peevish stars as to the size of their names in electric lights, jealousies and backbiting, listened to 'how will that go,' the 'what will she gross,' and 'they won't stand for that,' saw publicity and its methods, read facts and figures on salaries, rents, contracts, censorship and equity, investments, overhead, receipts, the box-office."[38]

Then he had been told that what he was looking for was not on Broadway but in the independent theater, the "New Theatre." He went to the independents and saw a lot of innovations, but he was not impressed by the elaborate props, for "why should the poor taxpayers give you a million dollars for that when it can be done so much better by reading the book, or by using the simple properties of children's games or the Chinese and Elizabethan theatres? Have not all the novels and poems and stories proved how superior is the mind's eye?" His idea of a New Theatre was "the theatre of imagination, of lofty common sense," which he had not yet found—"And so for the present I prefer books to footlights."[39]

Returning to the folklore project, Paul and Elizabeth went through the material they had gathered and began writing:

Gathered for the twenty-first anniversary of the Carolina Playmakers, 1940, are (*left to right*) DuBose Heyward, Clifford Odets, Paul Green, Frederick Koch, Barrett Clark.

We had this book divided [into] folk cures, folk religion, . . . folk medicine. And so, in the chapter on folk religion, that is, a religion that was a folk custom and had the . . . suspicion of scientific disbelief. . . . The whole thing was folk, the whole thing, in other words, a superstition. And all this idea of Jesus being able to be washed in his red blood and turning out white as snow, I put it down as a folk belief. And all this idea of you going to heaven and being happy there and purified forever more, it was a folk image. The same [for] hell.[40]

So Green went to see Dr. Howard W. Odum, head of the sociology department and a friend of the Greens, and shared his theory with the

Methodist deacon. He asked Odum, who had applied for a Rockefeller Foundation fellowship for this project, "Are you going to subsidize a fellow that's going to show—or intend[s] to show—that your beliefs are also part of the . . . folk superstition?"[41] Odum was saved by the fact that the Greens were unable to complete their work before going to Europe: "The book was never finished. The manuscript's up there [in the library], four or five hundred pages."[42]

NOTES

1. Paul Green, interview by Billy E. Barnes, March 1975, pp. 17-18, Southern Oral History Program Collection, Southern Historical Collection, Wilson Library, University of North Carolina at Chapel Hill (hereafter cited as Barnes interview, with appropriate date and transcript page number).

2. Barnes interview, March 5, 1975, pp. 15-16.

3. Paul Green, interview by Rhoda Wynn, February 1974, tape 7, p. 25, Southern Oral History Program Collection, Southern Historical Collection (hereafter cited as Wynn interview, with appropriate tape and transcript page number).

4. Paul Green, interview by James R. Spence, May 6, 1976, James R. Spence audio recordings relating to Paul Green, 1974-1979 (collection #5170), Southern Historical Collection (hereafter cited as Spence interview, with appropriate date).

5. During a subsequent interview, Green again talked with the author about this subject. Spence interview, October 24, 1976.

6. Barnes interview, May 1975, p. 56. During this same discussion, Green did say, however, that "I never felt it with my sister Mary. She was a sort of a mother."

7. It is not entirely clear why the funeral was not held at Pleasant Union Church. Family members say that Billy Green was not active in church during the last several years of his life, but there is no indication that he had withdrawn his membership. See the author's interview with Caro Mae Green Russell, October 2, 1976, James R. Spence audio recordings relating to Paul Green, 1974-1979 (collection #5170), Southern Historical Collection (hereafter cited as Caro Mae Green Russell interview). Buies Creek Academy changed its name to Campbell College in 1927. William S. Powell, *Higher Education in North Carolina* (Raleigh: State Department of Archives and History, 1964), 15.

8. Caro Mae Green Russell interview.

9. Spence interview, May 6, 1976.

10. Caro Mae Green Russell interview.

11. Samuel Selden, with Mary Tom Sphangos, *Frederick Henry Koch, Pioneer Playmaker: A Brief Biography*, University of North Carolina Library Extension Publications, vol. 19, No. 4 (Chapel Hill: University of North Carolina Library, July 1954), 29.

12. Wynn interview, tape 3, p. 12, tape 7, p. 10.

13. Spence interview, May 6, 1976.

14. The two letters from Barrett Clark, dated January 11 and 14, 1927, are in the Paul Green Papers (collection #3693, folder 84F), Southern Historical Collection, as is the letter from Heyward, dated February 2, 1927 (folder 86H).

15. See Burns Mantle, *Best Plays of 1926-27* (New York: Dodd, Mead, 1927), 325-326, and Agatha Boyd Adams, *Paul Green of Chapel Hill*, University of North Carolina Library

Extension Publications, vol. 16, No. 2 (Chapel Hill: University of North Carolina Library, January 1951), 34.

16. "Folk Drama from the South," *New York Times*, February 20, 1927.

17. Brooks Atkinson and Albert Hirschfeld, *The Lively Years, 1920-1973* (New York: Association Press, 1973), 51.

18. Adams, *Paul Green of Chapel Hill*, 37.

19. "Drama: A Folk-Tragedy," *Nation* 4 (May 1927): 510.

20. Paul Green, *Drama and the Weather: Some Notes and Papers on Life and the Theatre* (New York: Samuel French, 1958), 6-7.

21. Wynn interview, tape 12, p. 53.

22. "Charting the American Drama's Drift," *New York Times*, February 19, 1928.

23. Barnes interview, May 1975, p. 20.

24. Quoted in Adams, *Paul Green of Chapel Hill*, 37.

25. Barnes interview, May 1975, p. 34.

26. Green, *Drama and the Weather*, 15-16.

27. Barnes interview, May 1975, p. 35.

28. Brooks Atkinson, *Broadway* (New York: Macmillan, rev. ed., 1970), 250.

29. Paul Green Diary, June 10, 1928, Paul Green Papers (collection #3693), Southern Historical Collection (hereafter cited as Diary, with entry date).

30. Diary, June 11, 1928.

31. Ibid.

32. Ibid.

33. Diary, June 12, 1928.

34. Diary, June 15, 1928.

35. Diary, June 17, 18, 1928. *The House of Connelly* eventually appeared in Green's collection *The House of Connelly and Other Plays* (New York: Samuel French, 1931).

36. Diary, June 25-26, 1928.

37. Paul Green, "The New Theatre," preface to *One-Act Plays for Stage and Study*, fourth series (New York: Samuel French, 1928), vii.

38. Ibid.

39. Green, "The New Theatre," x, xii.

40. Wynn interview, tape 9, pp. 4-5.

41. Wynn interview, tape 9, p. 5.

42. Wynn interview, tape 9, p. 6. Folder 4496 in box 118 of the subseries 5.8 of the Green Papers contains numerous loose-leaf notes on superstitions, in various handwritings, and a typescript on "The Frank C. Brown Collection of Folklore: Its Organization, Classification, and Publication" for the Gen Lit Group of the MLA, NY, Dec 28 1944. But altogether there are not "four to five hundred" pages; the editor is not certain as to which manuscript Green is referring here.

17: The Guggenheim Fellowship

In March 1928 Paul Green received the news that he had been awarded a Guggenheim Fellowship, so on August 11, 1928, the Green family left Chapel Hill for Germany. "Off babies, baggage, books and all to N.Y. Nancy Byrd with fever of 104, vomiting. We two forlorn parents live like fools."[1]

The Greens stopped off in New York, where Paul conferred with Barrett Clark and the people at the Samuel French publishing house. "Let them exploit me if they wish," he wrote that night. "They are business men and at best I'm not much of a commodity. Barrett H. Clark though is the best friend a man ever had."[2] Whether he felt exploited or not, Green was willing to accept money (and did) from French and McBride because he doubted that the fellowship money was adequate. Green also met with Jimmy Light of the Provincetown Players about his plans for *Tread the Green Grass*, another play he had finished that summer.[3]

The Green family then crossed the Atlantic aboard the ship *Westphalia*, arriving at Hamburg on August 29 after a thirteen-day voyage. They took a train to Berlin and began searching for a house or an apartment: "Everything expensive, everything crowded."[4] They settled for a flat near Tempelhof Airport in Berlin. A newspaper reporter came to do an article about Green, and an artist to do a cartoon of him, both of which appeared in the *Berliner Zeitung*.[5] Green described his observations upon arrival: "When Elizabeth and I got there in 1928, the refugees that had flocked into Germany were all outside the edge of the city, living in wooden boxes, living in everything.

The city was disorganized. Inflation was rampant; jobs were few. . . . Everywhere, for the Jewish people, their times were great. They were buying up apartment houses, international banking. . . . It was just normal. . . . The Jewish people made more money."[6] He added to his observation about Jewish affluence, "When we were in Berlin, everything was Jewish: the university professors, all the psychiatric stuff was Jewish. The big department stores were Jewish. The drama and music [and] theater, and practically all our friends, were Jewish."[7]

According to Elizabeth Lay Green, she and her husband took different approaches to dealing with the language. She went out into the grocery stores and shops and got what the family needed by signs and expression, picking up words along the way. Paul, she later reported, "studied his grammar very hard" and did not speak unless he was sure he was correct. He did not like to "make a fool of himself." He trained himself to understand German, but he spoke infrequently.[8]

The Greens placed their children in school "at some church place. Cheap and somewhat pitiful from the looks of the poor children." Green wrote in his diary of exploring the city: "Uncommonly ugly. . . . What public buildings, what taste! What shapeless women and men! As far as the women are concerned one cannot tell whether it's beer or babies."[9]

One day Paul took Elizabeth and the children to Tempelhof Field to watch the airplanes. "We were so intrigued with this new form of travel . . . planes that came in from Moscow, from Rome, and were setting off into Norway. Passenger planes were really active, whereas in our country we were hardly started at all. . . . We just used to stand there by the hour and watch these planes land and wonder whether they would make it or not make it. . . . It was one way also to amuse the children."[10] On another occasion the Greens went to an air show at Tempelhof Field. "What a thrill," Green wrote in his diary, "the great world of daring. What is a dealer in words? Nothing. Action, daring the infinite of space and unforeseen change—autogyro the Bremen of Hunefield and the others, Lindbergh, Chamberlain, Byrd, the great world and the absolute thrill! Walked ten miles back and through the town, home weary and to sleep!" The following day he was in bed with a bad cold but then went to the air show again "to stand in the

Roanoke Island, 1938. Shown in front are Betsy and Janet Green; in the back (*left to right*) are Anna Lay (Elizabeth's mother), Byrd Green, Elizabeth Lay Green, Paul Green, and Dorothy ("Dottie") McBrayer Stahl.

cold and rain to see the planes take off—Paris, Prague, London, Dresden . . . Moscow."[11]

He and Elizabeth also amused themselves at the theater. Years later he wrote:

I went to many plays at different theatres. . . . Three opera houses were running, and I saw much opera, too. And there were playwrights everywhere—192 practicing professional ones in Germany at that time—according to a literary yearbook I read. And actors, singers, designers, and technicians were everywhere too. The plays ranged from Tolstoy's *The Living Corpse* to *Abie's Irish Rose*, and there was much emphasis on homosexual and neurotic themes in between. For all its activity, I found the German theatre a pretty sick one.[12]

The Greens were invited to the home of Herr Julius Bab, a leading theatre critic of the country and a lecturer on the theater who could command large audiences in Zurich, Vienna, and Prague. His wife was as involved in her husband's work as Elizabeth Green was in Paul's. Elizabeth Loos-Bab (this was the name she used on her stationery) was proficient in English, but her husband spoke only

German. "A quiet heavy man," Green wrote of Bab, "who showed in all his quietness that his work is about all that interests him. He continually pulled things from different places to show you even while conversation was at its height. He rates Shaw (as his book shows) as a more important person than I can conceive him to be—I for one."[13] Elizabeth Loos-Bab immediately took an interest in Green's work and was soon translating some of his plays into German.[14] Green read a lot of Joseph Conrad, wrote outlines for stories and plays, wrote letters, and studied German. He found a copy of *Ulysses* and began to read it.

Patron of the arts and philanthropist Otto Kahn came to Germany:

Somebody gave a big dinner for him. And he heard that I was in Berlin, and he suggested that they invite me to come to dinner. . . . I had a little money, and I bought a tuxedo. . . . They had all the opera singers and the stars. [German theater director] Erwin Piscator was there, the editor of *New Rundschan* was there, also the bigwigs. I was embarrassed [because] everybody was dressed to kill, with white tie and tails. I had my black tie on, and I felt so out of place; and then when the guest of honor showed up, Otto Kahn, he had a black tie and was dressed like me, so I recovered. . . .

Berlin . . . was riddled with suspicion and inflation and disappointment. In the evening a fight broke out among these people, these great stars. . . . They all got drunk and they called one of them a spy, and it was a free-for-all. The suspicion. So, I made for my coat in the hall, and there was Otto Kahn, and he said, "Green, this is no place for you and me, good Americans." . . . The next day it was in the *Berlin Tageblatt* about this furor.[15]

Paul and Elizabeth went to see a production by the Moscow Jewish Academy Theatre, which Alexis Granowsky, its director, had brought to Berlin. Years later Green wrote:

I went again and again, and I decided that if I had seen nothing else in Europe, this . . . would have been worth my coming. True, here again was much of the symbolism and constructivism of the confused new theatre followers back home. But there was more. Except for that impassioned and wonderful story of religious ecstacy [*sic*], and human love, The *Dybbuk*, I had never seen any modern plays that were more lyrical and intense in their productions. Such use of music, pantomime, acrobatics, masks even, and energized properties! And such rhythmic harmony of ensemble acting! It seemed as if the director had deliberately meant to fuse all the elements of theatre arts into one.[16]

Green made an appointment with Granowsky and called on him in his apartment. He recalled their visit: "Ah, the music," said the Russian, "that is it. Mine is first a musical theatre, last a musical theatre." Granowsky was not complimentary toward American musical comedy; in contrast, he said, "Our [Russian] plays are real, full of life; they say something." He told Green that Otto Kahn had "offered to guarantee" his troupe a few weeks in America. He was asking permission of the Russian government but was somewhat fearful of doing so.[17]

Green was so enthusiastic about Granowsky and his theater that he sat down and wrote Koch about him:

Well, here is the most astonishing folk theatre I've ever met! Marvelous to me. Grotesque and human, puppet-like, musicalized, stylized, unreal and other-worldly. I felt I must tell you about it! The plays are done in Yiddish, but the strange tongue but adds to its exotic charm. For once I have been satisfied with the conventions of the stage. Here it is a child's theatre, too—few properties, but all attention on make-up, ballet movements, mass formations, color, lighting—all submerged in and generating a strange dream-likeness, the artless (and yet fibered pattern) theatre of play, of the folk. During the last month I've wished many a time that you could see what Granowsky has done and tell me what you thought of it. You might not agree. But I do know that you would agree that something as new and full of "fine excess" could be done with the folk songs and customs of North Carolina. We must do that Virginia Dare sort of lyrical song-drama some of these days. And what we could do with the mountain ballads! I've always been interested in the relation of music and drama, and have always felt that opera was not the solution. Granowsky has reached a sort of solution which has given its own art forth, and it satisfied me.[18]

Perhaps Green's visit with Granowsky is what inspired him to stop being a tourist and get busy with his own writing. Near the end of October Green began work on the novel that he had promised to the McBride publishing house. It had not yet been named but eventually became *The Laughing Pioneer*.[19] He also "worked on *Tread the Green Grass*. Can't get the end to come right yet." Come November he was working on *The House of Connelly* and worrying about money: "Have to sweat with mortifications over another cable." He was trying to get some assistance from a publisher. A week later he was still "waiting for money, down to 3 marks." A few days later he worked out a deal with Oesterheld and Company for the publication of his plays in Germany. He cabled Samuel French, and French wired some money for him to Deutsche Bank. Written confirmation of the arrangements arrived by mail from French, so Green signed a contract with Oesterheld and "received 500 marks advance. Feel much safer now. Children don't cry in vain, philosophy and stomach both better."[20]

All his life Green had a great number of vivid dreams. Sometimes he immediately wrote them down. On occasion in his diary he would mention a dream; for example, "Worked at odds and ends. A DREAM."[21] He later confirmed that what he recorded was an actual dream, which is particularly enlightening as to the mind of Paul Green in 1928 as it relates to some of his later activities:

I am in jail sentenced to be hanged for a murder I did not commit. Tomorrow the execution takes place at one o'clock. Supper is brought, I eat heartily and strange to say, am sleepy. Dimly I think of that outside world— one—and myself here—the other one. I feel no resentment, rather a cold dumb proudness, a deep grief that holds its head up over the calamity that the world practices on those who die innocently and in vain, and something else keeps me calm, gives me hope and has given it all these weary months. Man may make mistakes but somewhere there is a justice, there is a reliable and to be trusted character in the universe. Considering that, I am again certain that I shall be delivered at the last moment. Dr. Chase comes quietly in with an enigmatic faculty-meeting smile. He alone of all the world comes and I cannot gather why he's come. I ask him to go to the governor for they both know I'm innocent. He smiles his smile, now grown unbelievably frank but he will say nothing—not a word. At last he takes his cane just so and goes away. I fall asleep and dream within this dream that the day has come, the sun has risen, people go along the street as usual— and I am to be hanged! And then I dream in that third dream that I fall asleep the morning of the execution and the hour passes, the clock ticks on by. Like a hovering form I float against the bars and see my real self sleeping on the iron cot. I say to my shadowy self that I will let no one wake him. But then I look at the clock down the corridor and the hour has not passed. It is ten minutes till one. The guards come with the keys. In vain I wish them not to wake that sleeping boy. But they open the door and pass quite through me and stir the sleeper. I see him wake, lift a haggard face.

I know what he feels, I feel what he feels, he is I and I he. They take him down the corridor, at the other end a door is open, the scaffold is seen! Beyond, a sea of human faces. I come behind him. So keenly do I feel his suffering that suddenly the distance between us is annihilated and I have become he and now his, that is my, suffering, is doubly intensified. All the woe of all the condemned becomes mine. . . . But at the bottom of this woe there comes another feeling, something that gives me a great peace—"I am now alone in the universe, single, completely subjected unto law and in that subjection and absolute singularity I am complete and master—one with the eternal processes of nature, immutable, inscrutable being—I am become as God." And then I felt a great pity for these two guards, for all those waiting the spectacle of my death. I fell to weeping over them and knew that those who saw me thought I was weeping for myself. I tried to say, "I forgive you for you know not what life is," but the words stuck in my throat. Then suddenly I felt the rope around my neck, the knot at my ear, and I said, "I am not afraid for I have already died," and I smiled at those about me. They looked at me strangely and I saw they thought I had gone mad. Then a guard springs the trap, and like a diver fighting his way up and up through suffocating billows I battled my way up through seas of sleep and awoke. For hours then I lay.[22]

The dream foreshadowed Green's later social activism in the battle against capital punishment, but at this time he was a writer and not an activist (though certainly a writer who addressed tough social issues).

Just before Christmas he finished and mailed both *Tread the Green Grass* and *The House of Connelly*. Barrett Clark had sold the latter script to the Theatre Guild:

Theresa Helburn, one of the directors of the Guild, . . . said to me, "Maybe you would like to work at it a little more. Maybe you can cut some." . . . The more I wrote, the worse it got, longer and longer. So, I finally sent a script that was two hundred and something pages. I thought that it was going to be big, but maybe they could do it in two nights or something. So, I got a wire from her or something, and it said, "For God's sake, quit writing. We'll get along with what we have."[23]

Green wanted to meet Max Reinhardt, and he was carrying a letter of introduction to the famous director. He explained his motivation: "In Germany I had seen his small productions and some of his big ones at the Grosses Schauspielhaus, the big theater. I was so taken with him that I wanted to see him in Germany, and I learned that he was living just outside of Salzburg."[24] Accordingly, on December 27

Green, along with an English friend named Wadsworth, took a train through Munich and over to Salzburg, Austria. After spending the night there he

got a cab to go out to Max Reinhardt's house. And there was snow all over the ground, and we drove out there, and here was this castle, kind of a castle. The man was a prince, just the prince of the theatre in Europe. And I sat there in the cab and looked at this thing, and the snow up the walk through the iron gates, as I remember, toward the house, was untrampled. And, I don't know, my heart failed me, and I finally turned around and went back, and I never did get to see him in Europe.[25]

The worst winter in seventy-five years began closing in. Inside the Greens' apartment it was so cold that the hatchet with which Paul cut kindling for his morning fire would freeze to the floor each night. Green recorded on Christmas Eve, "Paulie growing more and more sick, Nancy Byrd also, Elizabeth with sinus trouble."[26] As circumstances in Germany became worse, though, he stopped keeping a diary. Elizabeth's sinus infection ultimately required an operation. She felt quite uneasy in the German hospital, in which Roman Catholic nurses wore heavy black robes while assisting the surgeon. Black seemed so unsanitary. The operation was successful, but Paul Jr. had pneumonia, and Paul Sr. was depressed. During these illnesses,

We got busy trying to find somebody to help out, and we were so poor that we went to the church, thought maybe the church had people. And the Lutheran church nearby did have somebody, and so we asked them to send somebody over to be interviewed, and here came this lovely young woman, about twenty-five . . . in this immaculate white uniform. . . . She couldn't speak English, but we had some broken German and so we engaged her, and I remember walking with her to the *Untergrund*, the underground, the subway, and she was so charming and nice and so religious. Oh my, she carried a Bible and white gloves every Sunday and was very devout. Well, she was a real German. She took charge of these two sick younguns, and in no time she had them speaking German and cleaned them up and made them behave. They were so spoiled by us. . . . They became new children. So she stayed with us, and Elizabeth fell in love with her and she learned English slowly.[27]

In spite of this boon, Green's depression did not immediately lift. In a diary entry dated January–April 1929, he wrote: "Most difficult period!! Tried and tried and tried to write. But could accomplish nothing. The Berlin winter a gradual and descending frozen hell! Come spring, come before too long. Melt my deadened brain again into words!"

Perhaps to raise his spirits, he went to see *Dreigroschenoper* (*Three Penny Opera*) by Kurt Weill and Bertold Brecht, then so popular that it was playing in seven cities and generating great wealth for its creators. In Berlin the production Green saw starred Weill's wife Lotte Lenya, with whom Green would become friends. One night Green and a few others were with Granowsky when he announced that "his theatre had been dissolved by a command of the Soviet authorities, and his actors had been ordered back to Moscow." Green wondered if "[t]his was perhaps the answer he got for his request to take his troupe to America." Granowsky "moved to Paris" instead of returning to Russia.[28]

Surprisingly, given his poor spirits during the winter, Green applied for an extension of his Guggenheim fellowship, and it was granted (though the fellowship was not sufficient to meet his financial needs, and he had to ask for more advances from Samuel French). The Greens moved to London in June 1929, taking with them the German girl, whose name was Erna Lamprecht. There Green received introductions to various literary nobles (such as Rebecca West) by a fan of his work, Mrs. Frank Vernon, also an American living in London. She had translated Green's *In Aunt Mahaly's Cabin* for the Grand Guignol Theatre in Paris, and finding the playwright living in her new home city, hosted parties for the Greens.[29]

Green used a letter of introduction to get an interview with George Bernard Shaw. He immediately went home and wrote up the interview, but it was not published until 1953, after Shaw's death.[30] He did write Frederick Koch a letter about the experience of meeting Shaw, who

did about 99 percent of the talking. . . . [H]e asked me several questions almost simultaneously—about Chapel Hill, his friend Archibald Henderson, life in the South, O'Neill, and so on. When he found out I was interested in philosophy he tore loose and talked for half an hour by the clock without my saying a word or wanting to, for that matter. He reviewed the old dispensation—as he called it—before Darwin, the coming of the natural outlook, ending with the advent of Einstein on the scene. Then he talked about Einstein whom he admires greatly, told one or two anecdotes of their acquaintance . . . and then swung around to the present-day scene of thought in England—J. B. S. Haldane, Bertrand Russell, and others. Half the time he was jollying and half the time working at his words—but always with a terrific flow of words—never hesitating, never too involved. . . .

Finally I asked some questions that led around to the drama—by way of the modern religious feeling for science, especially in physics and astronomy, which so many dramatists and theatre artists are trying to use on the stage. . . . He is keenly alive to all sorts of possibilities and thinks— unlike most Englishmen I've met—that the Talkies have a tremendous future. Then followed lots of incidents about his speaking for the Talkies, experience in writing plays, etc., etc. From his talk at this point I had a feeling that he had in mind some grandiose, startling new dramatic work which would make use of some modern religio-scientific idea calling for the most stage devices in production of it. I didn't ask him, for it was none of my business of course, and he didn't tell me outright, but such was my feeling about it, my impression. Finally I rose to go, but he waved his hand and said he'd spare 5 more minutes. He began again and talked another 15 minutes with hardly a pause. Well I'll tell you in detail when I get back about our conversation—the many, many things he said or suggested. And I believe . . . he is the *youngest man in Europe* and about the only remaining hope for the English drama of the present period—still the Shaw drama, of course.[31]

Thomas Hardy had died in January 1928, but Green had a letter of introduction to Hardy's widow. He took a train to Dorchester, got a taxi to The King's Arms Hotel, wandered about the town talking to people about Hardy, and matching scenes with those from Hardy's books. The following day, a Sunday, he attended Stinford Church, where Hardy is buried. Later he met with Mrs. Hardy. The interview is described in "A Visit to Hardy's Dorchester," in Green's *Drama and the Weather*.[32]

The Greens invited Paul's sisters Erma and Caro Mae to visit them in London. Both came, and both took jobs there for a few months. Lots of Americans were traveling that summer, and many North Carolinians came to visit the Greens, among them Prof. William Olsen, a friend and Paul's colleague on the faculty, and Dr. James F. Royster, the man who had hired Green to teach a freshman English course when he was only a freshman himself. During the summer Green heard from J. O. Bailey, who requested an introduction to

Barrett Clark for his wife, Loretto, a determined young playwright. Green was glad to help. Later, Loretto wrote to the Greens, saying, "We saw Mr. Clark in New York and gave him the play."[33] Requests such as this one became more and more numerous as the years went by.

Green likewise received requests for his own written work. For example, a letter from Elizabeth Loos-Bab dated July 9 asked, "Are you still happy in England and how long will you stay there? We are all looking forward to Abraham in Frankfurt, and I want to ask you for something for propaganda reasons. Could you not send me an essay . . . about Negroes? Perhaps a little negro story would be good as well, and besides a small autobiography." She sent him a printed copy of her translation of his play. On the front in big letters was: "In Abraham Schoss von Paul Green." He heard from her again in August as she was translating some of his one-act plays. She was struggling to get the Negro language into German. Two months later she sent him copies of her translations, which she had prepared for the publisher. She was expecting word about when the rehearsals for *In Abraham's Bosom* would begin. She would then release publicity items to the newspapers. She said the publisher wanted to wait until after the production of *Abraham* before going ahead with a translation of *The House of Connelly*. She was looking forward to receiving Green's *Potter's Field* and *The Field God.*[34]

During all of his time in London Green had been attending theater productions. He wrote to Koch in October about his experiences:

The theatre here is, as usual, rather tame. No combining of forces, every manager on his own—clubs, subscription theatres, halls, carrying on individually, and with little inspiration or comprehension so far as one can see. . . . These producers won't organize, go on feeding rough recognizable pigs soft dove food. For the English theatre public is about like that of America—lively, healthy as a pig, and anxious for good trough feed as well as walking in the parlor, and like all publics, easily fooled by those whom they think superior. They will come running time without end to the rattle of an empty basket, hoping for corn and never getting it, and what they need of course is not sound and wind but something else. Maybe it will be provided. . . . Anyhow, I would say that a good organization somewhat like the American Theatre Guild is the only thing that will pull the present English drama out of its riveted coffin.[35]

But Green would not witness much more of English theater, for the end of October brought news that drew the Greens home. Caro Mae Green Russell later remembered clearly the headlines in London newspapers telling of the stock market crash in the United States. A few days later she received a letter from her employer, the Seymour School of Music in New York, saying that it was no longer able to stay open. She and Erma returned aboard the same ship at Thanksgiving. In spite of the problems of Wall Street, New York looked brilliant to her, greatly contrasting with the grayness of London.[36]

Paul and Elizabeth Green likewise soon headed home, but they were not able to bring Erna Lamprecht with them at that time—though all parties agreed that they would try to work it out later. They returned to a Chapel Hill that had been affected very little by the beginnings of the Great Depression, and Green resumed his place on the faculty. He felt that he had already been through a depression: he owed Samuel French, Inc., about $10,000 in advances.

NOTES

1. Paul Green Diary, August 11, 1928, Paul Green Papers (collection #3693), Southern Historical Collection, Wilson Library, University of North Carolina at Chapel Hill (hereafter cited as Diary, with entry date).

2. Diary, August 12, 1928.

3. Diary, August 13, 1928. *Tread the Green Grass* was eventually collected in *The House of Connelly and Other Plays* (New York: Samuel French, 1931).

4. Diary, August 31-September 9, 1928.

5. Agatha Boyd Adams, *Paul Green of Chapel Hill*, University of North Carolina Library Extension Publications, vol. 16, No. 2 (Chapel Hill: University of North Carolina Library, January 1951), 44.

6. Paul Green, interview by James R. Spence, May 6, 1976, James R. Spence audio recordings relating to Paul Green, 1974-1979 (collection #5170), Southern Historical Collection (hereafter cited as Spence interview, with appropriate date).

7. Spence interview, April 29, 1978.

8. Elizabeth Lay Green, *The Paul Green I Know* (Chapel Hill: North Caroliniana Society, 1978), 8.

9. Diary, September 14, 15-20, 1928.

10. Spence interview, August 9, 1979.

11. Diary, October 12, 13, 1928.

12. Paul Green, *Drama and the Weather: Some Notes and Papers on Life and the Theatre* (New York: Samuel French, 1958), 14.

13. Diary, September 28, 1928.

14. See the correspondence between Green and the Bab family in folder 108B of the Paul Green Papers, Southern Historical Collection.

15. Paul Green, interview by Billy E. Barnes, May 1975, p. 35, Southern Oral History Program Collection, Southern Historical Collection (hereafter cited as Barnes interview, with appropriate date and transcript page number).

16. Green, *Drama and the Weather*, 16-17.

17. Green, *Drama and the Weather*, 18.

18. Quoted in Adams, *Paul Green of Chapel Hill*, 44-45.

19. New York: R. M. McBride and Company, 1932.

20. Diary, October 26, November 4, 10, 15, 1928.

21. Diary, November 16, 1928.

22. Ibid.

23. Barnes interview, May 1975, p. 21.

24. Paul Green, interview by Rhoda Wynn, February 1974, tape 2, p. 23, Southern Oral History Program Collection, Southern Historical Collection.

25. Ibid.

26. Diary, December 24, 1928.

27. Barnes interview, May 1975, pp. 60-61.

28. Green, *Drama and the Weather*, 21.

29. Adams, *Paul Green of Chapel Hill*, 45.

30. See "The Mystical Bernard Shaw," collected in Green's *Dramatic Heritage* (New York: Samuel French, 1953), 112-132.

31. Green to Koch, October 27, 1929, quoted from Laurence G. Avery, ed., *A Southern Life: Letters of Paul Green, 1916-1981*, Fred W. Morrison Series in Southern Studies (Chapel Hill: University of North Carolina Press, 1994), 163-165.

32. Pp. 185-220.

33. See the correspondence with Bailey in the Paul Green Papers, folder 108. Loretto Bailey's play *Job's Kinfolks* had appeared in Koch's *Carolina Folk-Plays*, third series (New York: H. Holt and Company, 1928), and her play *Cloey* was published in his *Carolina Folk Comedies* (New York: Samuel French, 1931).

34. Loos-Bab to Green, July 9, October 22, 1929, Paul Green Papers, folder 108.

35. Quoted in Adams, *Paul Green of Chapel Hill*, 46.

36. This story is from the author's interview with Caro Mae Green Russell, October 2, 1976, James R. Spence audio recordings relating to Paul Green, 1974-1979 (collection #5170), Southern Historical Collection.

18: The Group Theatre

Green found that another Pulitzer Prize winner had come to live in Chapel Hill: Lamar Stringfield, who had won his award in music in 1928 for his suite *From the Southern Mountains*.[1] Stringfield had come to Chapel Hill as research assistant to the Institute of Research in Folk Music Development, an arm of the university. Green was a member of the Advisory Council of the organization. He had first met the musician in the army at Camp Sevier, South Carolina, during the war. Stringfield, who was a flutist, had come into conflict with the military and was working with a detail from the stockade (where he was serving a sentence of a few days). Meeting Stringfield again in 1930, Green was attracted by his enthusiasm for folk music, and they were soon collaborating. Green composed his own music for *Tread the Green Grass*, but he was limited in his ability to put it on paper. Stringfield wrote out the songs Green sang for him and then arranged the music for the orchestra.[2]

While some of this work was in progress, Green signed a contract for a New York production of *Tread the Green Grass* and made a trip up to confer about the matter. In March, Green received a letter from Francis E. Ferguson of the American Laboratory Theatre in New York saying that it had acquired the option for *Tread the Green Grass*. A few days later Ferguson came to Chapel Hill to talk about plans for the play.[3] Again, however, there was a delay, with nothing happening. On the European front, Green's earlier, more successful play was experiencing similar production difficulties: in May, Elizabeth Loos-Bab wrote, "Frankfort has postponed the representation of Abraham till the beginning of next season."[4] She did not know it, but that postponement was a death knell. Germany was rapidly moving into a new era that did not include sympathy for the aspirations of black people.

In July Green spoke at a seminar at the University of Iowa by invitation of E. C. Mabie, a man who ranked with Frederick Koch and George Pierce Baker as a pioneer in the noncommercial theater in America. Mabie had watched the progress of Green's work with interest and had produced *Unto Such Glory*, an early Green play about an evangelist who tries to steal a man's wife while she is caught up in his religious fervor.[5] While in Iowa, Green visited Norman Foerster, the teacher who had encouraged him to write his first play back in 1916. Foerster now held the position of director of the School of Letters at the University of Iowa. Soon after his trip to Iowa, Green wrote to Ferguson, saying that Mabie wanted to produce *Tread the Green Grass*.[6] It would be an amateur production and would not conflict with the New York presentation.

While that matter was in abeyance, rehearsals began for the American Laboratory production of the play. Jimmy Light, who had been one of the key people in the Provincetown Players, was directing. Green recalled: "I think they must have rehearsed about three weeks. The newspapers said something about the play was going to open so-and-so, and then it got crazier and crazier, and I think the backers . . . came and saw some rehearsals and threw up their hands. . . . Well, anyway, it never did open."[7]

In the meantime the Greens were reestablishing a social life in Chapel Hill. Paul organized another singing quartet, this time with Phillips Russell, a professor in the UNC Department of English who subsequently married Paul's sister Caro Mae; William Olsen; and E. E. Ericson as members. Short story writer Wilbur Daniel Steele, with his wife and two young boys, moved from Charleston into a house across the street from the Greens.[8] Green told of how he played poker with Steele and J. O. Bailey, among others: "We'd have a party [and] might sit up til two o'clock [playing cards]. The next morning at 8:30 [Steele] was at his typewriter." In retrospect, Green wondered, "why in the heck did we play poker so much?"[9]

But Green was writing, too: "I built myself a little cabin out behind [our] house in the glen. . . . I wrote a lot of plays in that place. . . . I was

At the glen house in Chapel Hill, 1931. *Left to right*: George Loy, Lamar Stringfield, George O'Neil, Philips Russell, Barrett Clark, and Paul Green.

in there working one day, and I heard this low muffled sound of an automobile. . . . I went out, and this fellow stepped out and said, 'I'm James Boyd. I just thought I would come in to see you.' Got to know him that way." Boyd, who lived in Southern Pines, was a novelist. "His wife [Kate] was the daughter of the secretary of the treasury under Cleveland."[10] Green had seen Boyd's historical novel *Drums*; later he saw the 5,000 cards Boyd had prepared in doing research for the work. Green told of how James Boyd

would come and visit us in that little old house [with] the electric light up in the ceiling. . . . Then . . . we went down and visited him and saw this forty-two-room mansion. . . . He was master of hounds. He had an Englishman there taking care of his hounds. . . . He had a hunt, and there Elizabeth and I were, out of the cornfields, and here were all these red coats and hounds and horses. . . . But Jim was such a wonderful guy. We got to be great friends over the years. We would read and talk about [writing]. He kept an open house. . . . Later on, Sherwood [Anderson] would come by every spring and spend three or four days with us and then go on down to Jim's. And Tom Wolfe would visit. Scott Fitzgerald visited down there. . . . In some ways [Jim and Kate were] the best friends we ever had—except [for] Barrett Clark.[11]

Jonathan and Lucy Daniels, too, became good friends of the Greens. The couples found common ground in their opposition to the

Old South, "in the cause of the New South," and in their various activities to promote social justice.[12] Occasionally the Boyds and the Danielses would come over to the Greens' house for a party. Entertainment might be provided by black singers with banjo and washboard, or by a local character named Bad Eye, also black, who would spin some of his yarns.[13]

Green's life as a teacher continued. According to Julian R. Meade, he had become "one of the most popular and influential professors on the campus."[14] Young people signed up for his classes, aware that they were getting a Pulitzer Prize winner and Guggenheim Fellow. They liked to pass along stories in the growing legend of Paul Green, they enjoyed his open friendliness, and they admired his tennis game. Many years later Walter Spearman, when he retired as head of the university's Department of Journalism, recalled being a student under Green and told William Friday that he was one of two teachers who most inspired him.[15]

In class, students found Green totally un-academic in manner but intense and persuasive.[16] They had no way of knowing that his conscience was bothering him about whether he was fulfilling his obligations to Horace Williams, thus motivating him to work harder, even though he was beginning to recognize that Williams's own studies were too narrow for himself:

Horace claimed to be a Hegelian, and he let it be known there was no use studying philosophy after Hegel. Hegel had said the final word. I got a lot out of reading Hegel, especially his four volumes on fine arts, especially the drama—I think that after Aristotle maybe Hegel was the greatest writer and interpreter of the nature of the drama. He had wonderful things to say. But Hegel's whole philosophy was a triad. Something happens . . . and that's the thesis. Something counters against it, and that's an antithesis. Then the two fight each other and emerge in a solution, and that produces a synthesis, and out of the synthesis comes a thesis. And the antithesis, and then . . . So it's the eternal marching of the triad. And to Horace, that's the last word to be said; you don't need any more.[17]

During the fall of 1930 Green, in addition to teaching, put in many hours on his novel *The Laughing Pioneer*.

In the meantime, Erna Lamprecht kept writing from Germany, and Elizabeth was anxious to bring her to the United States. The

Greens sent her enough money for passage. When she was to arrive, Green "went to New York to get her [in his] old Buick car. It didn't have a heater, . . . and it was wintertime. I . . . went to Ellis Island to get her, and . . . her name was called and they took me to see her, and she was behind bars."[18] The authorities would not release her without a $500 bond. Green

didn't have a dime. Maybe enough to buy gas back to Chapel Hill. So I said, "I haven't got any $500." "Well, she'll have to go back to Germany. She was born in Poland and has to be guaranteed while she is here." Well, I thought of my old benefactor, and the next morning . . . —she had to stay in jail overnight, or behind bars—so the next morning, I showed up at French's office and I said, "Mr. Sheil, I need $500." He said, "Do you want it now?" I said, "Yes, sir." He said, "Write him a check for $500." I said, "I need the cash." He said, "All right, we'll send to the bank.". . . So I go back to get her out, and by that time it is almost dark [and] cold as blazes. . . . I didn't have any [money] to get a place to stay. So, we set out for Chapel Hill, and all through Virginia there were no paved roads—it was all dirt and they were frozen. I was sure that at any moment we were going to have a blowout with some of these ragged old tires. And she sat there mile after mile, no heat, and I just froze. I said, "Erna, *Bist du Kalt?*" (Are you cold?) "*Nein, nein, Herr Green.*" So, along about daybreak I was practically dead, and I passed a filling station and there was a chimney with smoke roaring out of it. I pulled in there and knocked on the door, and there was a man in there that had a big fire, and I told him that we were two frozen people, and we went in there. Well, it finally got warm, and we finally got to Chapel Hill.[19]

As the year ended, Green felt terribly disappointed with his writing career. None of the work he had done during the preceding four years had gained acceptance. He decided to go to New York during Christmas vacation and see what he could do. Green made the trip, but it did not result in any progress toward getting a play produced. A few months later Green reported, "Miss Helburn said, 'We have a younger group that would like to use your play to get started, and we are willing to surrender the rights to them if you agree.' I said, 'Whatever you want to do.'. . . I went up and met with Cheryl Crawford, Lee Strasberg, and Harold Clurman. They were the directors of the new group."[20] The co-directors had been restless and dissatisfied in the Guild. They considered the policies of the organization too conservative. Soon they had twenty-eight actors, including Stella Adler, Franchot Tone, and Clifford Odets, who wanted to be a part of a new project. They began to call themselves the Group Theatre.

The Group Theatre directors told Green that they would take the company to the country for summer rehearsals and open the play in New York in the fall. He agreed to go and work with them. The Theatre Guild, which still held the option on the play, agreed to put up $1,000 for the summer encampment. More money was raised from friends such as Edna Ferber and Maxwell Anderson. Green joined them at Brookfield Center, Connecticut, at a country place with several houses and a big barn. Somehow they were managing to accommodate the twenty-eight—plus some spouses and children. Maxwell Anderson, who was in love with one of the actresses, was likewise there part of the time.

Lee Strasberg directed the play. He was using "The Method," which he had adapted from the Russian director Konstantin Stanislavsky. It was a technique that he and Stella Adler (as competitors) would make famous in America. The young actors responded to the direction of Strasberg, and he was something of a father figure to most of them—though not to Franchot Tone, according to Green: "In the Group Theatre [Tone] and I were aloof. I never quite subscribed to either their aesthetics or their sociology or politics. And he was like that. Maxwell Anderson came over. . . . The three of us were a little bit watchful. When I was invited to become a member of the group, I wasn't too cordial."[21] But Green did enjoy the companionship of Franchot Tone and Maxwell Anderson.

Many years after he worked with the Group Theatre, Green wrote of his experience:

The directors would take a particular actor or actress and say, "Here's . . . a little piece of a scene. Now, you go off over there by that tree and . . . do all you can to bring back a feeling, an experience in your life that is similar to what the scene is about—an emotion. . . ." Emotion was a great word with them. They hardly ever used the word "thought" or "reason"—just "emotion." . . . And often you'd see him weeping. I would hit the air with my fist and say, "What kind of business goes on here?"[22]

One night, in the barn they used for rehearsals, they were doing a scene for *The House of Connelly*. Green later described the evening in

The House of Connelly, by Paul Green, produced by the Group Theatre at the Martin Beck Theatre, 1931. *Left to right*: Rose McClendon (Big Sue), Fanny de Knight (Big Sis), Eunice Stoddard (Evelyn Connelly), and Stella Adler (Geraldine Connelly).

an essay titled "With the Group Theatre—A Remembrance": "so much emotionalism around that it resembled a Holy Roller meeting pretty soon. And I sat there and watched. They got so overcome by the emotions they felt flowing out of my poor lines that they couldn't talk. They broke down and wept. Some of them turned and laid their heads up against the partition and boo-hooed."[23] He spoke of it in negative terms as well:

It was the most circumambient or periphrastic organization I ever saw. They'd be all around the subject, and it looked as if they could never get to it. Cheryl Crawford was usually silent as the grave, but she had two associates who were as voluble and foamy-mouthed people as I've ever seen in my life: Lee Strasburg and Harold Clurman. They could talk for hours, and . . . the young people would sit around and just drink it in. It wasn't long before I was completely fed up with the whole thing. . . . They were a pretty left-wing outfit. I remember once Tamaris, a dancer, came over, and she was arguing for the New Day when the bourgeoisie would be down and out, . . .

and she said, "Yes, when the Revolution comes"—they used that word a lot—"when the Revolution comes, you're going to be on the other side, and it will give me great pleasure to cut your throat." The only answer I had for that was, "Well, honey, if you look at me with those wonderful eyes the way you do now, I'll die with joy." She had wonderful eyes.[24]

On the other hand, he has a positive memory of one of the actors there: "They had a young actor . . . Clifford Odets. He was twenty-one years old. . . . I would rewrite, and I remember that Cliff would come around and say, 'Could I have a copy of that?'. . . He was interested in writing."[25]

A dispute arose about the play's ending. *The House of Connelly* is about the difficulty of an aristocratic, slave-owning family in the South coping with the changes brought about by the Civil War. Green had decided that the tenant farmer's daughter who took over the plantation by marrying the weak young owner should die at the end because she had used foul means to achieve her goals. Cheryl Crawford and Harold Clurman wanted to show some hope for the South (and perhaps for the proletariat) and pressured him into changing to a happy ending.[26]

When the company returned to New York after twelve weeks (Green had gone back to Chapel Hill after a short stay), the board of directors of the Theatre Guild was quite disturbed about the change. They had promised to put up $10,000 for the New York production. Now they decreed that unless the ending were changed back to the original, their support would be cut to only $5,000. Not to be outdone, Cheryl Crawford obtained a $1,000 investment from Eugene O'Neill and a $4,000 investment from Samuel French, Inc.[27]—both without Green's knowledge—and went forward with the production.

The House of Connelly opened on September 28, 1931, at the Martin Beck Theatre. Franchot Tone and Margaret Barker played the leads. Cheryl Crawford later wrote of that night:

The opening night was torture. So much depended on the play's reception. Paul Green and I sat in the mezzanine lobby . . . pretending to converse. We were both listening for response from the audience. Paul's fawnlike face was masked, his usual eager, questing look gone. When the final curtain fell, I began counting the calls. When they reached sixteen and the audience began shouting "Author, author," I pulled Paul to his feet. "For God's sake, get up on that stage!" I said. He did. The curtain rose and fell twenty-two times. . . . At two A.M. I got the call. The reviews read to me were raves, the kind we had dreamed of, singing the praises of our company. We couldn't have written better ones ourselves. I called and relayed the news, then dressed and joined the party. By the time I got there someone had gone to Times Square to bring the papers back. Lee read them aloud to cheers and yells. Paul, a very tall man, pushed up the ceiling with one hand and quoted something appropriate from the Bible.[28]

NOTES

1. Agatha Boyd Adams, *Paul Green of Chapel Hill*, University of North Carolina Library Extension Publications, vol. 16, No. 2 (Chapel Hill: University of North Carolina Library, January 1951), 53.

2. Paul Green, interview by James R. Spence, August 9, 1979, James R. Spence audio recordings relating to Paul Green, 1974-1979 (collection #5170), Southern Historical Collection, Wilson Library, University of North Carolina at Chapel Hill (hereafter cited as Spence interview, with appropriate date).

3. Brooks Atkinson, who had not seen Green since his trip abroad, wrote on January 16, 1930: "Please save some time for me and call me up when you get to New York." See telegram from Atkinson in the Paul Green Papers (collection #3693), folder 108, Southern Historical Collection. The letter from Ferguson, dated March 3, 1930, is in folder 141 of the Green Papers.

4. Loos-Bab to Green, May 5, 1930, Paul Green Papers, folder 137.

5. This play is collected in Green's volume *In the Valley and Other Carolina Plays* (New York: Samuel French, 1928) and in his *Out of the South: The Life of a People in Dramatic Form* (New York: Harper, 1939).

6. Mabie's letters and Green's letter to Ferguson, dated September 4, 1930, are in the Paul Green Papers, folders 153 and 136; see also Laurence G. Avery, ed., *A Southern Life: Letters of Paul Green, 1916-1981*, Fred W. Morrison Series in Southern Studies (Chapel Hill: University of North Carolina Press, 1994), 173n.

7. Paul Green, interview by Rhoda Wynn, February 1974, tape 4, p. 36, Southern Oral History Program Collection, Southern Historical Collection (hereafter cited as Wynn interview, with appropriate tape and transcript page number).

8. Adams, *Paul Green of Chapel Hill*, 48-49.

9. Spence interview, August 9, 1979.

10. Ibid.

11. Ibid.

12. Ibid.

13. See Julian R. Meade, "Paul Green," *The Bookman* 74 (January-February 1932): 505.

14. Ibid.

15. Green reported to the author that he heard this from William Friday. Spence interview, April 29, 1978. William Clyde Friday (b. 1920) became president of the Consolidated University of North Carolina in 1956 and served as president of the University of North Carolina System from 1957 to 1986.

16. Adams, *Paul Green of Chapel Hill*, 48.

17. Wynn interview, tape 11, p. 37.

18. Paul Green, interview by Billy E. Barnes, May 1975, p. 61, Southern Oral History Program Collection, Southern Historical Collection (hereafter cited as Barnes interview, with appropriate date and transcript page number).

19. Barnes interview, May 1975, pp. 61-62.

20. Barnes interview, May 1975, p. 35.

21. Spence interview, October 24, 1976.

22. Paul Green, *Plough and Furrow: Some Essays and Papers on Life and the Theatre* (New York: Samuel French, 1963), 46.

23. Green, *Plough and Furrow*, 47.

24. Wynn interview, tape 3, pp. 16-18.

25. Barnes interview, May 1975, p. 35.

26. Barnes interview, May 1975, p. 36. See also Cheryl Crawford, *One Naked Individual: My Fifty Years in the Theatre* (New York: Bobbs-Merrill, 1977), 55.

27. Crawford, *One Naked Individual*, 55.

28. Crawford, *One Naked Individual*, 55-56.

19: The Southern Writers Conference

Perhaps it was his experience with the Group Theatre that prompted Green to gather together a group of writers for a writers' conference: "I was connected with trying to start a southern writers conference. I don't know whether I was the one who originated it or [whether it developed] in talking with some writers. I talked with Sherwood Anderson. . . . I wrote to William Faulkner. . . . I was interested in helping get [the group] together. We decided to meet at the University of Virginia. That's the old mother of everything, you know."[1]

Letters of invitation went out in September 1931 over the signature of Prof. James Southall Wilson, founding editor of the *Virginia Quarterly Review*.[2] Green drove to Charlottesville and took with him Helen Stallings, wife of writer Laurence Stallings and a poet in her own right, and Dr. Archibald Henderson, biographer of George Bernard Shaw. It was understood that Green would go directly to New York from Charlottesville and that he would take William Faulkner with him when the conference concluded. Thus, it was not surprising that he ended up driving Faulkner around during the conference as well.

Green made arrangements to meet Faulkner at the Monticello Hotel in Charlottesville, although he and his passengers were staying at the site of the conference, the Farmington Country Club, outside town. At the Monticello, on the morning of October 23, he telephoned Faulkner's room from the lobby. Green described his first glimpse of Faulkner: "Pretty soon, down he comes. He's wearing a Canadian airman's cap. He was in the Canadian air force, this little fellow. . . . Never had met him, never had seen him before."[3] Faulkner played a significant role in Green's recollection of the conference:

There were other writers there. We all go out to this place in the country, this big, beautiful inn where we're going to have our meeting. He had on some half-brogan shoes, I remember. Archibald Henderson and I had put up at this place. . . . Well, we have a meeting, and Sherwood Anderson, being a sort of a dean, we asked him to open the meeting. We had twenty-five or thirty writers from all around. Sherwood—unfortunately, his fly was open— . . . walks up and down with his hands in his pockets . . . talking about the greats getting together. . . . That was embarrassing. . . .

I had to go somewhere, and I came on back to my room—we had adjourned until the evening, and I guess I went back to the hotel. So I was back in my room in the late afternoon, and there was a knock on the door; Henderson came in. He said, "There's somebody in my bed in the next room." I said, "That's queer to me." He said, "Queer to me. He's there in my bed, and his shoes are sticking out. He's got his face covered . . . —must be some workman." So I go in with him and lift the cover, and it's William Faulkner. I don't know whether he was asleep or not. He had that way. He would play with you. . . . And he opened his eyes. . . . You could smell a little liquor. I introduced Dr. Henderson to William Faulkner, lying in the bed . . . —didn't bother William a bit in the world. He finally sat up and said, "I appreciate the rest" or something. . . . It's all right to tell these things because . . . after all, look what he accomplished. . . .

The next morning we had a meeting, and I went to pick up Faulkner at the hotel—he didn't have a way to get out there—but he'd already gone. So I went back and parked, and there he was talking to Josephine Pinkney. So I said, "We'll go into the meeting." We walked across this polished floor, this beautiful polished floor, and all of a sudden William Faulkner lets loose and vomits all over it. It didn't bother him a bit in the world. If it did he didn't show it. Here came the colored boys, rushing up to clean up. Bill looked around, didn't say sorry, nothing. We went on and had our meeting. . . . He attended, but he never did make any talks. . . . We really tore into the Old South. Talked about the New. . . .

The next morning I'm to pick up Faulkner at the hotel [to take him to New York]. I go to the hotel, and we can't find him. I come up, and I look down about fifty yards from the hotel and there's a little fellow sitting on the curb. I walk down there, and it's Faulkner. I said, "Bill, we're ready to start," and he looked up and said, "We can't do nothing till Messenus comes." And I said, "Messenus?" . . . I knew about Messenus, the great patron of arts. I said, "Who the hell is Messenus?" He said, "He's a black fellow, but he'll be here soon." And so I stand there, and he doesn't say anything. He's sitting on the darned curb, and he's got a little suitcase by him. . . . We wait and talk a little, but he won't say much. But he does say, "I've got a manuscript here in my suitcase I'm taking to New York. That's what I'm really going for, and I'm glad to ride with you." I said, "I've got an old car; I hope we make it." I said, "What is your manuscript?" He said, "*Light in August.* . . . Would you like to look at some of it while we're waiting for Messenus?" I said, "Sure." So he opened and showed me a sheet or two, all written in this beautiful little handwriting. . . . He put it back, and he said, "I don't believe Messenus is coming." I said, "I don't either." He said, "I know where he lives." I said, "Well, come on and get in the car and we'll go by there." . . . We get in the car. . . . So we drive, and he tells me to go down here and go down here into the Negro section, to a bootlegger. That was Messenus. And he gets—I guess it was a quart jar or a half-gallon of liquor.[4]

Joining Green and Faulkner for the trip to New York were Harrison Smith, who had published Faulkner's *The Sound and the Fury* in 1929 and, more recently, *Sanctuary*, and Milton Abernathy of Chapel Hill, who was launching a new literary magazine called *Contempo*. Faulkner was in the process of allowing Abernathy to publish some of his writings in his magazine.[5] Continuing the story of this trip, Green described Faulkner as having "an imp of the perverse in him. It was part of the drama of his living. Often you couldn't tell just what was meant, whether he was really serious or was joking. I've always felt that that Nobel Prize speech had a sense of the joke in it . . . this beautiful thing about man." This "perverse" streak showed itself during the drive, as well: "We set out, and every once in a while he would take a little sip. . . . We were riding along talking, and he said, 'I'm going to get on the back seat.' And I said, 'Well, why?' He said, ''Cause I don't like you.' I said, 'Well, go on, sit on the back seat.' So he sat on the back seat, and every once in a while he would sip."

Faulkner's drinking worried Green:

We'd stop at a filling station, and I'd say—it was Prohibition time—I'd say Bill, for God's sake, keep that liquor hid. "Well, okay, okay, anything to please you, your reverence," or something like that. Well, we got to Washington, and the old car began to sputter and cut up, and I was expecting it to conk out any time. I pulled in a garage—it was now dark, eight or nine at night—so I go to get the man to look at the motor, and he comes, and I turn around and look down there, and there's a cop standing by the car, and Bill is offering him this jar. Well, I said, "We're sunk now." But you know that . . . cop smiled and said, "Oh, no, oh, no." . . . That cop didn't do a thing to him.

Faulkner continued drinking until the bottle was apparently empty: "We got up there in New Jersey somewhere, and he said, 'I've got to have something to drink. . . . I used up this.' I said, 'We're in New Jersey.' He said, 'I know, but I can't do it. I've got to have something to drink.' I said, 'Well, I don't know where in the world you can find something to drink.' But he said, 'I've got to have it.' Evidently he did, so we pulled in a place somewhere, and I don't know how it happened, but he got . . . another small bottle of liquor."

Green dropped Faulkner off at his hotel, the Century: "He had reservations at a hotel, and I left him there and went on to my Old Bristol up on 48th Street. The next morning the . . . man at the hotel called me. He said, 'This gentleman, your friend'—I was there when he registered—. . . 'Your friend down here is in trouble with us. You've got to come and do something.' And I said, 'What's he done?' He said, 'Why he's pulled a pistol on the maidservant, and we don't know what to do with him.'"

Green wasn't worried, for Faulkner had told him of putting his pipe under a handkerchief and pretending it was a gun. On the other hand, Green recalled another story Faulkner had told him of "how he'd tried to kill a doctor [who] wouldn't come and treat his little sick child on the weekend. I don't know whether he was spoofing or not. But he said the pistol snapped, didn't kill him." So Green went to Faulkner's hotel to check on things: "So they gave me the key, and I go up there, and the door's unlocked. I open the door, and Bill [is] lying there, a little fawn character, naked in the bed. I said, 'Bill?' No answer. And I touched him. 'Bill?' No answer, and I know darn well he's awake. I'm just sure. I noticed the old pipe over on the table. So I went down and told the man, '. . . He plays jokes. I'm sure he's alright. He's sleeping now. He'll be alright.'" Green concluded the episode incredulously, "The next day there's a news story in the *New York Globe*—picture of Faulkner arriving in town. . . . He had a new novel."

Faulkner may have tried to make amends for his behavior— offering to go see *The House of Connelly*—but once again he ended up insulting his fellow southern writer: "He was nice—said, 'I'd like to see that play,'" but then, as they came upon a flower shop on the way to the play, "He goes into the flower store, comes out with a bunch of roses, and he bows and says, 'I present these roses to you.' Made me feel sore as a devil, made me feel like a woman. I think that's exactly what he meant me to feel. . . . We go on down to see the play. He never did say a word of praise or anything for it." Faulkner did tell Green "that he had a play coming on. He didn't at all, but he said he did, from *Sanctuary*. He said, 'I've dramatized *Sanctuary*. I'm going to produce it. I'm acting in it.' Then he said, 'Ha, ha, ha, ha.' He had a way of, little whickering laughter. I said, 'What part are you going to play, Bill?' He said, 'I'm going to play the corncob.'" In spite of such offensive conduct, the author of *Sanctuary* was the hottest property in the literary world, a fact that probably did not escape Faulkner's notice after a few days in New York. Sinclair Lewis, Theodore Dreiser, and H. L. Mencken came to call on him.[6]

Green was likewise making a name for himself. About that same time, Green, now back in Chapel Hill, received a telephone call from a Hollywood agent named Hunter Lovelace asking him to come out and do a film script for Warner Brothers from H. H. Kroll's novel *Cabin in the Cotton*. It would be an eight-week contract, and the pay would be $5,000.[7] Green's recollection some years later was that his annual salary at the university at that time was $2,750. With his head in the clouds, he went over to see Horace Williams about another leave of absence from teaching.

As further confirmation of Green's growing reputation, during the fall of 1931, Julian R. Meade had been working on an article about Green for publication in *The Bookman* early in the coming year. In preparing the article, Meade contacted Thomas Wolfe, whose *Look Homeward, Angel* had been published just before the Greens returned from England. (Wolfe too had recently returned from Europe, where he, like the Greens, had been residing with the aid of a Guggenheim Fellowship.) Meade wrote: "His friend, Thomas Wolfe, recalls that even as a college student Paul Green was concerning himself with paths that were forbidden and unexplored, that even then he was amazingly farseeing and mature. Yet he never made a self-conscious gesture. In him there was nothing of the aloof and unsocial intellectual. Though he was never a back-slapping collegian, he was interested in people and was affable and kind."[8]

Former classmates Green and Wolfe had seen each other in New York (Wolfe did not visit North Carolina for a while after the publication of his autobiographical novel). Green recalled that the last time I saw Tom here in Chapel Hill before he went away, he said, "I'm not coming back here till I'm famous. Some words like that . . . I saw him once or twice in New York. . . . I don't know what the reason was, but we were to meet. I knew where he lived, and we were to get together about something, so I picked him up. Went by his place, and, you know, he went very disheveled, shoes and all. So we came to Scribner on Fifth Avenue, and he says, 'Oh, I've got to go in here. . . . Come on in here and I'll introduce you to my editor, Max Perkins.' I said, 'Fine.' . . . So we went on in. I didn't know it, but Tom was going in [to] get a little money. . . . So he introduced me to Perkins."[9]

Green may have been impressed by the signs of Wolfe's success, but his own continued as well. Samuel French published another collection of Green's plays, *The House of Connelly and Other Plays* (1931), which encompassed *The House of Connelly*, *Potter's Field*, and *Tread the Green Grass*. The title play of this volume did not win a Pulitzer and, in spite of the high praise of critics, had a run of only ninety-one performances.[10] Long before its closing, however, it had gained the attention of people throughout the theatrical community. It had brought Green more admirers than any of his previous work and was no doubt a factor in his opportunity to go to Hollywood.

NOTES

1. Paul Green, interview by James R. Spence, August 9, 1979, James R. Spence audio recordings relating to Paul Green, 1974-1979 (collection #5170), Southern Historical Collection, Wilson Library, University of North Carolina at Chapel Hill (hereafter cited as Spence interview, with appropriate date).

2. See Joseph Blotner, ed., *Selected Letters of William Faulkner* (New York: Vintage Books, 1978), 51.

3. Spence interview, August 9, 1979.

4. Ibid. The description of the trip that follows is all excerpted from this same interview.

5. Blotner, *Selected Letters of William Faulkner*, 55.

6. Blotner, *Selected Letters of William Faulkner*, 53.

7. Paul Green, interview by Rhoda Wynn, February 1974, tape 1, p. 10, Southern Oral History Program Collection, Southern Historical Collection. The Warner Brothers contract, dated December 28, 1931, is in the Paul Green Papers (collection #3693), folder 196, Southern Historical Collection.

8. See Julian R. Meade, "Paul Green," *The Bookman* 74 (January-February 1932): 506.

9. Spence interview, August 9, 1979.

10. Cheryl Crawford, *One Naked Individual: My Fifty Years in the Theatre* (New York: Bobbs-Merrill, 1977), 55.

20: Hollywood

Of the many well-known writers who went to Hollywood in the 1930s, none went with higher hopes for motion pictures than did Paul Green, who was fascinated with the medium. He first saw a movie about 1904 and then described his experience in an essay called "The Theatre and the Screen":

I stood with my father in a side show [sic] and saw a miracle happen on a screen. A little man in a top hat was shown diving from a high platform into a swimming pool and then springing backwards out of the water and up onto his perch again. The tent that day was crowded with farmers and their wives and children who had come to see the sword swallower and the wild man from Borneo. But when for the last act this jerky little figure came walking along the side of the tent as it were, made his manikin bow to us the audience and then went twirling down from his high perch into the water, and zoop! back again the way he'd come, we thought no more of smoking knives or bloody meat that day. Later at night the farmers, their wives and children, all on the roads that led home like lengthening spokes from the bright city to the rim of darkness were talking of this wonder.[1]

Green had another memorable theater experience in 1915 when he went to Raleigh with Gordon Long, a neighborhood friend, to see D. W. Griffith's *The Birth of a Nation*.[2] (Several years before, he had read *The Clansman*, the book on which the movie was based, by fellow North Carolinian Thomas Dixon.) Green recalled the trip to Raleigh:

We broke down on the way to Raleigh to see this show. We got there just a few minutes late and got a seat on the balcony. It was packed. They had a traveling orchestra with it. . . . I have never seen such excitement in people, the audience. There was a sort of climactic scene where the Little Colonel on a horse is summoned into the Ku Klux Klan, and then there is a shot to the bugler in the Ku Klux paraphernalia blowing this call, the Ku Klux call to assemble. And this woman in the seat right in front of me sprang up and shouted, "Kill them, kill them," and fell in a faint.[3]

Green felt that the woman's outburst reflected "the power of music" and believed that a silent movie without background music would have had a different effect: "And without the trumpet note I doubt she would have fainted. So right there lies the mystery to me— the power of music in the theater and the marriage of that image on the screen with the sound of the trumpet made a powerful expression which neither one separately could have had."[4]

But Green understood that music was not the only source of the movie's power:

The effect of *The Birth of a Nation* was doubly strong in that it was a darned good dramatic story. It was well done. It had pathos, heartache, fervor, antagonism, even hate in it. The power of the drama was such that the spillover effect was not spiritually healthy. After you had gone through the experience of seeing this thing and appreciating it, there was this hangover of antagonism. There's no question about it that . . . when you came out from it and [saw] a black man, you didn't feel more like embracing him, but you felt more like pushing him away.[5]

Indeed, as Ralph Ellison wrote in 1949, "[I]t was this film that forged the twin screen image of the Negro as bestial rapist and grinning eye-rolling clown—stereotypes that are still with us today. . . . [I]t resulted in controversy, riots, heavy profits and the growth of the Klan. . . . [I]t became a further instrument in the dehumanization of the Negro."[6] Surprisingly, Green admired the film and was sorry that "the effect, the aesthetic effect, was swallowed up in its social significance. And that's a great pity. . . . I've never seen art used with more fervent result than that picture. . . . He had a great picture, unfortunately."[7]

Green added:

In the picture there were also examples of friendship and love between the races—as in *Gone with the Wind*. . . . Even though it might have had this racial strain and stress in its result . . . all in all the picture was, well, say, healthy because [of] all the heartache, the tragedy of the Civil War, the sympathy, the understanding that came out of that war [between] people on opposite sides who actually at heart were brothers. . . . Well, you could almost say the cleansing power of the tragic depiction of a tragedy—the Civil War, [the] suffering of the people, and so on—was of such consequence and importance that it outweighed, to my way of thinking, the racial touch.[8]

Green disagreed with Ellison's opinion of the film's influence, deeming it an "exaggeration," and elaborated on his view of the movie's effect on its audience, which he viewed as ultimately positive rather than negative:

I found . . . the whole thing, when it was over, a depiction of man, human beings, black and white, in a crisis of the human spirit, so that all in all it had this cleansing power. . . . But for Ellison and others to say that it did all this harm . . . is, I think, an exaggeration. As you know, Aristotle spoke about tragedy and the catharsis, the cleansing power of tragedy [that] creates in the spectator or auditor a sense of sympathy so keen and strong in good tragedy that the listener . . . wants to do something. . . . He cries out, "This ought not to be." . . . [It] makes him want to give himself to help this situation, makes him a better man because it brings out the noblest feeling in the human beings, this love that loves to give.[9]

Four years after viewing *The Birth of a Nation*, Green enjoyed another significant movie experience while serving in France: in 1919 he saw Charlie Chaplin in *Shoulder Arms* and included the memory of that viewing in his "Theatre and the Screen" essay as well:

Chuckles and gales of laughter swept through the hall at the antics of the little man, and for a while the memory of air raids, whining 75's, snipers, stink and filth was forgotten. He was the divine magician playing with the bauble of our souls for an hour. And some weeks later, when I saw the likeness of Charlot hauled through the streets of Paris and followed by a great crowd of hurrahing boys and girls, I joined in the procession which led to a moving-picture entrance. And from that day to this I have followed wherever he leads.[10]

Given Green's early recognition of the power of the motion picture screen, it is not surprising that he jumped on the opportunity to participate in the process of making movies. When Green went to Hollywood, talkies had just emerged, and the transition from silent film was still going on. Silent-film stars were struggling to find their way, and studios were scrambling for new talent to write the lines that now had to be spoken. Green was just such a talent. He remembered his arrival in Hollywood:

When I arrived, the agent [Hunter Lovelace] met me at the train and took me over to . . . First National at Warner Brothers at Burbank and took me in and introduced me to a little dynamic man—struck me as being rather little—behind a desk, named Darryl Zanuck. While I was being interviewed by Mr. Zanuck, in came a man named Jack Warner, one of the Warner brothers, and I was introduced, and Jack said, "Oh, yes, I've heard about you. You're the boy from the cotton fields." I never have liked that kind of introduction. . . . I got to know Zanuck very well during my stay there. . . . We used to exchange a lot of talk. . . . He told me how he got in the motion picture business. He tried out as a writer and brought in some stories to Warners or somebody, and they said, "Oh, no, we can't deal with that. Bring us a published book, and we'll look at it." "So," he said, "Green, you know what I did? . . . I went off and wrote a whole batch of stories and had them published." He gave me a copy. . . . "So," he said, "I march in with this book, and I hand it in, and so they look at me with some respect. So they hired me."[11]

Like Zanuck, Green surveyed the situation early in his tenure in Hollywood in order to learn how to be a success in that new arena. Hundreds of acres of buildings housed the "dream factories." He went to the cutting rooms, the wardrobes, the construction departments, and the sets. He familiarized himself with how the movie camera was used on those sets. He read everything he could find, both European and American, on the movies:

And the more I learned the more enthusiastic I became. Here indeed was the creation of the machine age which was the equal of the Word as spoken by men of old. Here was a medium infinite and universal in its power, able to depict anything—whether in heaven, or earth, or in hell; whether of man's relation to man or man's deepest submerged self. For the first time in history a completely democratic art form was available, capable of answering any vital demand made upon it by the imagination of any human being.[12]

Then Green got started: "I got an office and . . . in a short time, maybe a couple of weeks, I had a thirty- or forty-page treatment, a good outline with some dialogue, and took it in to Mr. Zanuck and left it."[13] A few days later Zanuck called him in and gave his enthusiastic approval to the work Green had done. Green thereupon

set to work on a script, put it into dialogue, shots and so on, and in four or five weeks I turned in the script—and sat and waited. And then the phone rang one day, and I was in a cold sweat, I am sure. . . . I was told to go in, and Zanuck had Mike Curtiz, the director, and Hal Wallis and a few other people, and they had all read this *Cabin in the Cotton* script. And Zanuck said, "We like it, Professor Green." He called me Professor then. Then he turned to Curtiz, Wallis, and some other fellows I don't remember, and he said, "I want this script shot without changing one word." So I went away so thrilled.[14]

It was during this time that Green met the creator of *The Birth of a Nation*:

There was a fellow, and I would see him sitting around a lot, and sometimes coming home in the afternoon I would pass him on a park bench. . . . I got to know him, and it was D. W. Griffith. I would sit down and talk with him. He didn't talk much. He couldn't get a job. He was down and out. . . . I used to talk to some of the movie people, "Why in the world can't they do something for D. W. Griffith? He is a great pioneer." . . . I was at MGM, I think, another time, and I noticed a writer in the next office and went in to call on him, and it was Buster Keaton. Buster was down and out, and they hired him as a writer. He didn't write anything. I thought that they could do something for Griffith.[15]

While Green's concern about Griffith may not have been heeded, he was consulted for his expertise in farming. Being the only farmer around, he became something of a technical adviser for *Cabin in the Cotton*, and, since he was supposed to know the type of people in cotton country, he was designated to help Mike Curtiz pick the cast: "So I went down the first morning with Curtiz, and there, in front of the gates . . . a mob of people. And so we opened up and we started tryouts. And one young lady trying out, a sort of freckle-faced girl, struck me as very good, and we needed kind of a lively young lady for the lead, the landlord's daughter. . . . I told Curtiz I liked her, and he said, 'Well, we'll cast her'—and her name was Bette Davis."[16]

Bette Davis later wrote in her autobiography about getting the part of "the southern girl in . . . an extremely interesting screenplay by Paul Green. It was an excellent part, mine—that of a rich, vixenish belle. . . .

The director, Michael Curtiz, did not want me for the part and made it clear. But Mr. Zanuck did and made it clearer. My director made my life hell every day." This was Davis's tenth movie but her first starring role, and she made the most of it, in spite of the "pressure." She recognized the importance of the role of Madge, which she called "my first downright, forthright bitch," and also wrote of the play, "One of my very favorite lines was in this picture": "'Ah'd love to kiss you, but ah just washed mah hair.'"[17]

Davis played this role opposite Richard Barthelmess, who "had been a great silent star"; his role was his last big Hollywood film appearance. Davis wrote that "Barthelmess was easygoing and kindly" but noted that his wife was often "sitting beside the director appraising our love scenes," adding to the pressure Davis felt. Furthermore, she remarked, "When his face was not being photographed, he relaxed in his dressing room," leaving his co-star to act her part in a close-up love scene without him. Davis wrote, "Mr. Curtiz, with a glint in his eye that could only have been borrowed from the Marquis de Sade, made me writhe toward the camera and kiss into a vacuum." Green, who was on and off the lot, was unaware of the suffering of the (at that point in her life) ingenue, and Davis "refused to let [Curtiz] get [her] down. The part was that good."[18]

For the film's setting, the studio brought in, all the way from Texas, a boxcar load of mature cotton plants with white open bolls to be replanted in the studio lot. Green had written a scene in which the black mothers bring their babies to the field and leave them on pallets in the shade, sucking small pieces of cloth filled with simple syrup or sugar water, called "sugar tits." Green recalled the scene: "I'll never forget the morning that here came all these black mothers with these little teeny babies—and they were howling and cutting up, but Mike Curtiz was a patient fellow. . . . Curtiz worked . . . a whole day trying to get them quiet. . . . Finally he threw up his hands and said, 'Take 'em out of here, take 'em out!' So that scene never appeared in the show."[19]

Another of the actors in this movie was Henry B. Walthal, who played the part of a poverty-stricken white tenant farmer afflicted with tuberculosis. Coincidentally, he had played the glamorous Little Colonel in *The Birth of a Nation*. One day on the set Green heard someone ask Walthal what he thought of the script and heard the response, "It won't make a dime."[20] The box-office fate of the film was of minor concern to Green, however, as he left for a brief visit to Chapel Hill. He was elated with what he was doing—with his earnings and with the artistic freedom he had been given.

At one point Green received a call informing him that Winfield (Winnie) Sheehan at the Fox Film Corporation wanted to see him. Fox wanted someone who could write for Will Rogers. Green recalled his interview with Sheehan, a movie mogul who had been secretary to the New York police commissioner Grover Whalen:

I went over to the writers' building—beautiful building—and met with [Julian] Johnson, the story editor, a good, stout, quiet man who had been married to Texas Guinan and had been divorced. . . . So he called up Sheehan's swank offices and took me up to Sheehan, but Sheehan wasn't in. The secretary said, "He's in the barbershop. He'd like to see you." So I go in with Johnson, and Sheehan is lying back getting a massage. . . . So he holds an interview right there. . . . They put the towels on his face, and he talks through the towel and asks me about myself and so on.[21]

Green described Sheehan as "a short, pudgy man, a good-hearted fellow, as I later learned, but woefully ignorant of the things I was interested in."[22] Following the barbershop interview, Sheehan showed off his huge, high-ceilinged office with a giant imported rubber plant and tempted Green with a much larger salary and a beautiful office in the new Writers' Building.

With the blessings of Warner Brothers, they came to an agreement, and Sheehan put Green to work on a script for *State Fair*, advising Green, "'The old bastard [Rogers] will try to bother you. Don't talk stories with the old bastard.' That's exactly what he called him. . . . 'He'll try to rewrite your stuff.'" Green was not worried about interference with the script. He wanted to get help wherever he could. He settled into his new office, and the "next morning . . . I heard this voice: 'Gre-een, anybody around here named Green?' I stuck my head out, and here come this fellow with boots and all. It was Will Rogers, who asked Green, 'How're you and the old bastard up there getting along?'" Green noted the coincidence that Rogers used the "same word" to describe Sheehan that Sheehan had used to describe Rogers. According to Green, Will Rogers "never once made the least suggestion on that film to me except one thing. I talked it over with him, and I wanted him to be a family man and sit in the evening with his newspaper and his pipe. He said, 'Now, wait a minute. Pipe? No smoking. No alcohol.'" But he did agree, finally, to use the pipe without tobacco.[23]

Green reported that he "saw a lot of Will. We'd have lunch together [and] talk. He was always public image. . . . When we'd get in the office alone he'd let down, but most of the time he was Will Rogers the actor."[24] Green admired this actor: "Will was fifty-five years old [and] didn't have an ounce of extra flesh on him." He was "athletic—played polo" and invited Green to watch. Green reported simply, "He was terrific." Green also noted that Rogers "chewed chewing gum all the time, and I often felt he was chewing gum rather than smoking. . . . I admired the fellow. I've always admired people who take care of their bodies."[25]

Indeed, Green and Rogers liked each other immediately. It was easy for Green to write in the folksy style that Rogers used. He admired Rogers not only for his good health but also for his talent, his common sense, and his friendliness. On a couple of occasions, however, he saw an aspect of Rogers's personality that baffled him:

I remember once having lunch with him in the lot café. Will Hayes, who was head of the censorship office, walked by, and Rogers called out and said, "Hey, Will, come over here." So Will Hayes came over. And Rogers said . . . "Will, we both like money, and I have figured out a scheme where we both can make plenty of money." Will Hayes said, "How is that, Will?" Will Rogers says, "I'll get a cage, and I'll put you in it, and I'll exhibit you throughout the land as a remarkable specimen, and I'll do the spiel. And we'll get rich." And Will Hayes turned sharp on his feet and went away. And I looked at Will Rogers and I couldn't figure that. . . . He sort of said something [like] "Stuffed shirt. . . . He has no more interest in morals."[26]

On another occasion Rogers had invited Green to be on the set for the shooting of the film *Judge Priest*, and Green witnessed another scene that did not place the actor in a very good light:

A woman came up—one of the extras—with a little teeny boy who was in the film as one of the crowd, and she said, "Mr. Rogers, Tommy would just love to have your autograph." So Tommy hands up the book to be autographed. Will takes it—I was standing by Will—and Will gets a pencil from the boy and "writes" in the book quite a bit. He doesn't make a mark at all. He just "writes," and he closes it up and hands the boy back his book. And he says, "How old is Tommy?" The mother says proudly, "He's eight . . . and he's in the third grade." I'll never forget what Will said: "Well, from the looks of it, he'll be in that grade a long time to come." He said that, and I couldn't figure that. So now Tommy opens his book to read the wonderful thing that Will had written, and there's nothing written. And the boy looks at Mr. Rogers and hands that book to his mother, and the mother looks at it, and then she looks at Rogers, and they turn quick away. . . . Will said to me, "You know, they just bother you to death."[27]

In spite of such disconcerting moments with the actor, writer and material were well matched for the script of *State Fair*: Green would always get excited when he talked about going to the North Carolina State Fair in Raleigh when he was a boy. He recalled what it was like for a teenage boy to meet on the fairgrounds a girl from some other part of the state and fall in love for a day. He knew how it was with young people who were coming with their families to display prize calves and see outlandish sideshows.

One day while Green was working on *State Fair*, he was shown the final version of the film *Cabin in the Cotton*. He wrote of his dismay:

Whatever touch of inspiration I thought I had in writing it was gone. On referring to my script, I found a bit here, a bit there, this end of a scene, this key line of a scene changed or left out. Somebody had been there while I was gone. I discussed the matter some days later with another writer. . . . "Yes," he said, "they gave your script to me to look over. I hope you don't mind. We often have to do that."

"Do what?" I asked.

"Well, smooth things up. You see, your script leaned too much toward one of those cussed artistic productions, and that's a thing no studio will allow. There's not a cent of money in them."

"How do you know there's not?"

"Listen, this is a business out here, not an art."[28]

Rewriting occurred with *State Fair*, too, and this time Green knew more about how it came about:

After I had finished that script and they had shot it, they had a studio run-through—you know, all the bigwigs, the directors, and so on. . . . Well . . . there was a fellow named Sol Wurtzel [who] had just appeared as one of the family out of Hungary or somewhere. He could hardly speak English. . . .

Rogers was there, and I was there watching it. They had a consensus and some person said, . . . "I think we have a family picture." Great glee, you know, if you can get a family picture that would suit everybody in the family, you got something. . . . I'll never forget what Sol . . . said, "Naw, *nein*—if we have more sex—*jah*! Yes!" I can see Will Rogers throwing his old hat down on the floor and grunting. Anyway, they had a meeting after we had gone, and they decided to put more sex in the film. . . . And of all things, the boy and girl in bed together, but of course, never show it. . . . But you knew they were in bed.[29]

Following that incident, Green had excused himself from the project, and Rogers had no more to do with it; but the studio hired another writer, Sonia Levine, to do the scene, and it was added.

In spite of Green's early defection, in the fall of 1932 he received a letter from Julian Johnson on the stationery of Fox Film Corporation Studio: "I have never written you my appreciation of your splendid performance on this lot. I feel that you did a job that very few men could do—and when I say that, I don't mean men merely writing in motion pictures, but dramatists or novelists anywhere. Your compression into a compact, pictorial scenario of the life and color so vividly suggested in the novel *State Fair* is an achievement of which anyone might be proud."[30]

NOTES

1. Paul Green, *The Hawthorn Tree: Some Papers and Letters on Life and the Theatre* (Chapel Hill: University of North Carolina Press, 1937). This passage opens the essay, which is also included in Green's *Drama and the Weather: Some Notes and Papers on Life and the Theatre* (New York: Samuel French, 1958).

2. In the aforementioned essay "The Theatre and the Screen," Green likewise wrote about this trip to Raleigh to see the movie.

3. Paul Green, interview by Billy E. Barnes, March 1975, p. 86, Southern Oral History Program Collection, Southern Historical Collection, Wilson Library, University of North Carolina at Chapel Hill (hereafter cited as Barnes interview, with appropriate date and transcript page number).

4. Paul Green, interview by Rhoda Wynn, February 1974, tape 1, pp. 4-5, Southern Oral History Program Collection, Southern Historical Collection (hereafter cited as Wynn interview, with appropriate tape and transcript page number). Green also spoke with the author about "how music fitted this thing." Paul Green, interview by James R. Spence, August 9, 1979, audio recordings relating to Paul Green, 1974-1979 (collection #5170), Southern Historical Collection (hereafter cited as Spence interview, with appropriate date).

5. Spence interview, August 9, 1979.

6. This passage is quoted from the title essay in Ellison's book *Shadow and Act* (New York: Random House, 1953), 275. The actual essay "The Shadow and the Act" originally appeared in *The Reporter*.

7. Spence interview, August 9, 1979.

8. Ibid.

9. Ibid.

10. Green, *The Hawthorn Tree*, 40.

11. Wynn interview, tape 1, pp. 10-13. The book to which Zanuck is referring is his *"Habit" and Other Short Stories* (Los Angeles: Times-Mirror Press, 1923).

12. Green, *The Hawthorn Tree*, 42.

13. Wynn interview, tape 1, p. 11.

14. Wynn interview, tape 1, pp. 11-12. Warner Brothers produced the film *Cabin in the Cotton*, based on the novel by Harry Harrison Kroll, in 1932.

15. Barnes interview, March 1975, p. 88.

16. Wynn interview, tape 1, p. 17.

17. Bette Davis, *The Lonely Life: An Autobiography* (New York: G. P. Putnam's Sons, 1962), 134-136.

18. Davis, *The Lonely Life*, 135.

19. Wynn interview, tape 1, pp. 17-18.

20. Wynn interview, tape 1, p. 19.

21. Wynn interview, tape 1, p. 23.

22. Wynn interview, tape 1, p. 28.

23. Spence interview, October 24, 1974; Fox Film Corporation produced the film *State Fair*, based on the novel by Philip Stong and with screenplay credit to Sonia Levine and Green, in 1933.

24. Spence interview, October 24, 1974.

25. Spence interview, April 29, 1978.

26. Wynn interview, tape 1, p. 35.

27. Wynn interview, tape 1, pp. 35-36.

28. Green, *The Hawthorn Tree*, 43-44.

29. Wynn interview, tape 2, pp. 10-11.

30. Letter dated October 5, 1932, Paul Green Papers, folder 202, Southern Historical Collection.

21: Social Activism

Even as he pursued his writing career in Hollywood, Green entered upon the social activism for which he would also be remembered. In April 1932 he was first publicly identified as a person who had an interest in social justice that went beyond his writing. On April 1 Green received from the National Committee for the Defense of Political Prisoners a letter bearing his own name on the letterhead[1] and signed by Theodore Dreiser and three others, asking him to help raise $10,000 for the defense of the "Scottsboro Boys"—the nine illiterate black youths accused of raping two white mill girls while they all shared a freight car ride between Chattanooga and Scottsboro, Alabama.[2] An Alabama trial court had sentenced the young men to death. The convictions of the defendants had been upheld by the Alabama Supreme Court and were then being appealed to the Supreme Court of the United States. Green responded on April 11 with "An Open Letter to Theodore Dreiser." He said that even if he were able to contribute, he would not do so because he did not believe it would do any good. He went on:

Mr. Dreiser, I also have written, agonized, talked and prayed over the Scottsboro case just as you have, and each day I have seen these boys twenty-four hours nearer death. And did you know that one of the reasons why they are so set and bound for the electric chair is that you and your ignorant but well-wishing friends continue to hang your political theories around their necks. . . . You keep on stirring up trouble by linking your half-baked Marxism and social therapies to the race question, and thereby prepare seven blind and dumb but suffering victims for more certain sacrifice. . . . Ten thousand dollars are needed at once you say. Well, let me tell you that ten times ten thousand and ten times that won't pull these boys loose from the communistic symbolism in which you and your friends have sought to "frame" them. You and they seem determined to make it appear that they are political prisoners. They are not such and never have been. They are prisoners to a Southern—yes, a local attitude of ignorance, prejudice, hate and fear if you will. . . . The judgment levied against these boys has nothing to do with capital or labor or with any workers' government or system of politics and economics whatsoever. They are condemned to die because as Negroes they attacked Southern white women, or were supposed to.[3]

He concluded the letter by declaring that "it would be an ever-lasting sin for you to use the bones of seven Negro boys to hammer the drums of a social revolution."[4]

With this letter Green was not running for cover. If he had been afraid that his name and reputation would be tarnished by being on the same letterhead with Dreiser's and others, he would have resigned from the committee—but he did not. He was genuinely angry with the Communists for using the accused young black men to promote their cause, and he wanted to make it clear that their cause was not his cause. His approach, then and in later fights, was to save the individual, without regard for long-range social goals. It is also evident that although Green enjoyed his art-related friendships with the great and near-great, he was willing to offend them when he felt that they were endangering the lives of the Scottsboro defendants.

Also in 1932, Green took a break from his Hollywood writing to devote additional time to his own playwriting, as well as to his social concerns. In July Green and Lamar Stringfield went to the University of Iowa to work on E. C. Mabie's production of *Tread the Green Grass*. Green called the play a "folk fantasy." Like *The Field God*, it was about the conflict between "natural" human beings and an "unnatural" local religion. In the play, Tina, a sensitive farm girl, meets a carefree boy named Davey. She develops normal sexual desires that are immediately in conflict with her religion. She is unable to reconcile the two, and it finally drives her mad.

Tread the Green Grass was the first of Green's plays in which he was able to fully integrate music, dance, and drama. He was remembering the work of Alexis Granowsky. Green told of how Stringfield had put together an orchestra of about twenty-six pieces. . . . There was a horse in it, an old horse that gets down in the road, and the preachers pray over it. It was a real folk piece. And with the music that Lamar had arranged, the unbelievable became believable. You know how . . . with music [the audience] can often accept something that in the cold prose you wouldn't accept. So on the opening night it turned terribly warm and they had no air conditioning in this theater. It was jammed with people. . . . In the middle of the scene where the old horse gets down and they pray over him, to our surprise, he didn't get up. The prayer didn't help him. . . . The stage hands rushed out on the stage and opened [the horse costume]. . . . The temperature [was] 106 in the auditorium, and [they] had passed out. We had to get 'em outa there and resuscitate 'em and announce to the audience that the prayers didn't help [the horse]. The audience enjoyed . . . the joke, and we went on with the play.[5]

Barrett Clark came from New York for the performance. In reviewing the play for the *New York Times*, Clark said that it "marks an important point in this playwright's artistic development."[6]

A letter Elizabeth wrote to Paul while he was in Iowa reveals that he was then negotiating with Warner Brothers to do another script but was holding out for his price. She encouraged him in that stand. She said that her father was getting very feeble and had "remarked it was probably his last Communion Sunday. . . . Pa wants us to have our two youngest baptized, and I am planning on it for next Sunday, if you don't object." She reminded him who had been godparents to their first two children and made suggestions about godparents for the second two. "I hate to bother you with sech [*sic*], but I think we owe the gesture for Pa's peace of mind."[7] Green later said that by this period of his life he was "totally pagan," but he obviously continued to have certain contacts with churches as a matter of courtesy to his relatives. The fact that neither of the two youngest children had been baptized when they were newborn, as well as Elizabeth's assertion that the matter was a "gesture for Pa's peace of mind," suggests that Elizabeth herself was not pushing the matter out of personal conviction.

A final paragraph of the same letter is revealing as to the Greens' personal relationship, particularly during these periods when Paul's work took him elsewhere to live: "Honey, ol' man, do you realize you will receive this on our wedding anniversary. We have had our dark moments but pulled through rather well so far. When I consider how glorious you are I wonder that I am able to endure my happiness. You . . . are my life, sweet, and when you are gone everything is stale and unprofitable." It was their tenth anniversary. In spite of her remarks about their time apart, Elizabeth Green had learned that there were numerous demands upon her popular husband that would take him away from home or otherwise consume his time.

Indeed, Paul Green continued to receive a large volume of mail from people who wanted something. Bobbs-Merrill Company sent a novel, asking if it had movie possibilities. The Macauley Company sought comment on a book it was bringing out. A student editor at Queens College wanted a contribution of some writing for a student magazine. There were offers of honorary memberships in various literary societies and book societies. A man named J. Percy Bond wrote from New York about becoming a student at the University of North Carolina. He said he had played the lead in In Abraham's Bosom when it was produced at Howard University and had met Green in Iowa. A lawyer named G. W. Chamlee of Chattanooga wrote, saying that he and a group were forming a southern committee to aid in the Scottsboro defense. He asked for Green's support and the use of his name. Green responded affirmatively.[8]

Even in Hollywood he was called upon to undertake responsibilities other than writing. When Franklin D. Roosevelt, running for the presidency in 1932, paid a visit to Hollywood, "there was a reception committee set up. . . . Lionel Barrymore called me up and asked me [to] serve as one of the writers. They had these fellows from different committees—actors, writers, designers, and so on. He was sort of a leading arranger of things. I told him I would be glad to serve on the committee. So the committee goes to the Hollywood Bowl. . . . [Roosevelt] made the tour inside the Bowl, drove all the way around, . . . and people cheered him."[9] Roosevelt was riding with Charlie Chaplin, who was very popular at the time, "and he makes a speech, and he promised nothing except change—no details [as to] how it was going to be done."[10] Green was not impressed. He also recalled seeing Roosevelt in Hollywood: "I remember in Hollywood . . . once seeing the picture of Franklin Delano Roosevelt come on the screen and there was applause, and then Joe Stalin's picture came on the

The glen house, Chapel Hill, ca. 1929.

screen—and tremendous applause! . . . I didn't applaud this Joe Stalin. I had already for my own self decided this was another one of those dictators, a killer, a man who was ambitious and ruthless."[11]

Shortly afterward, Green received a telegram from Mrs. Florence Bowers of the Thomas-for-President Committee (Norman Thomas was the presidential candidate of the Socialist Party). She asked him to sign a letter of support that had been drafted by Elmer Davis and co-signed by Heywood Broun and others. He responded by telegram: "CONSIDERING THE POLICIES ADVOCATED BY HOOVER, ROOSEVELT, AND NORMAN THOMAS THERE IS NO DOUBT IN MY MIND THAT THOMAS IS THE BEST SUITED TO BE PRESIDENT OF THE UNITED STATES STOP I AM GLAD TO GIVE MY SIGNATURE TO ANY LEGITIMATE MOVEMENT IN HIS BEHALF."[12] Green explained that he

had met Thomas, I remember, here in Chapel Hill. We lived down in that glen. And one day there was a knock on the door, and there stood Norman Thomas. He was in Chapel Hill. . . . He didn't call up or anything. He said, "I just came out. I thought maybe you would be at home." . . . He came in and sat down, and we had a fine talk, and I was very much impressed by him.

"I built myself a little cabin out behind [our] house in the glen. . . . I wrote a lot of plays in that place," Paul Green wrote.

And I talked with him some about our capital punishment cases in North Carolina and so on. . . . I liked his ideas. I knew he didn't have any chance to getting to be president, but I thought he would have made a very good one. . . . Even in conversation, how eloquent he was.[13]

Green's concern about social issues continued to find its way into his writing, prompting a reviewer of his first novel, which R. M. McBride and Company published in September 1932, to contrast his depiction of the South with the popular moonlight and magnolias image. Reviewing *The Laughing Pioneer* in the *Saturday Review of Literature*, Mariston Chapman wrote:

It is a picture of life in the North Carolina plains country done with the vividness of an etching. The illusion of reality is maintained so skillfully that a reader contemplating the picture awakes with a belated shock to the realization that he has seen more than his nerves can well bear. Accustomed as we are to novels of the Southland as pretty-pretty, day-dream romances that distract the mind, or as revealing treatises composed by unripe realists, it is good to come upon one which . . . points the way of escape from that artistic lethargy which has fallen upon folk literature in the last decade.[14]

The Laughing Pioneer includes some unforgettable scenes, such as one in which a robed member of the Ku Klux Klan marches up the middle aisle of a country church to present a Christmas offering. But the core of the novel, as in *Tread the Green Grass*, is the conflict between human passion and the local religion. Miss Alice Long, a spinster who has devoted her life to caring for her aging father, is sexually attracted to a wandering young farmhand who comes to live at her home. Her religious beliefs deny her this relationship (even though the community and the Klan think otherwise), but her torture causes her to develop what the neighbors call "brain fever," which ultimately kills her. In spite of critical praise, the book was not a best seller. Paul Green would have to continue his more lucrative writing in Hollywood.

NOTES

1. Two years before, Green had received from Forest Bailey, director of the American Civil Liberties Union in New York, a telegram asking him to join a committee "of 100 more or less of persons uncompromisingly opposed to state censorship." The committee would have a nucleus of prominent writers. Green replied, "Accept membership on committee absolutely opposing state censorship of drama." Transcripts (in pencil) of both telegrams, dated only 1930, are in the Paul Green Papers (collection #3693), folder 136, Southern Historical Collection, Wilson Library, University of North Carolina at Chapel Hill. A short time later, when Green was asked to become a member of the National Committee for the Defense of Political Prisoners, he signed on along with such illustrious members as Sherwood Anderson, Malcolm Cowley, Theodore Dreiser, Langston Hughes, Claude McKay, Edna St. Vincent Millay, Lewis Mumford, Upton Sinclair, Mary Heaton Vorse, and a number of others. (For a sample of the committee's letterhead, which lists these and other notables, see a letter from Elliot E. Cohen to Paul Green dated September 19, 1932, in the Green Papers, folder 199.)

2. Letter dated April 11, 1932, Green Papers, folder 200.

3. Laurence G. Avery, ed., *A Southern Life: Letters of Paul Green, 1916-1981*, Fred W. Morrison Series in Southern Studies (Chapel Hill: University of North Carolina Press, 1994), 201-202.

4. Avery, *A Southern Life*, 202.

5. Paul Green, interview by James R. Spence, August 9, 1979, James R. Spence audio recordings relating to Paul Green, 1974-1979 (collection #5170), Southern Historical Collection (hereafter cited as Spence interview, with appropriate date).

6. Quoted in Agatha Boyd Adams, *Paul Green of Chapel Hill*, University of North Carolina Library Extension Publications, vol. 16, No. 2 (Chapel Hill: University of North Carolina Library, January 1951), 53.

7. Elizabeth Green to Paul Green, July 6, 1932, Paul Green Papers, subseries 4.1: Elizabeth Lay Green Papers, folder 4078. The use of folk words such as "sech" was an affectation that the Greens had picked up in their college playwriting days.

8. Letter from Bond, dated January 6, 1932, Paul Green Papers, folder 198; from Chamlee, July 23, 1932, Green Papers, folder 224.

9. Spence interview, August 9, 1979.

10. Spence interview, October 24, 1976.

11. Paul Green, interview by Rhoda Wynn, February 1974, tape 4, pp. 1-2, Southern Oral History Program Collection, Southern Historical Collection.

12. Both telegrams, dated September 23, 1932, are in the Paul Green Papers, folder 198.

13. Spence interview, August 9, 1979.

14. "A Tale of the Southland," *Saturday Review of Literature* 9 (September 24, 1932): 123-124.

22: Affluence

As the Great Depression worsened, economic conditions were particularly difficult in rural Harnett County, and during the spring and summer of 1932 Paul Green made loans to his brother Hugh to get him through the growing season. Fall crop sales were devastating, however. Cotton that had been 26 cents a pound in 1926 sold for 5 cents. Tobacco that had been 25 cents sold at 12, with buyers ignoring lower grades altogether.

In January 1933 Paul's half brother John wrote, saying that he was simply unable to pay back what he had borrowed. Hugh wrote just a week later, also asking for money, and noting, "and if I ask for it you may know that I'm bound and compelled to have it and there is no other way. I do hope you will still have a job and plenty money for it is a consolation for someone in the family to have some."[1] A few days later it developed that Pleasant Union Church needed to borrow some money. Someone got the idea that native son and former member Paul Green, now a rich Hollywood writer, might be willing to make the loan. Deacon Hugh Green was designated to make the request, which he did. Native son politely declined.

An article written by Lee Shippey and published in the *Los Angeles Times* in the spring of 1933 offers a contemporary glimpse of Green in Hollywood:

Paul Green is one of those serious Southerners. He looks at life very earnestly, almost as earnestly as he does at Paul Green.

When he joined the staff of Warner Brothers a few weeks ago, story after story was submitted to him, all of which he read intently and rejected. "I think they would all be merely wasting my time," he said. So the studio

Hugh and Mable Green with two of their babies.

turned these stories over to other men to write, and Green is writing a story
for George Arliss around the great character of Voltaire.

He considers Paul Green's time much too valuable to waste.

He has demonstrated "the importance of being earnest" even in
Hollywood. Last year he came out here, but declined to do certain things.
Unless he could write a story sincerely he declined to write it at all, no
matter if the salary per week was several times as much as he had received
before. So his contract ended. This year he was recalled to finish unfinished
work in his own way. Which comes pretty near to establishing a record.[2]

While Shippey may have idealized Green somewhat, it was true
that Green had made enough of a name for himself in Hollywood to
be matched with a very appropriate project. The film producer
Darryl F. Zanuck had a manuscript devoted to the life of eighteenth-
century French philosopher and author Voltaire that had been written

by two of his friends. He needed a movie script from it to star George
Arliss, an ideal assignment for Paul Green, a philosophy professor
who was also a playwright. Green met with Arliss, the sixty-five-year-
old silent film star who had already made a successful transition to
sound movies.[3] The actor laid down a minimum of rules: "'I never try
to dictate to a writer what to do . . . but I never allow any birds or
animals in my pictures, [and] I never allow any vulgarity or
profanity.'"[4] Those restrictions did not bother Green, who had
worked with Will Rogers and had witnessed Mike Curtiz chasing the
movie dog Rex off the set of *Cabin in the Cotton* when he couldn't get
the animal to perform according to the script.

When Green finished writing the manuscript and Zanuck's
committee approved it, it was given to Arliss just as he was going on
vacation to Palm Springs. The following day Green got a call from the
actor saying that he wanted to come back from his vacation
immediately. They met at the Champs Élysées Hotel. Arliss liked
Green's script, but his tongue could not speak the lines as written by
the southerner. He told Green, "'I've studied your script thoroughly
and, as I said before, I like it. But in saying the lines to myself I find
that your'—I think he used the word 'vernacular'—'is such that I
can't say some of the speeches . . . and I would like to go through the
script with you, line by line, and wherever it needs turning into my
idiom, let's do that.'"[5] The two men, joined by Arliss's secretary,
made the changes over a period of several days. Green developed a
great admiration for the movie star because he was such a meticulous
artist. Later, during the actual filming, Arliss insisted upon redoing
one particular scene twenty-seven times.

Sometime during the making of *Voltaire*, Green got into a
discussion with Zanuck about how much power Hollywood had and
how it should be producing more movies like *Disraeli* (also with
George Arliss), which Green had just seen. He said that this film
proved that the public would accept good movies, but Zanuck replied,
"You are so wrong. That picture has not made any particular money
for us." Zanuck reached under his desk blotter and took out a list of
Warner Brothers productions. "Here is the Arliss picture that is
making us money," he said. "It is called *The Unexpected Father*. Now,
that's making money." Green commented that he had heard of that

one and that the standards were much lower than in *Disraeli*. "That may be true, Mr. Green," Green recalled Zanuck responding, "but my business is to make pictures that the people go to see, and that's what I'm doing for Warner Brothers, and I'll continue to do it." Green later remembered that because of their different outlooks, "a coldness sprang up between Zanuck and me."[6] As a result of that coldness, he went over to Fox and wrote another script for Will Rogers, *Doctor Bull*, from the James Gould Cozzens novel *The Last Adam*, and later, also for Rogers, *David Harum*.[7]

Green's contract to write the latter screenplay came at a good time, for Hugh had written at the end of May, complaining, "It's been such a long time since I heard anything from you, I feel like I'm trying to write to a stranger." Brother Paul apparently felt guilty, so when he signed a $7,500 contract with Fox for the *David Harum* script, he sent Hugh an unsolicited check. The response: "A thousand thanks. . . . It came just when I was racking my brain."[8]

Hugh's financial woes may have persisted, but Paul's success continued. Within a week after signing his Fox contract, he had a meeting with Samuel Goldwyn: "So on that particular day I went over to [Goldwyn's] studio [MGM]. And he had a lunch and he had a whole lot of people there to this luncheon, sort of bigwigs in Hollywood. . . . And I kept wondering, 'What the heck goes on? Why should he give me this luncheon?' And after the luncheon he showed me around the studio and then went into his office, and he said, 'I want you to work for me.' . . . He said, 'I'll give you two thousand a week.' I was making fifteen hundred a week."[9]

It developed that MGM was shooting a film based on Tolstoy's *Resurrection*, starring Frederic March and Anna Sten. Goldwyn had recently brought Sten from Poland with great fanfare. The script-writers had been unable to come up with an ending for the film, and Goldwyn was under pressure because Frederic March was planning to leave for the South Seas aboard his yacht. Green reported the rest of the story:

I went over, and there was another fellow came in named Thornton Wilder. . . . I had met Thornton years and years before at the McDowell Colony, and I admired his writings greatly. Then it turns out that he and I both had been asked to write this ending for this play. . . . Evidently, Goldwyn had got the idea of both of us and thought, "Now if I put them both together, maybe the two of them could come up with the right ending." . . . I said, "I know what the problem is. You can't afford to let this woman end the play as an unredeemed prostitute." [Goldwyn] says, "Exactly." . . . I said, . . . "How're you going to satisfy the folks, say, in Kansas?" And he said, "That's the problem." . . . So Wilder and I went to work together on this ending. And we worked out something, and we turned it in, and he called us in the next day, and he said, "Fellows, it won't do. This is not right. It's just not right." Well, we tried another one, and we sent it in—"It's not right." He didn't know what was right, but he would have recognized it if he'd ever get it. So he made us an amazing proposition. Time was running out, and he said, "Gentlemen, I propose this. If you two fellows will agree not to leave this studio till you find the ending, I will send food in." . . . So I looked at Wilder, and Wilder looked at me and—"Okay, okay." So we went to work. And I remember that particular night, we worked on, and Wilder walked around . . . . And finally Wilder said, "I've got it, I've got it, I believe." And then he ran over there to the table and scribbled something, and he said, "We will adapt the story of Jesus. . . . Jesus, through suffering, gets crucified."[10]

When they handed in the script, Goldwyn said, "'Fellows, you got it, you got it! That's exactly what I've been wanting. . . . This is going to be wonderful.'" Green concluded this story: "Well, you had to admire the guy. He knew what he wanted, and he could recognize it when it showed up.[11]

Like Zanuck, Goldwyn confided in Green about his own past, before he was the success he had become:

Mr. Green, I've had one of the greatest experiences. I was in New York the other day, and I walked along a street—I don't remember what street it was—but I suddenly remembered that it was right here that I walked with my mother and father when we were immigrants. I was a boy, and we'd just landed and were walking along this street, and I was looking at this great city. The other day I remembered it so clearly, and you know what I did, Mr. Green? . . . I stopped right there and I cried. I just stood on the sidewalk and I cried. I was so happy to think what this great country has allowed me to do . . . me, a poor immigrant boy.[12]

Green likely understood, being a poor southern boy himself and seeing, in contrast to his own good fortune, his brother Hugh's struggles. At about the same time, Green sold to Fox the screen rights to *The House of Connelly*. He was so delighted with all of his good fortune that he mailed checks as presents to several members of the family. Hugh wrote back, "It's just too good of you to send the check as you did. . . . Allie [their half sister Alda] was dumbfounded and said she didn't know what to do with hers and I told her to go to town and spend it and get some enjoyment."[13]

Paul Green did not just send money home. He also made brief visits there, during one of which his mentor Horace Williams offered him some advice on how to invest his wealth: "Mr. Williams, Horace, came down to see me and . . . he was so patient. He let me go to Hollywood and still kept me on the faculty. He said, 'Paul, I understand that you've got a little money.' Well, . . . he wanted me to go in with him and buy Negro property and make forty percent income. That's when I told him that I hoped I would die and burn in hell before I would ever do it. He laughed and said, 'Well, you owe it to Elizabeth and the children.'"[14] Green's banker advised him to buy two hundred acres of land just east of Chapel Hill that his institution owned as a result of a foreclosure. After some initial skepticism, he purchased the tract, and he and Elizabeth began dreaming of building a new house on it.

In the meantime, he moved his family to California for a few months. He rented a house at 7647 Mulholland Highway, Los Angeles. Green described it:

A driveway up in the hills—ran along the ridge of the hills. You could . . . see for miles and miles over Burbank and that valley overlooking Warner Brothers. We just couldn't find any place to live. We didn't want to get this place, but . . . see, it was Depression. . . . It was a splashy place. The dining room must have been forty feet long, . . . all furnished. Mr. Parker, the owner, . . . he'd fallen into hard times. It was such a big house, he couldn't rent it. He finally came down to two hundred dollars a month. . . . Mahogany doors . . . rooms for the children, a wishing well in the front yard . . . a pirate's den behind the edge of the cliff . . . a trout pool under . . . live oaks.[15]

Green was a bit embarrassed by the place, which was so ostentatious that "when James Boyd came out, this rich man with a forty-two-room mansion, he came to the back door," and when Green opened the door for him, Boyd "took off his cap and said, 'Please, suh, can I come in?' . . . Then he asked me, 'Could I sleep in the garage?'"[16]

The House of Connelly, by Paul Green. Photograph from the WPA Federal Theatre Project of New York City. *Left to right*: Rose McClendon (Big Sue), Fanny de Knight (Big Sis), Margaret Barker (Patsy Tate), and Franchot Tone (Will Connelly).

Elizabeth's mother likewise visited. Winnie Sheehan, head of Fox Studios, took Mrs. Lay and her daughter up to his mansion in the hills to see his roses and told them how he had bought the ceiling from an Italian villa and had shipped it over. They visited movie lots and toured the area.

From home, Hugh wrote that he was in need of some money for the crop. In response Paul enclosed a check and said, "I am sorry to have to mention it but I will just have to have these loans back in the fall. I guess the other will have to wait."[17] Even after acquiring the two hundred acres of land near Chapel Hill and enjoying a measure of high living in Hollywood, he could see that his funds were not limitless.

The entire family returned to Chapel Hill on August 1, 1933. In a story that appeared in the *Charlotte Observer*, reporter Robert W. Madry wrote, "When he roared into town the other day with two large motor cars, one of them a brand new machine, the neighbors began to wonder if he hadn't come home to show off. But when they saw how many were in his party and how much baggage he carried, it was clear enough that he needed the cars." Madry hastily assured readers that fame and money had not turned Green's head: "He is the same plain, modest type of chap he was when he left the Harnett county soil 16 years ago to enter the university." He described how Green, since his arrival, had been "taking his workouts with the baseball team that represents one of the local restaurants," and how he was still pitching ambidextrously.[18]

In spite of any misgivings, Green was still highly optimistic about Hollywood. He told Madry, "'It is my sincere conviction that the movies constitute the most powerful art form we have today. They have their abuses, of course. For one thing the sex stuff is still emphasized too much. But they are improving all the time.'" Madry then cited an example Green had shared: "'The movies afford an opportunity that is not to be found on what is called the legitimate stage. . . . George Arliss, for instance, would like to return to the London stage . . . but he feels that to do so would be throwing away the opportunity of reaching a much larger audience, an audience that includes almost the whole world.'"[19]

Green luxuriated in the beauty of home and resumed keeping a diary: "Found a yellow bill cuckoo's nest in exploring around our contemplated farm homesite—situated about nine feet from the ground in a little pine. . . . Walked through woods and back through Battle Park with the children. Noticed a touch of autumn now and then. . . . Black gums and sycamores showed yellow and even brown leaves here and there." Paul and Elizabeth explored their land, found a witch hazel bush by the branch, the remains of a rock chimney on an old house site. They identified seventy-one "different kinds of trees." Another day they found a muscadine vine with large black grapes and "a well-fruited 'simmon tree."[20] They noticed large patches of goldenrod and blue asters.

Paul and a helper began clearing out the spring on his new property. He wrote: "In the evening a little picnic with the children by the spring, cooked hotdogs, steaks, swung with them. Returned about 8 P.M., climbing the hill with an array of lights, blankets, bottles and baskets. Al Smith [the family dog] along sniffing about and growling at imaginary spectres."[21] A few days later there was another night picnic, with Proff Koch and his wife and Freddie B. McCall (of the law school faculty) and his wife Adeline in attendance. (Adeline was a niece of Koch and had been Caro Mae Green's roommate in New York.)

After a morning of working on *David Harum*, Green joined friends for golf at the Hope Valley Country Club, which he had recently joined. A new class of freshmen arrived on campus, but he still had no specific plans to return to teaching. He played tennis with his friend Bill Olsen. Though the socializing was enjoyable, Green was agonizing over the script. When he got stuck on *David Harum* he would write on other projects, but visitors interrupted. For example, a man from Richmond came with a personal true story of his time on a chain gang. And there were others: "Next came Reverend Henderson about Robert Griffin, the colored boy whom I'd tried to help. Promised what I could. At noon Robert came. Gave him $25 and a good suit of clothes. Returned his lynching story."[22]

Though Green was being drawn back into his North Carolina home, Hollywood continued to call. On September 25 Hunter Lovelace at Fox sent a wire indicating that Green needed to come out and help the studio with the production of *The House of Connelly*— "at regular salary which will cover expenses."[23] Green had turned down Lovelace's offer to write the film script, but Fox apparently nevertheless needed his advice on the production.

Before Green left for California, *Doctor Bull* arrived at a Raleigh movie theater. On September 28 Paul took Elizabeth, Caro Mae, and his two eldest children to see it, but they caught only the last half. Green's verdict was: "Rotten! Rogers no good, the director, John Ford worse. Remember Ford's telling me last summer of the hard time he was trying to get Rogers to act my lines. But I know all the fault was not Rogers'. Discouraged about ever making an interesting vehicle out of *Harum* for Rogers."[24] But he would go to Hollywood and try.

Upon arriving in Los Angeles, Green checked into the Roosevelt Hotel, and Hunter Lovelace came bearing offers from Fox and others; but by then Green had decided he was going back to Chapel Hill as soon as he could finish his duties with *House of Connelly* and *David Harum*.

While there, however, Green went by to see his friends Laurence and
Helen Stallings.[25] Helen was the daughter of Dr. Hubert Poteat,
president of Wake Forest College. Laurence was a well-established
playwright and novelist and had gained particular attention with
What Price Glory, which he had co-authored with Maxwell Anderson.
Stallings "was a great friend to everybody in Hollywood, and he was
always telling me what to do. . . . He was going to make a lot of money
and go back" home to North Carolina. Green explained that after
some successful writing, Stallings would say, "No more Hollywood.
I've got enough money," but then his money would run out and he
would stay. Stallings was Marxist in his beliefs but succumbed to
luxury. Once he came by with a new, luxurious automobile and told
Green, "I got a tremendous new contract with Paramount." Green
respected this other North Carolina writer as a capable writer and as a
fellow veteran. Stallings had lost a leg in the battle at Chateau-
Thierry but had maintained his "enthusiasm."[26]

At the studio, Green talked with Will Rogers, who, he recorded,
"looks more harassed and busily lonely than usual." Rogers said that
Doctor Bull had not killed him, but the shooting wasn't all over yet.[27]
To ease his own loneliness, and since it appeared that he was going to
be on the West Coast longer than he intended, Green sent for
Elizabeth. On October 19 she wired him from Memphis to notify him
that she was on her way to join him.[28]

NOTES

1. John Green to Paul Green, January 2, 1933, and Hugh Green to Paul Green, January 8,
1933, Paul Green Papers (collection #3693), folder 246, Southern Historical Collection,
Wilson Library, University of North Carolina at Chapel Hill.

2. Quoted in Agatha Boyd Adams, *Paul Green of Chapel Hill*, University of North Carolina
Library Extension Publications, vol. 16, No. 2 (Chapel Hill: University of North Carolina
Library, January 1951), 58.

3. Warner Brothers produced the film *Voltaire*, based on a novel by George Gibbs and
E. Lawrence Dudley, in 1933. Credit for the screenplay went to Green and Maude T. Howell.

4. Paul Green, interview by Rhoda Wynn, February 1974, tape 1, p. 26, Southern Oral
History Program Collection, Southern Historical Collection (hereafter cited as Wynn
interview, with appropriate tape and transcript page number).

5. Ibid.

6. Wynn interview, tape 1, p. 15.

7. Fox Film Corporation produced the films *Doctor Bull* and *David Harum* in 1933 and
1934 respectively.

8. Hugh Green to Paul Green, May 28, June 11, 1933, Paul Green Papers, folder 246.

9. Wynn interview, tape 2, p. 14.

10. Wynn interview, tape 2, pp. 16-17.

11. Wynn interview, tape 2, pp. 18-19.

12. Wynn interview, tape 1, pp. 33-34. Green may have remembered Goldwyn's story inaccurately, or Goldwyn may have told it inaccurately, for Goldwyn did not arrive in America with his parents.

13. Hugh Green to Paul Green, June 13, 1933, Paul Green Papers, folder 246.

14. Paul Green, interview by Billy E. Barnes, May 1975, p. 74, Southern Oral History Program Collection, Southern Historical Collection.

15. Paul Green, interview by James R. Spence, August 9, 1979, James R. Spence audio recordings relating to Paul Green, 1974-1979 (collection #5170), Southern Historical Collection (hereafter cited as Spence interview, with appropriate date).

16. Ibid.

17. Paul Green to Hugh Green, July 1, 1933, Paul Green Papers, folder 246. Green also discussed these loans with the author. Spence interview, April 29, 1978.

18. Robert W. Madry, "Paul Green Plans to Continue to Live in State; Not to Teach," *Charlotte Observer*, August 6, 1933. Green likewise discussed with the author his family's return to Chapel Hill, specifically how he needed two cars in which to transport all of them and their things. Spence interview, April 29, 1978.

19. Madry, "Paul Green Plans to Continue to Live in State."

20. Paul Green Diary, September 7, 18, 1933, Paul Green Papers (hereafter cited as Diary, with entry date).

21. Diary, September 8, 1933.

22. Diary, September 14, 1933.

23. Telegram, Lovelace to Green, September 25, 1933, Paul Green Papers, folder 241.

24. Diary, September 28, 1933.

25. Diary, October 2, 3, 1933.

26. Wynn interview, tape 5, pp. 16-17.

27. Diary, October 4, 1933.

28. Telegram, Elizabeth Green to Paul Green, October 19, 1933, Paul Green Papers, subseries 4.1: Elizabeth Lay Green Papers, folder 4078.

23: Keeping Hollywood at Arm's Length

Paul Green's stay in California in the fall of 1933 was the end of his innocence about the nature of Hollywood and his relationship to it. He was concerned about the direction in which filmmaking was going and was willing to jeopardize his income and risk blacklisting by publicly stating his points of view. He prepared an article on the subject for publication in the *New York Times* in early February 1934.[1] In the meantime the world premiere of *Carolina*, Fox's version of *The House of Connelly*, was scheduled for January 24 in Charlotte. Winnie Sheehan had talked to Green about his reason for buying the script. Green later recalled this conversation:

I can see Mrs. Connelly with diamonds on her hands, smoking cigarettes. . . . I thought about the Connellys, all poverty-stricken in the play—how could—but I guess maybe it was because of talk like this that I didn't want to adapt it. . . . So the next thing I knew this fellow who had written the script of *Cavalcade* named Reginald Berkeley—and Reginald had been a member of the House of Parliament, an Englishman, so I was told—. . . called me up one day in the studio and says, "I'm adapting your play *The House of Connelly*, and I'd like to talk to you." He said, "I don't know a damned thing about tobacco and things like that." So I met with Berkeley quite a lot and just became a sort of a technical adviser on the whole thing with him, but I didn't get my credit. I didn't want any. . . . One day coming to the studio I came over the hill from Santa Monica, and there on the hill in the lot was this great southern mansion, been built overnight—great columns and so on.[2]

Green said of Sheehan, "Doggone it, he was sort of a likable fellow—ignorant as he was, and he always liked me, for some reason," but of the final film, Green remarked, "Oh, it was pitiful, I thought. Rather pitiful."[3]

The mayor of Charlotte invited Paul and Elizabeth to attend the world premiere. Green recalled that he "didn't want to go," but he accepted the invitation when encouraged to by his former Paris roommate: "one reason I went was that Joe Blythe of Blythe Brothers Contracting Company— . . . old Joe and I had been in the army together and we'd slept in the same bed in Paris. . . . He called me up and he said, 'Now Paul, you've got to come up here and be present for this premiere. . . . The town is doing you honor.'"[4] Green relented. He and Elizabeth went to Charlotte and checked into a hotel. When he began to dress for dinner, he found that he had forgotten to bring black socks and studs for his tuxedo shirt. He went to the dinner with his shirt pinned together and wearing light-colored socks. The mayor was there, as was the lieutenant governor and other dignitaries, and photographs were made. The next morning there was a picture in the newspaper of Green sitting between the VIPs with his white socks showing.

Four days later, on a Sunday night, he spoke to a crowded house at the Playmakers Theatre and read the audience the article (mentioned previously) that would be published a week later in the *New York Times*. In the article he reviewed his long interest in movies, the side-show film he had seen as a boy with his father, the first time he saw *The Birth of a Nation*, and his discovery of Charlie Chaplin films in France during World War I. Then he told of his experiences in Hollywood, from which he had concluded that

[m]aking pictures . . . is a business, an industry. . . . This simple and first fact is the source of all the trouble that befalls anyone interested in the art of the cinema. . . . The studios have a product to sell to the masses of the world, and in order to sell to everybody they think they must strike a common denominator of general illiteracy and bad taste. . . . There is hardly any place on the globe so full of unhappy would-be artists—writers, musicians, actors, and poets. They are surfeited with hush money, but many of them cannot hush the gnawing that wakes them up at night.[5]

In spite of his criticism of Hollywood, Green told his audience that he looked forward to an imaginative cinema, which he believed would develop. It would recognize that the art of the cinema is not the art of the theater. It would use "an invention which eradicates all the material difficulties of depiction which beset the stage."[6]

The following day the *Daily Tar Heel*, the campus newspaper, said that Green had "delivered a smashing indictment of Hollywood and its methods."[7] After the article appeared in the *New York Times* on February 4, the Raleigh *News and Observer* reprinted it.[8] The honeymoon was over. Green would continue to do work in Hollywood from time to time, but the relationship would never again be the same.

A few days after his article appeared in the *News and Observer*, Green took time to make a personal appearance at Shaw University, a black institution in Raleigh. His friend Loretto Bailey was directing the Shaw University Players, who were performing three one-act Carolina Folk Plays, including Green's *The Man Who Died at Twelve O'Clock*. The playwright made a "curtain speech" for the occasion.[9]

Green also turned his attention to a local black man who was not nearly so fortunate as to be attending college. Quite the contrary: he was sentenced to die on March 23 for killing his landlord. On March 5, 1934, an Associated Press story from Durham reported that "Paul Green, noted North Carolina playwright, has joined a committee which has been organized to save Spice Bittings, Person county Negro, from the electric chair." The newspaper story also noted a parallel between this man and Green's Abraham McCranie, the lead character in his Pulitzer Prize-winning play.[10] Bittings had been convicted and his case reviewed by the North Carolina Supreme Court, but questions had arisen that aroused new interest in the matter, including Paul Green's. The press reported that the committee had appeared that day at Negro churches in Durham and begun "a drive to raise funds and bring Bittings's case before the public." A new lawyer, M. Hugh Thompson of Durham, was hired and soon obtained a temporary stay of execution.

Serving on the committee along with Green were two black members—R. H. Austin, editor of a Durham "Negro paper," and Louis J. Spaulding, a real estate agent—and two white members—Dr. Phillips Russell of the University of North Carolina (and Green's brother-in-law) and Bruce Crawford, editor of a Virginia newspaper. Jonathan Daniels and Dr. Frank P. Graham, president of UNC, were interested but would not serve on the committee because of their positions.[11] At that time, it became necessary for Green to go to Boston about the production of one of his plays, but Bittings's new lawyer kept in touch with him while he was at the Hotel Somerset there.[12] Then Green had to go back to Hollywood, but from there he wrote to North Carolina governor J. C. B. Ehringhaus: "As a citizen, interested along with you in the welfare of the people of North Carolina, no matter of what race, color or creed, I am making a plea for clemency for the negro in case he is not granted a new trial."[13]

Not atypically, Green was needed in several places at once. He was trying to finish commissioned work for both Fox and MGM because his play *Potter's Field* was being prepared for a New York production. Green recalled meeting with Samuel Goldwyn before leaving California: "One day he pulled out a document and said, 'I've got a contract here I want you to sign, $200,000.' . . . I said, 'Well, I was thinking about going back to New York. I've got a play I want to put on up there.' He said, 'Oh, well, we could work it out.' So I put it in my pocket and took it home"—their Hollywood "home," that is: Elizabeth and the children were with him during this period. Paul told Elizabeth, "'Here's a contract with Sam Goldwyn for $200,000, but I'm not going to sign it.'" Green reported how his wife "always said" to do what he thought was right. "So I took it back, and he called a conclave of notable people for a luncheon and had this luncheon for me. So after luncheon I went in his office. He said, 'Well, are we fixed up?' I said, 'No, I can't sign it.' He said, 'Well, it's not enough is it? Not enough money?' I said, 'Yes, the money's alright, but I just can't do it.' He was really flabbergasted."[14] It seemed to Green that this contract was the ultimate temptation. He had seen some of his writer friends who had become addicted to Hollywood money. They had allowed themselves to become accustomed to expensive automobiles and big houses, and now they had to have them. He did not want to get in that position.

On July 3 another Associated Press story, this time originating from Raleigh, was headlined "Daughters Seal Doom of Father." It reported:

Two young Negro girls, who declared that they would "tell the truth regardless," today sent their father, Emanuel "Spice" Bittings, nearer death in the electric chair at state's prison.

The daughters of the doomed Negro, brought here in a state truck from Durham county to allow Parole Commissioner Edwin M. Gill to question them, corroborated in nearly every detail the testimony that caused a Person county jury to convict their father of the first-degree murder of his landlord, T. M. Clayton.[15]

Hugh Thompson wired Green the bad news and followed it with a letter, but just when everything seemed hopeless the execution was delayed to July 20.[16] On July 9 Green wired Thompson, suggesting that Bittings's relatives had been "intimidated," and followed it up the next day with a letter that deemed Bittings's family's sudden "loyalty to truth . . . at the expense of the condemned man . . . downright suspicious."[17] On July 10 Green wired to Mrs. Maude Wilson at Chapel Hill: "THERE SEEMS TO BE A CHANCE OF SAVING BITTINGS FROM THE ELECTRIC CHAIR[.] PLEASE GO DOWN TO MY HOUSE AND GET ALL BITTINGS MATERIAL FROM THE FILES AND SEND TO ME BY AIR MAIL."[18] He dispatched copies of that correspondence to Jonathan Daniels and others. Through the various efforts, the execution was again postponed to September 28.

In the meantime, Green finished the movie he was working on, *Broken Soil*, which would star Gary Cooper as a writer who is working alone in a farmhouse. His meals are being furnished by a nearby Polish family; so when the mother gets sick, the daughter (played by Anna Sten) brings his meals, and they get acquainted. One day as the writer is reading a portion of his manuscript to the daughter, a blizzard traps them together for the night. Goldwyn apparently liked the plot, as Green later recalled:

Well, when that goes in to Goldwyn, that part of it, he rubs his hands so gleefully. I remember what he says. "Aw, Mr. Green, we got a million-dollar situation, a million-dollar situation." . . . Well, I guess a kind of bassackwards or all-awry Puritanism in me fought against the economic. Well, maybe Sam was a broader-minded person. But . . . it bored me and made me tired to exhibit and purvey public sex like that. People can love and so on, and sure, the human race has got to go on, and it's all marvelous and all, but to sell it to the public is a land of whoredom.[19]

In early September Elizabeth took the children back to Chapel Hill. Her husband finished his Hollywood work and left for New York for the *Potter's Field* rehearsals. Thompson kept him updated about the Bittings case.[20] When the company of *Potter's Field* went to Milwaukee, Green joined them. On September 26, two days before the scheduled execution, Elizabeth went with Phillips Russell and a few others to Raleigh to meet with Governor Ehringhaus and Commissioner Edwin Gill about Bittings; but they were not successful, and Green received from Elizabeth a telegram that read: "BITTINGS EXECUTION FRIDAY."[21] There was nothing else to be done but go back to work.

While the acting company was in Milwaukee, *Potter's Field* was renamed *Roll, Sweet Chariot*. The name change was purely a commercial decision by the producer, Margaret Hewes, perhaps at the urging of one or more of her backers. She had obtained part of her financing for the venture from Warner Brothers because of her company's association with Green. The name *Potter's Field*, according to Hewes, would not appeal to the public. Green opposed the change because *Potter's Field* was the actual name of the Negro community near Chapel Hill that had inspired his play.[22]

Potter's Field, now *Roll, Sweet Chariot*, had begun its history as the one-act play *In the Valley*. Green wanted to expand that material.[23] The idea for it had come to him as he walked through the black area at the edge of Chapel Hill: "I decided to try to write a play about this Negro settlement, with its teeming, upboiling life, its intense emotions, superstitions, frustrations, hopes, and accomplishments, its grievings and dark humilities. I would write not about a single protagonist and antagonist, but about the whole village."[24] The play is about the plight of the people in the settlement, trapped by their own hates and jealousies but also at the mercy of man-made forces over which they have no control. Progress, in the form of a new highway, is coming to destroy their little world, and they are power-less to stop it. They can only lash out at one another.

After Green returned from Germany with new ideas on how to fuse music and drama, he went back to the same material for a much larger play:

In controlling and handling these many characters as they played out their story, I felt I was in something of the same position as a composer driving forward his composition for some eighty or one hundred instruments, or even as the conductor directing the orchestra which played that

composition after it was written. . . . In trying to express the inner lives and
their meanings in my Negro community, I found that I was having to call
upon about every element available in modern theatrical art. Folk song and
poetry were needed, also dance, pantomime, sound effects and chorus
voices.[25]

He added masks, lights, and the voice of God—"And always there
was music." He did not like the terms "music drama," "ballad opera,"
"festival drama," or "lyric drama," but felt "'symphonic drama'
seemed right . . . a 'sounding-together' in the true meaning of the
Greek word."[26] It seemed to fit best, and Green adopted both the term
and the form.

When the play opened at the Guild Theatre in Milwaukee, Green
was so busy that he neglected his correspondence. On September 28
(the day of Bittings's execution), Elizabeth wired him: "HAVE YOU
FORGOTTEN YOUR FAMILY AND FRIENDS[?] AWAIT
WORD FROM PLAY AND YOU."[27] Just a few days later, on October 2, the production opened at the Cort Theatre in New York. Green
remembered that

The place was packed, and I was nervous as a witch. . . . I had God's voice in
the play, and God was supposed to speak from way up in the loft, and a fuse
blew. When God got ready to speak, he just squealed, . . . and the audience
kind of laughed. Well, the whole thing went to pieces. We drove right
through without intermission. And I was pacing up and down in the
lobby. . . . A fellow came out blowing, and his name was Bob Benchley. And
Benchley said, "Well, Green, I don't know what your play is about, and I'm
going to smoke anyway. Why the hell you want to do it without
intermission?"[28]

Although Brooks Atkinson wired Green, praising the production,
most reviews were unfavorable. Warner Brothers, which had invested
in the production, had a representative in New York named Klawans,
"so I thought I better go down and call on Mr. Klawans. I went down
there to his office, and he was sitting at his desk and had a pistol lying
on the table. And he looked up with kind of bloodshot eyes, I guess.
And I said, 'Mr. Klawans, what in the world are you going to do with a
pistol there?' And he said, 'I'm thinking of blowing my damn brains
out for backing your play.'"[29]

Green also went to see a Mr. Shubert, from whom they had rented the theater: "I go over to see Mr. Shubert because the announcement goes out [that] he's going to close the play. And he's sitting back there with his big undertaker's collar and black tie and all that . . . I think . . . that embalming fluid was in his veins. . . . I was pleading for another week. Maybe the thing would catch on. He made it clear he was going to close Saturday night because . . . 'We're going to put something in there they will understand—it's going to be a nice leg show.'"[30] At the closing a few days later, Green later recalled, "Mrs. Hewes said she had no money to finish the payroll, so I furnished the balance myself. It didn't amount to too much, maybe $2,000, $1,500, or something like that, that I just put in the kitty and never got anything for it. It wasn't a loan. It was a gift because she was closing. So I just paid it up. I never expected to get it back."[31]

Edith Isaacs ignored the box office problem and wrote in *Theatre Arts Monthly* of the "thrilling experience of coming unexpectedly on a great production. . . . *Roll, Sweet Chariot* is a great new thing *done*, not worthily *tried*, but beautifully *done*. . . . For years there has been a looking forward to the time when someone would make a play of words and music, not separately but jointly, so that the music should be as integral a part of the play's sound and meaning as the words. *Roll, Sweet Chariot* achieves all this."[32] Isaacs's praise foreshadowed the success of Green's later symphonic dramas, in spite of the failure of this first one.

During this period, too, while Green was ending his Hollywood work and turning his attention back to his own drama and to social concerns within his own home state, he also took time to help with a project at Campbell College. Evelyn Snider, an English teacher there, looked about the campus for a place to stage a May Day production. She selected a site where she envisioned that a small outdoor theater might be constructed. During the 1933-1934 school year, Green went to Buies Creek with Dr. H. R. Totten of the University of North Carolina botany department to begin the planning.[33] Dr. J. A. Campbell, at age seventy-two, was still the active president of the institution, but he died in March 1934. Work on the project continued through that year and into the fall of 1935. J. Winston Pearce, a student at Campbell at the time, later wrote in his history of the college, "I have always cherished the memory of . . . see[ing] Paul Green, Pulitzer Prize winner, Guggenheim Fellowship participant, . . . and academically oriented Dr. Totten in overalls and muddy shoes with blistered hands, using shovels, rakes, and hoes as they supervised and led in the manual labor required for the construction of the beautiful little theatre!"[34]

Green likewise recalled the construction project:

Talk about an example of the People's Theatre. This was it. . . . I remember Lonnie Matthews. Lonnie was a tenant farmer. He came and saw us working there, saw me and Mr. Totten and some of the students digging with hoes. . . . I knew him from years back. He came over to me and said, "Paul, what is this?" And I told him. He said, "Can I help some?" I said, "Lonnie, you sure can." He was a strong fellow, so the first thing you know, Lonnie was digging away and helping to shape up things. You know how much money we spent to build that amphitheater? Two hundred dollars: that's what it cost. Person in Dunn gave . . . seed. We tried to get dogwood and little trees from every historic spot we could find around the Cape Fear valley. We went down to the old locks where they . . . tried to canalize the river. We got some rocks there and brought them up to build a little retaining wall for the front of the stage. . . . We went over to Flora MacDonald's home site and got a dogwood. And we tried to make it a real little historical center architecturally, as well as subject matter for the drama to sort of memorialize the people who lived in this region. It was just interesting to see how everybody . . . contributed everything. They were glad to do it.[35]

On October 16 a big dedication of the new facility took place. Master of ceremonies for the occasion was Leslie H. Campbell, son of the founder, new president of the college, and member of the singing quartet Green had formed prior to the war. For the occasion, Lamar Stringfield brought the North Carolina Little Symphony (originally a WPA project that had developed into the North Carolina Symphony) and performed musical selections from Green's *Tread the Green Grass*. Loretto Bailey brought the Shaw University Players and performed Green's *The Man Who Died at Twelve O'Clock*. Campbell College students sang folk ballads and demonstrated folk dancing. And speakers included Frederick Koch and Green's old teacher Hubbard F. Page. Green recalled:

On opening night I was standing at the back. The theater seated about 700 people. Everybody sat on cushions on the grass. . . . Lonnie was back there. There he was to see this play. And during intermission Lonnie says, "This is the first time I ever seed a theater." He meant the play. . . . He said, "Paul, I like this. I like this fine." I said, "Lonnie, we owe a lot to you." It was really one of the finest examples of all the people working together.

Now in Harnett County today we have a regional theater. They produce Broadway plays and do all kinds of things down there. . . . The greatest thing is they feel self-fulfilled. They feel needed.[36]

NOTES

1. "A Playwright's Notes on Drama and the Screen," *New York Times*, February 4, 1934. This essay is the same one mentioned in chapter 20, n. 1. Green later included this essay in his *The Hawthorn Tree: Some Papers and Letters on Life and the Theatre* (Chapel Hill: University of North Carolina Press, 1937) and in his *Drama and the Weather: Some Notes and Papers on Life and the Theatre* (New York: Samuel French, 1958).

2. Paul Green, interview by Rhoda Wynn, February 1974, tape 2, pp. 5-6, Southern Oral History Program Collection, Southern Historical Collection, Wilson Library, University of North Carolina at Chapel Hill (hereafter cited as Wynn interview, with appropriate tape and transcript page number).

3. Wynn interview, tape 2, pp. 5, 7 respectively.

4. Wynn interview, tape 2, pp. 7-8.

5. Green, *The Hawthorn Tree*, 44-46.

6. Green, *The Hawthorn Tree*, 48.

7. H. N. L., "Self Justification," *Daily Tar Heel* (Chapel Hill), January 3, 1934.

8. Paul Green, "Dimes vs. Art," *News and Observer*, February 7, 1934.

9. See letters dated March 7 through August 13, 1934, from William Stuart Nelson, president of Shaw University, thanking Green for his appearance and discussing Loretto Bailey's work with the student theater company. Paul Green Papers (collection #3693), Southern Historical Collection, folder 325. *The Man Who Died at Twelve O'Clock* is included in Green's *In the Valley and Other Carolina Plays* (New York: Samuel French, 1928).

10. "See Parallel in Paul Green Play: Playwright's Defense of Spice Bittings Recalls 'In Abraham's Bosom,'" *News and Observer*, March 5, 1934.

11. Graham's interest is mentioned in a letter from defense attorney M. Hugh Thompson to Green dated July 5, 1934; Daniels's interest is expressed in a letter of the same date from Daniels to Green. Both letters are in the Paul Green Papers, folder 284. See also another letter from Daniels to Green on the Bittings case dated March 21, 1934, Green Papers, folder 289.

12. See telegram, Thompson to Green (at the Somerset), April 13, 1934, Paul Green Papers, folder 283. The play requiring Green's presence in Boston was *Potter's Field*, which received favorable reviews for its production at the Plymouth Theatre. It is included in Green's collections *The House of Connelly and Other Plays* (New York: Samuel French, 1931) and *Out of the South: The Life of a People in Dramatic Form* (New York: Harper, 1939).

13. Laurence G. Avery, ed., *A Southern Life: Letters of Paul Green, 1916-1981*, Fred W. Morrison Series in Southern Studies (Chapel Hill: University of North Carolina Press, 1994), 234.

14. Paul Green, interview by James R. Spence, October 24, 1974, James R. Spence audio recordings relating to Paul Green, 1974-1979 (collection #5170), Southern Historical Collection (hereafter cited as Spence interview, with appropriate date).

15. *Durham Morning Herald*, July 3, 1934. See also "Daughters' Story Brings Death Nearer to Father," *News and Observer*, July 4, 1934.

16. Telegram, Thompson to Green, July 2, 1934, and letter, Thompson to Green, July 5, 1934, Paul Green Papers, folder 284.

17. Avery, *A Southern Life*, 238.

18. Telegram, Green to Wilson, July 10, 1934, Paul Green Papers, folder 284.

19. Wynn interview, tape 2, pp. 32-33.

20. Telegram, Thompson to Green, September 17, 1934, Paul Green Papers, folder 284.

21. Telegram, Elizabeth Green to Paul Green, September 26, 1934, Paul Green Papers, folder 299.

22. Spence interview, September 9, 1979.

23. The expanded play, *Roll, Sweet Chariot: A Symphonic Play of the Negro People*, was published in 1935 by Samuel French.

24. Paul Green, *Drama and the Weather: Some Notes and Papers on Life and the Theatre* (New York: Samuel French, 1958), 23.

25. Green, *Drama and the Weather*, 26-27.

26. Green, *Drama and the Weather*, 27.

27. Telegram, Elizabeth Green to Paul Green, Paul Green Papers, folder 299.

28. Wynn interview, tape 4, p. 11.

29. Wynn interview, tape 4, p. 12.

30. Ibid.

31. Spence interview, August 9, 1979.

32. Edith J. R. Isaacs, "Critics' Pleasure: Broadway in Review," *Theatre Arts Monthly* 18 (November 1934): 813.

33. See J. Winston Pearce, *Campbell College: Big Miracle at Little Buies Creek, 1887-1974* (Nashville, Tenn.: Broadman Press, 1976), 147-148.

34. Pearce, *Campbell College*, 148-149.

35. Spence interview, August 9, 1979.

36. Ibid.

24: Interlude at Chapel Hill

During the textile mill strikes that swept North Carolina in 1934, an incident occurred that soon caught the attention of Paul Green. At the E. M. Holt Plaid Mill in Burlington at three o'clock in the morning on September 14, there was a dynamite explosion within a fenced area near an unused section of the mill. The blast broke some windows, which the defense later contended were worth twelve dollars. Seven men were soon indicted and convicted, including John Anderson, president of the Piedmont Council of the United Textile Workers. His sentence was eight to ten years in the State Penitentiary. Green wrote a letter to a newspaper, noting the severity of the punishment. He soon received a call from one of the defendants, J. P. Hoggard, who was out on bail. Hoggard came to see Green and brought with him the mothers of some of the other defendants. Green noted how "They looked so pitiful in their sunbonnets, . . . but [they] were really eloquent in their complaints. The language would just pour out."[1]

Green attended a meeting of the Workers' Defense Committee in Durham on January 10, 1935.[2] The defendants had asked for help from the International Labor Defense. A lawyer for that organization, who had been in Burlington two days investigating the matter, assured the crowd that the entire case was a frame-up. Some of the defendants rose to tell their stories. The lawyer stated that three of the defendants were still in jail. The mother of one of the defendants (one of the women who had come to see Green) said that her son was so distraught about being in jail that he had "tried to commit suicide." Green recalled, "Well, he was such a pitiful thing, and his mother—

Elizabeth and I signed his bond for $4,500 to get him out. And he went down the road and robbed a store. . . . He got tried for that and put in the penitentiary."[3]

Undeterred by such problems, the Greens were soon participating in an organization known as the Chapel Hill Defense Committee for the Burlington Workers. Elizabeth was treasurer of the group. Her husband was the largest contributor.[4] An attorney obtained a court order giving the defendants more time to appeal. The National Committee for the Defense of Political Prisoners helped with fund raising by sending out letters of solicitation signed by Dr. George S. Counts of Columbia University (Green's name was still on the letterhead, in spite of his earlier blast at Dreiser). A representative of the committee asked Green to come to New York on April 17 to speak to a meeting sponsored jointly with International Labor Defense.[5] He declined.

On that night, Green hosted a gathering at his home. In his diary he indicated that the group met "to discuss formation of Southern liberal group to fight against the many acts of injustice occurring in the [S]outh."[6] The same diary entry mentions that the "leading spirit" of the meeting was a Mrs. Olive Stone. Some of the others present were W. A. Olsen, UNC Press founder W. T. Couch, J. O. and Loretto Bailey, Muriel Wolfe, North Carolina historian C. C. Crittenden, and Newman I. White. Green and Olsen discouraged the establishment of another organization. They were outvoted, and the group formed the Southern Committee for People's Rights, which decided to continue work on the Burlington case and to investigate three other cases that had been reported in the press. It also agreed to send delegates to the Trade Union and Civil Rights Conference, to be held in Chattanooga in May, in order to hear about workers' needs.

The author's reputation as a social activist brought a visitor to the Greens' home during that period, and the story the visitor told ended up in Green's novel *This Body the Earth*:

A fellow called me up from Charlotte, a newspaperman, and he wanted to come down and see me . . . so we set an appointment. . . . He had some photographs in a manila envelope, which he had in his hand, and he held them for a while and he talked and then he pulled them out and handed them to me. And I looked at them. There was a picture of two Negro men, each one sitting in a wheelchair and his feet bound up, on the ends of his legs.

He didn't have any feet, . . . and I said, "What in the world happened?" and he said . . . "Those two fellows have had their feet amputated. . . . They were on the chain gang . . . and they committed some misdemeanor, and out on the road they often have these steel cages on wheels, a good big kind of caravan thing, and when they're not able . . . to bring the convicts . . . back to the center they used caravan vehicles. . . . They were put for the night in this place . . . and the captain . . . tied them up, stood 'em against the bars of this caravan vehicle, and tied their hands up there and left them for a certain number of hours in that position. . . . [He] went off and he got drunk, and he forgot about these fellows, and it turned awful cold during the night, and these guys were tied up there, and when the morning came and he finally got back from his drunk, their feet were frostbitten. And so they lost their feet."[7]

Green could not resist such an appeal for assistance. He very quickly became involved in an effort to obtain compensation for the two prisoners: "So I go over to the governor and show him these pictures and say, 'Here is something terrible that has happened.' He said, 'What is that, Paul?' . . . So I tell him the story. . . . He said, 'Oh, Paul, that's just terrible.' . . . I said, 'Well, Governor, what are we going to do about it?' He said, 'Well, there is nothing we can do. . . . We can't accept responsibility or agree that we are liable. They can't sue the state.'" Following additional discussions without progress, "I said, 'I know the Paramount News man in Hollywood, and when I get home I'll call him in Hollywood, and tomorrow or the next day we'll have a team of photographers here, and we'll photograph these boys. We'll cover the whole United States with their pictures. . . .' He said, 'No, no. You can't do that.' I said, '. . . I'll even make a speech.' So he got busy then, and out of that they pensioned them."[8]

Inspired to find out more about conditions for convicts, Green did additional personal research: "And about that time I met a fellow named Matthews, Thaddeus Matthews, who was a convict guard. Thaddeus came over to see me and wanted me to recommend him as a writer for the WPA. . . . He wanted to write. He said, 'I kept some notes while I was a convict guard.' So I talked to him a lot about it."[9] But Green also went to see for himself:

They had a convict camp over here at Hillsborough. . . . I went over there. It had barbed wire and all, and I talked to the boss man, and he was very nice and said, "Look around. We've got some bad guys in here. In fact, I've got

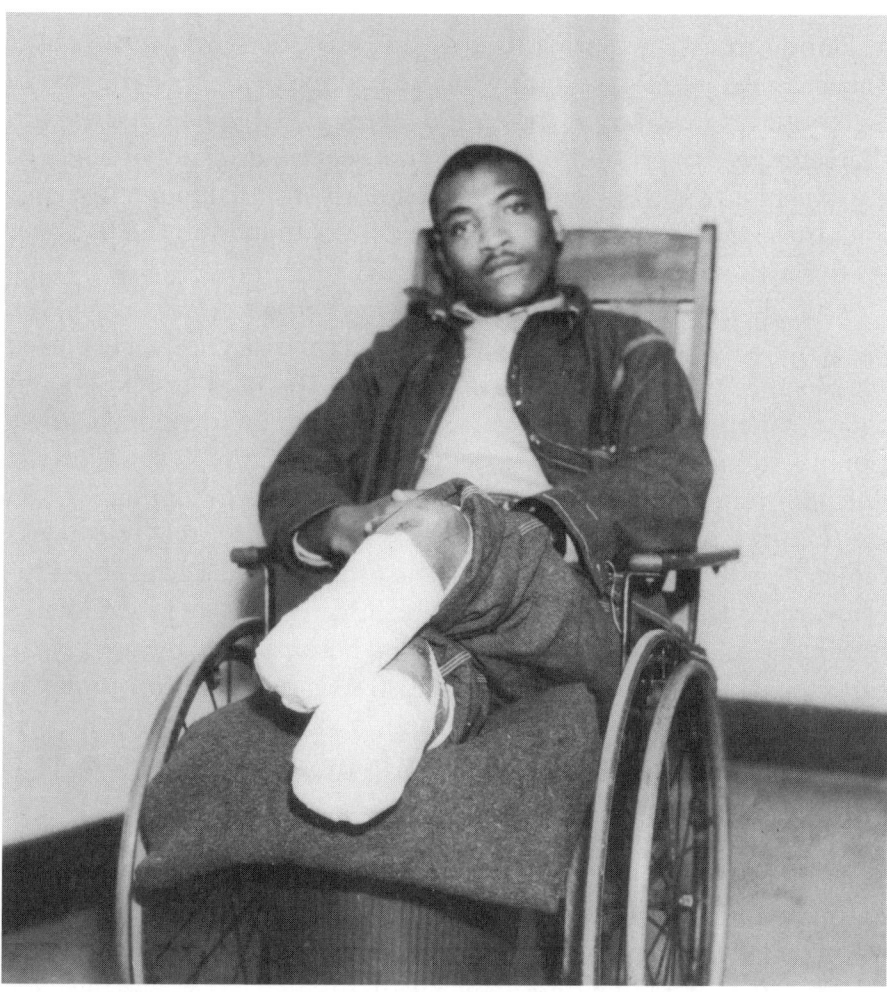

In the mid-1930s Paul Green, already pondering the formation of a southern liberal group to fight against the many acts of injustice occurring in the South, received a visit from a Charlotte newspaperman who showed him photographs of two African American members of a chain gang whose feet had been amputated as a result of frostbite incurred by the negligence of a white captain. Green not only became involved in efforts to compensate the prisoners but also familiarized himself with general conditions under which convicts were held in North Carolina. This photograph from the Paul Green Papers shows an African American member of a chain gang whose legs have been amputated below the knees.

one guy in there in the potato house now who is a bad character, but I'm sweating it out of him." . . . So I went down to this potato hill thing, kind of dirt with a grill or bar thing, and he was back in there. They had a kind of tin roof or something, and I bet that it must have been 150 degrees in that place.[10]

During that same spring, Green was working hard on his novel *This Body the Earth*. Based on what he had learned about the prison farm system, Green wrote the section of the novel in which the main character goes to prison for a time. That section does not actually fit into the plot of the book and was apparently inspired more, it seems, from the author's recent real-life experiences than from the fictional events in the novel that lead up to it.

Though once again finding himself busy with both writing and the concerns of his community, Green still had time for family. He played with Paul Jr. and his friends on "the farm," the land he had bought outside Chapel Hill. He took his son with him on a trip to Harnett County, stopping on the way to let the child examine the airplanes at Raleigh Municipal Airport (just as they had done in Germany). On another day he was at the farm with his children making hawk-callers—perhaps using the same method that he had learned from his black friend Rassie during his boyhood. One night Green attended a Boy Scout celebration at Kenan Stadium because Billy Johnson was a participant. Billy was the son of his sister Mary and Alton Johnson. Green also liked working on the land, and, with his black helpers Leander and Willis, he planted onions, beans, corn, strawberries, Irish potatoes, watermelon, and cantaloupe.[11]

When Green received a request from Hollywood to come out and write a script based on Rachel Field's novel *Time Out of Mind*, he postponed giving an answer while working furiously on his own novel, once from midnight to six in the morning. In mid-May he accepted the offer but wrote "Dread it" in his diary.[12] Green may have finished his novel, but his concern about convicts (those wrongly accused, as well as those badly treated) did not wane. He went to the penitentiary to visit Red Hendricks, a prisoner whose case had been identified by the group that had met at his house. Following the visit, he wrote, "An innocent man, but victorious in captivity." The next day he recorded: "Liberal group meeting at my house. As usual, wanted to investigate round the world."

Green apparently focused his own concern on those oppressed locally. And with his attention focused locally, he found it hard to get interested in *Time Out of Mind*: "Worked on Field's book. Hard earned money." "Worked on *Time Out of Mind*, no inspiration at all." Nevertheless, he "finally finished it and mailed script"—less than sixty days after he had written the first line.[13]

With the movie off his mind, Green immediately began working on his own play *The Enchanted Maze*, a satire of the academic world.[14] He took time out to go to New York for conferences with representatives of the Group Theatre and *Harper's* magazine and followed up with the former by later sending a synopsis of *Enchanted Maze* to Harold Clurman, who was very anxious to produce another Green play.[15] Since Green was then in New York, he missed an unusual presentation of *Roll, Sweet Chariot*, which opened on August 9 in Birmingham, Alabama. The production was sponsored by the Park and Recreation Board of Birmingham under the leadership and direction of John McGee and included a cast of two thousand. The board built a "Negro Village" in the middle of Legion Field with scenery 200 feet long. A "street" led into the "Village." In one scene of the play, a small red automobile was driven down the "street" and into the "Village" as the audience looked on from the bleachers. Fifteen hundred singers chanted songs from the play.

Between September 11 and 14, Green wrote *Hymn to the Rising Sun*, which he believed might be the finest work of art he had written.[16] It was a play about the cruelty of the chain gang system, inspired not only by what Green had witnessed and heard recently about actual chain gangs but also by his war experiences, for what he witnessed at the convict camp had brought back memories: "I got to thinking more about the convict boss, and I remembered a top sergeant that I had during the war."[17] The chain gang captain in his new play became Captain Hough, based on the character of the top sergeant Green had served under during World War I. There was no Shropshire or Barnes, the men who had lost their feet to frostbite, but the cruelty they had suffered was very much on his mind as he wrote.

With *Hymn to the Rising Sun* written, Green spent the afternoon in conference with "Prof. Koch, Sam Selden, Harry Davis, wife, and Bell about government drama relief."[18] Events had been unfolding that would affect the lives of all of them, Green most of all. Harry Hopkins, head of the U.S. Works Progress Administration (WPA), had decided that unemployed theater people needed jobs just as much as did unemployed factory workers. He created the Federal Theatre as an instrument to deal with that widespread unemployment; hired Hallie Flanagan, former director of the Vassar Experimental Theatre, to head the project; and announced his undertaking on July 26 at the National Theatre Conference at Iowa University. Paul Green's old friend E. C. Mabie had been chosen as regional director for the Midwest at a salary of one dollar per year. Now Frederick Koch had been approached about undertaking a similar position in the South.[19]

Green was skeptical of the government organizing and managing thousands of theater people, even though Harry Hopkins had said in Iowa, "What we want is a free, adult, uncensored theatre."[20] Following his meeting with Koch and the others, Green wrote: "The longer we talked the harder it became for us to find any reasonable point of view to hold. When one has to beat his head for an idea to justify his actions something is wrong."[21] In spite of Green's misgivings, Koch was soon appointed head of the Federal Theatre project for the entire South.

On October 22 *This Body the Earth* was published. In his diary entries, Green was usually self-deprecating about all of his writings, never satisfied. Of the novel, he had commented back in June, "Book seems dull, slow." One day as he was revising the proofs he wrote, "Why can't I ever get it right? I remember how Thornton Wilder writes a line, then paces around the floor and eyes it from every angle. Back again, a change here, there. Result—style. I have no style." On publication day, he wrote, "Oh, that it were a great book."[22]

The reviews were better than he had anticipated. In the *New York Times Book Review*, J. Donald Adams wrote, "Mr. Green has written a good book: moving, sincere, permeated by a strong love of the land and of the people on it; a book that Americans who love their country will do well to read and think about. If it moves them to act, it will then have served its purpose."[23] Edward Larocque Tinker wrote for the *New York Herald Tribune*'s Books section, "This book is a tragic one and a powerful arraignment of the whole tenant-farmer system of the South, as Green sees it. . . . The author makes Alvin the prototype of all his class to show that even a man so superior to his kind in ambition and industry cannot break through the system." There was another aspect of the book that interested Tinker: "[H]e has achieved a real American document—a graphic detailed picture of the folkways and minutiae of living—the revivals, harvest bees, hopes and thoughts—of a class that are a numerically large slice of the South. . . . In spite of the mountainous accumulation of minute detail which fills its 422 pages, 'This Body the Earth' is a really fine, interesting novel of American soil."[24]

Although Green had broken the structure and pace of his novel by putting in the chapters in which the main character is on the chain gang, reviewer Hamilton Basso, writing in *The New Republic*, was unconcerned about such literary problems: "The chapters of this book that are likely to receive most attention are those exposing the penal system of North Carolina—the whippings, the chain gang, the 'sweat box.' . . . Paul Green has written a brave, honest, eloquent book—his most important performance since 'In Abraham's Bosom.'"[25]

At present, with the problems of the chain gang and the tenant farmer largely forgotten, one can read the novel not as a protest piece but as a sensitive story of people and their conflicts. A lot of Green himself is in *This Body the Earth*: "I was this Alvin Barnes fella," he admitted, "and his granddaddy was my granddaddy."[26] Alvin is likewise inspired by the legend of Green's grandfather, who was supposed to have been a very brilliant man. There is the wandering farm worker modeled after the man Jim Faulkner who lived in the Green home when Paul was a teenager. There is Alvin's burning desire to be somebody, a theme preached by Green's mother. Green never set up inherently good people to occupy one class and bad people to be their masters or servants. He showed the system and the good and bad of all classes playing out their roles within it.

In addition to the problems of convicts and sharecroppers, Green was observing individual tragedies resulting from racial segregation. A week after the novel was published, he took time to record his thoughts about a particular young black man whom he had helped the year before:

He has grown hopeless, he says, and wants to return north. His efforts at work among his own people have failed. One might expect that around the University he would find a higher type of Negro, but actually the colored section here is about the worst he has ever seen. . . . [His] great dream—his all night working as an orderly in Watt's [Watts] Hospital, and his going to school in the daytime, his struggles to put himself through Lincoln University, his Phi Beta Kappa, his smiles, bows, courtesies to the white folks—roll themselves up into a wrinkle across his forehead and nothing more. "Yes, but there was Booker Washington and there is Moton." But that asks too much of the individual and too little of the system if we would view the matter with any justice.[27]

And once more Green recalled the quiet words of Phillips Russell: "We will have more and more of these cases."[28]

Drawn back into the Burlington case, Green became concerned that a conservative supreme court of North Carolina establishment type might not receive kindly the brash young Jewish lawyers that were being sent down by the International Labor Defense: "We met with them [these lawyers], and I told Bill Couch, 'Listen, these guys are going to ruin the whole thing if we let them get up and plead this thing.' So we talked with them, and they promised that they would go to the hearing but that they would say nothing."[29] On November 21 headlines in newspapers throughout North Carolina proclaimed that the state supreme court had sustained the convictions of six of the seven defendants.[30] These men received active sentences totaling twenty-six years. One got a two-year suspended sentence. The fight for the Burlington group continued for years with various attempts to obtain pardons for them or have their sentences reduced. And Green continued his social activism in his civic as well as in his writing life.

NOTES

1. Paul Green, interview by Jacquelyn Hall, May 30, 1975, Southern Oral History Program Collection, Southern Historical Collection, Wilson Library, University of North Carolina at Chapel Hill, p. 18 (hereafter cited as Hall interview, with appropriate transcript page number).

2. A twenty-six-page typescript of notes from this meeting is in the Paul Green Papers (collection #3693), folder 4517, Southern Historical Collection.

3. Paul Green, interview by James R. Spence, October 23, 1976, James R. Spence audio recordings relating to Paul Green, 1974-1979 (collection #5170), Southern Historical Collection (hereafter cited as Spence interview, with appropriate date).

4. An unsigned copy of a listing of contributions to the organization (the original presumably signed above the typed name "Mrs. Paul Green"), dated May 30, 1935, is in the Paul Green Papers, folder 4517.

5. See Alfred H. Hirsch to Green, March 1, 1935, Paul Green Papers, folder 351.

6. Paul Green Diary, April 17, 1935, Paul Green Papers (hereafter cited as Diary, with entry date).

7. Paul Green, interview by Rhoda Wynn, February 1974, tape 4, pp. 25-27, Southern Oral History Program Collection, Southern Historical Collection.

8. Hall interview, 52-53.

9. Hall interview, 55.

10. Hall interview, 55-56.

11. Diary, April 14-17, 1935.

12. Diary, May 16, 1935. Green dictated (sometimes as much as 15,000 words a day) into an Ediphone machine with wax cylinders, from which Elizabeth typed a rough draft. Sometimes he would dictate for six hours in the morning and then leave the house to walk the fields and woods. While he was gone, Elizabeth would take the material off the cylinders, often completing the typing while he was away. "I began to think of myself somewhat as Mrs. Tolstoy," she later said. Elizabeth Lay Green, *The Paul Green I Know* (Chapel Hill: North Caroliniana Society, 1978), 6.

13. Diary, May 22, 23, June 3, 7, July 13, 1935. Universal-International Pictures produced the film *Time Out of Mind* in 1947.

14. *The Enchanted Maze* was published by Samuel French in 1939.

15. Diary, August 8, 28, 1935.

16. Spence interview, October 24, 1976. *Hymn to the Rising Sun* was published by Samuel French in 1936.

17. Hall interview, 230.

18. Diary, September 20, 1935.

19. See Hallie Flanagan, *Arena: The History of the Federal Theatre* (New York: Benjamin Blom, 1940).

20. Flanagan, *Arena*, 28.

21. Diary, September 20, 1935.

22. Diary, June 11, July 3, October 22, 1935.

23. "Paul Green's Novel about Sharecroppers," November 10, 1935.

24. "Grim Novel of the Southern Farmer," November 3, 1935.

25. "Nemesis in the Cotton Belt," November 13, 1935.

26. Spence interview, October 23, 1976.

27. Diary, October 29, 1935.

28. Ibid.

29. Hall interview, 22.

30. See, for example, "Six 'Dynamiters' to Serve Terms, One Wins Appeal," *News and Observer* (Raleigh), November 21, 1935; "Conviction of Six Defendants in 'Dynamiting' Case Is Upheld by Decision of Supreme Court," *Greensboro Daily News*, November 21, 1935; "Mill Dynamiters Start Sentences," *News and Observer*, January 4, 1936.

25: The Big Broadway Musical

In November 1935 Paul Green owed Warner Brothers a script, and the film company kept sending him wires, trying to pressure him into fulfilling his contract. The problem was not that Green was unwilling to work. Warner Brothers simply had not offered him a story that he was willing to accept. As his money got lower, however, he realized what he had to do: "I had to finish . . . *Enchanted Maze*; I had the last act to do. But I had to get to Hollywood. . . . [T]hey said, 'We have to start on such and such a date.' So I set out for Hollywood and wrote on the train, all the way across the country, and mailed it back to Sam [Selden] in installments."[1] Green revealed in his diary that he would "[r]ather take a beating" than make the trip.[2] After his first conference at Warner Brothers concluded, Green recorded, "All their promises about marvelous stories to choose from died down to the same old <u>Green Light</u>" (an allusion to the novel of that name by Lloyd C. Douglas, which was being adapted for film).[3]

Green was not interested in that project, but he did respond enthusiastically when someone from Warner called to talk about doing an opera with Max Reinhardt.[4] Sometime after Green had gotten as far as the gates to Reinhardt's estate in Germany but then could not get up the nerve to call on the idol, the renowned director had arrived in America and received a great welcome. The *New York Times* had pondered the impact Reinhardt might have on the film industry and Broadway, and Hollywood had met him with grand reception parties and signs along the highways bearing the word "Reinhardt."[5] The famed director had immediately gone to work on creating a movie adaptation of *A Midsummer Night's Dream*.

Green, already an admirer, was hopeful about this man with such a reputation and so much influence doing Shakespeare. Conscious of his own relationships with Hollywood, however, he wondered whether even so great a man as Reinhardt could effect much change: "[If] he could take a play, *A Midsummer Night's Dream*, and make it into a great commercial success—and I thought also, God bless him—if he could do that, if he can take a Shakespeare play, that one especially, and put it across for the American people, certainly he will help develop Hollywood toward the sort of celestial-city philosophy that I had hoped for and believed in."[6] At that time, Reinhardt was in New York working on a stage production of Franz Werfel's *The Eternal Road*. Green was quite excited about the possibility of doing an opera with Reinhardt, but before the day was over his Warner contact called back to say that nothing could be done on the project until Reinhardt returned from New York.[7]

When word got around that Green was in town, other studios contacted him, offering to pay him more than Warner, but, as he wrote to his wife, he was bound to honor his contract.[8] Under those circumstances, he went to work on *Green Light*. He reported how he "got a dictaphone, holed up in the Hollywood Hotel, and I started on Monday morning and I got a couple of secretaries to take it off [i.e., transcribe his recorded dictation], and Thursday afternoon I finished. . . . And I got it over to Warner Brothers on Thursday night. And they were quick too. They read it, and so the next day they called me up and said, 'We like it. Come by and get your check.' . . . I got on the train and got back in time for Christmas."[9] In his diary, Green mentioned that the studio people had said the script was great, but added, "Great my ass, I thought, but here's to meat and bread and the great movie I'll do someday."[10]

Meanwhile, in Chapel Hill, the Carolina Playmakers were preparing to perform Green's *The Enchanted Maze*. The idea for the play had come to Green during a visit to Ohio University: "I remember one day . . . I looked under the Ph.D. theses in the catalogue, and I was amazed at the subject matter for some of the theses. So I early got the idea that the modern educational system is just full of this crap and nonsense, just like the motion pictures. So I decided I'd try to write an attack on this kind of education. . . . I thought about rats in a maze and that the professors were going round and round in a maze, with their nonsensical verbiage and so on."[11] Following the play's opening on December 6, 1935, Frederick Koch telegrammed Green in Hollywood: "Play great success. Reverberations and explosions still roaring."[12] After the play's second performance, Koch wired Green again to "TELL [HIM] THAT THE SECOND NIGHT WAS A THRILLING ADVENTURE. . . . MEMORIAL HALL WAS WELL FILLED BY AN EXCITED AUDIENCE OF 1100 PEOPLE, ACCORDING TO THE ESTIMATE OF OUR TICKET TAKERS; AND WE ARE LOOKING FOR A BIG CROWD AT THE REPEAT PERFORMANCE TONIGHT."[13]

In stark contrast with Koch's enthusiasm, however, UNC dean Robert B. House criticized Green's play before an assembly of students and advised them not to take it seriously, declaring, according to the newspaper coverage, that it was a "[p]oorly [e]xecuted [p]iece of [w]ork" and that Green's psychology was of "the pre-Elizabethan blood-and-thunder type and has not reached the Shakespearian stage of logical thought."[14] Others saw in the play's satire on big donors an attack on heavily endowed Duke University. A few weeks previously, Duke's football team had defeated the best team Carolina had fielded in many years, causing unusual tension between the two institutions. The situation delighted Frederick Koch, the master publicist of the Playmakers. All the major North Carolina newspapers, as well as the *New York Times*, covered the controversy.[15]

Apparently undaunted by the contretemps, Green on December 19 completed the script he had begun at the beginning of the month. Arrangements were made for him to meet Max Reinhardt in New York on January 2, 1936, and he left for home, noting with regret that he did not have time to accept an invitation to conduct a series of lectures at the University of Miami, which would have paid him $500. On Christmas Eve he wrote, "Arrived at Greensboro—noon. Elizabeth there. . . . Ground covered with snow—and now home again, and I could weep. At night the filling of stockings, whispers, tiptoeing about—and Elizabeth happy." A week later he was on his way again—his daughter "Byrd's accusing eyes staring after me"— spending New Year's Eve on the train. The following night he and his sister Erma (who lived in New York) went to three movies.[16]

Green joined Max and Helen Reinhardt for dinner the next evening. Reinhardt was "a gentle appearing kindly man of about 60" who insisted on speaking in his native language. There was news of several of Green's friends who had fled Hitler's Germany. Alexis Granowsky, Reinhardt said, was enjoying exile in Paris with a wealthy French lady.[17] One refugee, Kurt Weill, was in New York writing the music for Reinhardt's super spectacular *The Eternal Road*. Reinhardt asked Green if he would be "interested in working with him on a Negro Everyman story . . . that he had produced in Salzburg, and make it into an American Negro morality play."[18] They agreed to correspond and to meet again.

Green had a conference with director Harold Clurman, who told him that his play *The Enchanted Maze* was "not ready" to be produced.[19] He met with members of the Let Freedom Ring Acting Company at the Civic Repertory Theatre, who were readying a production of three one-act plays, including Green's *Hymn to the Rising Sun* and his *Unto Such Glory*. While watching Will Geer play the part of Captain Hough, Green "realized the director had directed him wrongly. There were [two] long speeches . . . in that play, and Will delivered them in the same rhythm, the same emphasis. . . . I took him aside . . . and just used the example of a good evangelical preacher. He builds up. . . . His second speech has got to be more intense and powerful and convincing than the first one, [so] I urged him to change the delivery of the second speech and make it more intense, so the audience wouldn't say, 'I've heard this before.'"[20]

Green attended a matinee of Clifford Odets's new play *Paradise Lost*, which was being produced by the Group Theatre. He "found some of it theatrically effective though its human story marred by the narrowed down propaganda material." His judgment was confirmed by the critics, and Odets, who had previously turned down an opportunity with MGM, accepted a Hollywood offer from Paramount. Later, he and Green would continue their friendship there. Elizabeth traveled to New York to join her husband, and they went to see *Porgy and Bess*. Green "felt always the pull of Negro life on Gershwin which he refused to yield to . . . kept skirting along the periphery and clinging to a Semitic preconception."[21]

Since there was nothing more to be done with Reinhardt or Clurman at the moment, the Greens went back to Chapel Hill. There Paul read Brooks Atkinson's *New York Times* review of the three one-act plays at the Civic Repertory Theatre, in which the critic called *Hymn to the Rising Sun* "an overwhelming piece of work."[22] The day after the review appeared, Green recorded in his diary, "One of the communist Jew boys down from New York to investigate the South—How many have passed this way during the last year! Think 'Tobacco Road' has impelled many of them this way. Oh, no, not racial, simply political, even when they kindly call long distance on one's telephone and then forget to mention the toll, or ask to be taken by auto somewhere, etc. etc. and then a little loan on the side. So far I have never received one cent in repayment—Now a strangled subsiding of charity, for this is past seventy times seven."[23]

Green may have been losing patience with intrusive outsiders, but his own interest in issues of oppression continued. His thoughts were often with those suffering hardship. When the thermometer dropped to four degrees in Chapel Hill, he wrote: "People in Potters Field must be bedding close tonight." And he often commented in his diary upon executions at the State Penitentiary; for example: "Once more the old announcement of the southern indoor sport—execution of more Negroes. Ours tomorrow is to be played in the new gas chamber at Raleigh. Incredible to think of the life and death power our 2 x 4 politicians have. Like the dreadful power of procreation resting in the loins of anything called a man." In contrast to his criticism of those in power, he wrote of the condemned man: "Of the thirty people there the best man of them all was the Negro who stepped straight and willingly to his death." He wrote that the man had winked at a reporter and said, "Yessah, I fou't Joe Louis onct."[24]

At the end of January Harold Clurman came to Chapel Hill for more conferences on *The Enchanted Maze*. Green and Clurman went out to the study on the farm, started a big fire in the fireplace, and spent many hours cutting, revising, and adding to the script and exchanging ideas.[25] Indeed, Green had numerous visitors who called upon him in his study. He recalled, for example, that one time he "was in that studio working, and Grant Wood, the painter, knocked on the door. . . . I remembered him from the Iowa paintings he had done.

We spent a good time talking together. And I remember other days when someone would knock on the door. . . . Now and then people would find their way out, and we would talk and talk." People continued to want not only to talk to him at his home but also to call him away from it to share his expertise elsewhere: "I remember," Green later recalled, "one day a group of fellows appeared, and they were from Princeton. They said they wondered if I would be interested in coming to Princeton and teaching creative writing at Princeton. I was very highly honored, but I said, 'I have to keep knocking on the typewriter.'"[26]

Green probably did not know it yet, but he was about to embark seriously on a project perhaps most significant to his career. In April the Greens made a trip to Roanoke Island, North Carolina, at the invitation of D. Bradford Fearing, secretary-treasurer of the Dare County Chamber of Commerce, a trip that would renew Green's interest in writing about the Lost Colony. Green had been interested in the "lost colony" for a long time: "Back in 1921, I was writing folks plays, . . . and I got to reading about Sir Walter Raleigh. So I went down to Manteo."[27] He later wrote, many years after the event, "I set out from Chapel Hill and traveled by bus and train to Beaufort, thence up Pamlico Sound by mailboat, and finally made the latter part of my journey across the open inlet by hiring a fisherman and his little motorboat—in all a distance of some three hundred miles."[28] Green reported that by the time he "got into town, . . . I had fifty cents left. . . . I went to the bank next morning and I said, 'I'm broke, and I want to cash a check.' And the fellow said, 'You got a blank check?' I said, 'No.' He said, 'Here's one.' Never did ask me who I was. And I wrote it out for ten dollars, and he gave me the ten dollars."[29]

Green's written account continues:

I . . . started walking up the sandy road through the forest toward the place known as Fort Raleigh four miles away. I plodded along in the ankle-deep sand, and . . . got to the little grove of pines and live-oaks on the edge of Croatan Sound and stood beside the small squat stone erected by a local historical group in 1893 to Virginia Dare, the first English child born in the new world. This stone was the only mark to tell that this was Fort Raleigh and the site of the perished colony. I wandered around in the woods. I idly plucked some sassafras twigs and chewed them, and thought upon that band of hardy pioneers who, three hundred and thirty-four years before, had come to this spot to build a fort, a bastion, a beachhead for the extension of the English-speaking empire across the sea.[30]

Green remembered that upon his return from his 1921 journey, he wrote a draft in which he "had Virginia Dare marrying Manteo's son in the end in the forest. And then I laid it up and went on with other things"; he felt that the draft "wasn't any good particularly." The subject emerged again in the early 1930s, when W. O. Saunders, editor of the Elizabeth City *Independent*, "came to see me. And he'd been over in Germany and seen what he called the *Oberammergau* play, the outdoor religious play, and he said, 'We've got to have something like that down at Manteo because we're having—soon coming up—the 350th anniversary and want to do something.' Maybe he heard that I had written something—so we started."[31]

There was talk of a nationwide contest to select a girl to play the part of Virginia Dare. Soon local congressman Lindsay Warren got a bill passed in Washington setting up the Roanoke Island Congressional Commission. A big meeting was held on the island, after which the Roanoke Island Historical Association was reactivated. A man from Norfolk who was in the plumbing business was at the meeting and offered to put up $200,000. Green recalled another "fellow, the Right Reverend Peacock, and we had a meeting in Raleigh with the governor and the Right Reverend was there. . . . This Right Reverend . . . had written many plays. . . . He wanted to write the play with me, he said. We had a fellow over there, came up to be the manager, and he had a pretty girl on each side, and he had Roanoke Island divided into lots, the whole island."[32] The WPA had constructed a replica of the fort, chapel, and village in 1932, but there the project stopped. The pledges for money vanished in the gloom of the Depression, and plans for a pageant were shelved.

In the fall of 1935, however, D. B. Fearing and others began trying to revive the project for a possible 1937 production. Fearing met with Gov. J. C. B. Ehringhaus (a native of the coastal town of Elizabeth City and therefore quite interested in the plans), North Carolina's U.S. senator Josiah W. Bailey, Congressman Warren, and others. He wanted Green to write the play and Koch to direct it. At a dinner meeting held at Manteo on April 12, 1936, W. O. Saunders revealed

Shown studying a possible site for an amphitheater at Manteo are (*left to right*) Paul Green, Melvin Daniels, W. O. Saunders, Frederick H. Koch, Chauncey Meekins, Martin Kellog, D. B. Fearing, and Ike Davis.

the latest version of his ambitious scheme. He wanted to "bring millions of tourists from all parts of the world just as millions are attracted to Oberrammergau in the hills of Bavaria." He proposed that Roanoke Islanders affect Elizabethan speech and let "their hair . . . grow long," as worn in the Elizabethan period. He suggested that "every spare room could be rented" to tourists, even as "the primitiveness of the island [was] preserved." Green did not agree with all of Saunders's grandiose plans and rose to voice his opinion. A reporter present somehow got the idea that Green was opposing the entire project. As a result, the Raleigh *News and Observer* ran a headline saying, "Green Opposes Island Pageant."[33]

The following day, in an editorial, the same newspaper said there should be some "middle ground between [the] Roanoke Island Historical Association and Paul Green." The writer agreed with Green that there should be no long hair or affected speech but counseled that tourists were "not only welcome but wanted" and that Roanoke Island was a true historical asset. On April 16 the *News and Observer* clarified the situation with a story quoting D. Bradford Fearing, now secretary of the Roanoke Island Historical Association,

"'Paul Green . . . promised us his wholehearted support,'" said Fearing, "'in production of a pageant in 1937 at Fort Raleigh.'"[34] By that time, Paul and Elizabeth Green were on a leisurely trip through eastern North Carolina, making notes to be used in another novel for the New York publisher McBride.[35]

Green was also preparing to start work on another project with the Group Theatre. On his trip to Chapel Hill, Harold Clurman had learned for the first time about Green's World War experience, which reminded Clurman that Kurt Weill had mentioned that he would like to do an American play similar to *The Good Soldier Schweik*, a Czech novel that had become a successful stage production in Berlin.[36] When he returned to New York, Clurman reported that Green was interested in the idea, and the director Cheryl Crawford adopted the project. Crawford later wrote, "I phoned [Green] and asked if Kurt and I could come to talk with him at his home in Chapel Hill. He seemed delighted. So off we went, Kurt and I."[37]

Actually, according to Green, Weill came down alone on the train in May:

Well, somebody in New York he met told him to get off at University. *The University* is a little old siding station out in the woods here beyond Carrboro. . . . I went to Durham to meet the train, and the train pulled in and no Kurt Weill. . . . So I finally came back home and wondered what had happened and tried to call New York, and I got Lotte Lenya or Cheryl or somebody. They said, "Well, he left here; he's supposed to be down there." Well, in the late afternoon the telephone rang, and it was Kurt. He had walked to a farmhouse and found a phone and called me. . . . So I got in the car and went over there in the woods, and there stood this little man by an old shack. . . . It was summertime and hot. The first thing I noticed [was] he had on a wool suit and very baggy trousers. So we met and talked, and we came over here and talked and talked. And so we got started on the idea of this antiwar play.[38]

Green's impression was that Weill, who had made a lot of money in Germany, had escaped with practically nothing.

Cheryl Crawford and Dorothy Patten (a member of the Group Theatre) soon arrived, and the three visitors stayed a week. "Worked night and day on comic play idea," Green wrote.[39] Crawford, Weill,

A scene from a 1971 production of *Johnny Johnson*. Photograph by Bert Andrews Photography, New York.

Patten, and Green spent days in the University of North Carolina library reading newspaper articles from the World War period. Then they worked out "a rough scenario."[40] Green "wrote to the War Department in Washington and asked what was the most common name in the American Army" during the war. The answer was that there had been "more than 5,000 John Johnsons" in the American Expeditionary Forces ("and the second name most common was William Smith"). Green gave his lead character the name, which likewise became the title of the play—*Johnny Johnson*.[41]

From the beginning Green wanted his play to have an antiwar theme, but he did not want it to be propaganda. He wanted to "just do it as a human document."[42] Johnny Johnson is a peace-loving country boy who is fired up by Woodrow Wilson's speech and enlists. When the army doctors give him psychological tests, he thinks they are playing with him and fires back the riddles that a real Mr. "shoes-untied" Johnson (see chapter 7) had related to young Paul Green on his way to school. The title character is soon at the front in a trench

A scene from a 1971 production of *Johnny Johnson*. Photograph by Bert Andrews Photography, New York.

drinking tea with English soldiers and chasing snipers in a no-man's-land. One sniper hides behind a statue of Christ, such as the one Green had seen standing in the destroyed town of Albert. There is a meeting of generals, such as that observed by Green at Buire Woods division headquarters, in which there are cold discussions of the 30,000 to be killed and the 100,000 to be wounded in the coming battle.

Green would envision a scene and its music and describe it to Weill, who would then put his own creativity to work: "I explained [that] I had a scene that later came on as brotherhood. We had an old hymn down there in Harnett County that we sang, 'Blest Be the Tie That Binds,' and I sang it for Kurt, and he would—it would always go through this alchemy . . . through his psyche, and it would come out Kurt Weill's stuff. He was an artist."[43] They were now far enough along that *The Enchanted Maze* project had been shelved. The visitors went back to New York, where Weill would continue his composing while Green worked on the play and lyrics.

Cheryl Crawford had arranged for the Group Theatre company to live for the summer at Pine Brook Camp near Trumbull, Connecticut. Green and Weill went by train from New York to Bridgeport, where Crawford met them and drove them to the Barlow Moffette House, which was within walking distance of the camp. This house was to be a brief home for five people—Kurt Weill, Lotte Lenya, Crawford, Green, and a maid named Doris.[44] Lenya and Weill had been married, but she had divorced him in Potsdam, Germany, in 1933. Then, in September 1935 they had arrived together in New York aboard the SS *Majestic*. They were living together and would remarry in January 1937. (Lenya is best remembered by a later generation by the inclusion of her name in Weill's song "Mack the Knife" and for her roles in the movies *From Russia with Love* and *Cabaret*.)

Cheryl Crawford later recalled that in the Moffette House Weill worked at his piano immediately below her bedroom and that "the songs were drilled into my head day and night"; nonetheless, "[t]he script progressed slowly."[45] One of Green's recollections suggests that he felt pressured by the close proximity of everyone: "Kurt was sitting there with all his talent boiling in him and waiting for some sort of script. . . . What a sort of dismal thing it was for me. There I was with all these people waiting with their tongues hanging out." Yet, he did enjoy the company of these people: "Kurt and Lenya . . . how wonderful they were. There they were, so far as I [k]new, poverty-stricken after all their glamour and glory in Europe . . . and never a complaint. . . . So they were a great inspiration."[46]

Green had given the group a script and was "trying to write lyrics too, and I even called on Elizabeth back in Chapel Hill to get busy to try to write a lyric or two, which she did." Not atypically, Green was not happy with the results, though Harold Clurman was: "I said to myself, well let's wait until Harold tells the people that it's so sorry and we got to hunt for another play this summer. But, bless his heart, he said, 'Folks'—or whatever he called . . . his disciples—'Paul is doing us a fine script, and we're going to have a big opening in New York.' . . . It was just like a weight had come off of me. I looked at Kurt, and old Kurt smiled. So we went back with renewed energy and worked on."[47]

Green went home for a few days to check on the construction of their new house.[48] There he discovered that a check had arrived from the U.S. government, a bonus that had finally been paid to World War veterans. Embarrassed to take the money, he described himself as a "shamed dog"; but he needed it to pay bills on his house and so did not return it.[49] At one point, he recalled,

The contractor called me up and wanted me to meet him at the bank. So I met him at the bank. He said, "We've checked on your bank balance here, and we're concerned about our investment in your building." . . . I said, "I haven't had a bill." He said, "I know, but we're committed here. We've ordered lumber and all sorts of things." . . . I was terribly embarrassed. . . . I think he wanted two thousand dollars or something. I put in a call right there to Samuel French. I said, "Mr. Sheil, . . . I need five thousand dollars. Could you just charge it to my account, please?" He said, "You want me to wire it or mail it?". . . I turned around to these fellows, the banker and all, and I said, "Mr. Sheil wants to know whether to wire it or mail it." Well, that really impressed them. They said, "Aw, mail it."[50]

Back in Connecticut the pressure was still substantial, but Green took a break each afternoon and played tennis to ease the tension. One night he left his writing long enough to watch as some of the actors performed Clifford Odets's play *Awake and Sing*. Another evening he went over to hear Lotte Lenya sing. He commented about her in his diary: "Nice mimicry around a chair in 'Miss Otis Regrets.'" He made a second trip home to try to help Elizabeth with problems involved with the new house; he stayed two weeks but was back in Connecticut on August 2. One night *Johnny Johnson* was read to the company. Green wrote, "Harold C. lets loose for a long hysterical harangue pointing out obvious little values in script, etc. etc. No wonder Group actors are so whipped down and full of psychoses—listening to this sort of thing for five years."[51] Green found that there were advantages to working near the actors. They had suggestions about the lines they were speaking, and some of their suggestions were quite good.

After two weeks of rehearsals the company had to leave Pine Brook, and Green went back to Chapel Hill. Green's Connecticut housemates took an apartment together in New York to economize. Lenya got a job in the huge cast of *The Eternal Road*. More money had to be raised to meet the $60,000 budget for the production of *Johnny*

Johnson (a quite substantial amount at that time), but Crawford obtained it from the financier John Hay Whitney.[52] Green then went to New York and took up residence at the Hotel Bristol as rehearsals began. He had trouble working out the ending to his play. One day he left the theater and went to bed trying to think of a solution: "I just lay there and figured and figured, and they were over there in the theater rehearsing, and Cheryl Crawford came over, knocked on the door, and I feebly said, 'Come in.' She came in and sat by the bed. And I had everything dark as pitch, and me there in my misery. And she said, 'How're you coming with the ending?' And I said, 'Oh, my God, Cheryl, what the—' and so on. Well, she was very patient."[53]

Adding to the pressure on Green while he was working at the hotel,

a fellow came . . . and he had repossession papers [for my car]. I had gotten behind with my payments to Johnson Motor Company in Durham. I had all this land. I could have gotten some money. It was stupid. . . . They took the car, and I came back on the train, and I went right over to Johnson Motor Company and bought it back. I went by the bank and got some money and went right over there and bought the same old car, right there. . . . I was so ashamed. . . . I just forgot it. Neglected it. They'd been writing me, and I was up there putting on a play, immersed in it. I forgot all about it—that I owed him any money. Mr. Johnson was just as nice as he could be. Said, "I've spent more time trying to get money out of you."[54]

Besides writing the play's ending, there were other problems. Rehearsals had been held in a small theater, but the only place available for the actual production was the 44th Street Theatre, which was very large. Harold Clurman wrote:

Our actors' voices sounded so small they were occasionally inaudible; Donald Oenslager's sets, which had been designed larger than I anticipated, now appeared monstrous; the performances now looked amateurish. . . . The first two previews of *Johnny Johnson* were the most distressing experiences I have ever gone through in the theatre. The large production— nineteen sets—and the orchestra had not had sufficient time for rehearsals (dress rehearsals are costly). The actors were lost. After the first five minutes of the first preview half the audience left. By the end of the performance there were no more than twenty people in the auditorium.

The panic that ensues on an occasion like this has nothing to do with art. It is hysteria that combines the fear and shame of economic ruin with the humiliation attendant or a blow to one's pride.[55]

There were also letters from loyal friends of the Group Theatre asking its members not to open the play for fear that it would be their ruin. Clurman "felt as if everything was giving way underneath me— not only the production, but six years of work."[56] The directors struggled to opening date. On November 19 Elizabeth Green joined her husband at the Hotel Bristol. There were "best wishes" telegrams from the four Green children, from Proff Koch, and from several others. Harold Clurman's telegram said, "Your beautiful spirit shines through your play. We are happy that we were able to work on it."[57] The cast, which included John Garfield, Lee J. Cobb, and Elia Kazan, rose to the occasion. Bad rehearsals were forgotten as the performance went perfectly. The audience responded warmly, and there were many curtain calls. The playwright was urged forward, and Green appeared on stage for brief remarks. Everyone felt that the play was a hit. But then the reviews came out. They were called mixed, but Green thought they were mostly bad. Within days everyone went on half pay, including Weill and Green.[58] More money was raised to keep the play going.

NOTES

1. Paul Green, interview by Rhoda Wynn, February 1974, tape 3, p. 23, Southern Oral History Program Collection, Southern Historical Collection, Wilson Library, University of North Carolina at Chapel Hill (hereafter cited as Wynn interview, with appropriate tape and transcript page number).

2. Paul Green Diary, November 24, 1935, Paul Green Papers (collection #3693), Southern Historical Collection (hereafter cited as Diary, with entry date).

3. Diary, November 30, 1935. Warner Brothers released the film *Green Light* in 1937.

4. Diary, November 30, 1935.

5. See *New York Times* articles such as "Two Strikes on the Bard" (with byline D.W.C.), about Reinhardt's "guid[ance]" of a Warner Brothers production of *A Midsummer Night's Dream*, February 17, 1935; "Reinhardt Tribute Is Led by Einstein," June 29, 1935; Curt L. Heymann's "Herr Reinhardt Likes the Movies," July 7, 1935; "Reinhardt Is Here to Produce Play," October 4, 1935; and "Reinhardt Fete at Fair Is Urged," October 9, 1935.

6. Wynn interview, tape 2, p. 21.

7. Diary, November 30, 1935.

8. Telegram, Paul Green to Elizabeth Green, December 1, 1935, Paul Green Papers, folder 348. "AM TRYING TO ESCAPE GREEN LIGHT BUT MUST FULFILL WARNER CONTRACT," he wrote, along with a request for her to wire him money.

9. Wynn interview, tape 2, p. 36.

10. Diary, December 6, 1935.

11. Wynn interview, tape 3, p. 22.

12. Quoted in "Green's College Drama Appears again Tomorrow," *Daily Tar Heel* (Chapel Hill), December 8, 1935.

13. Telegram, Koch to Green, December 9, 1935, Paul Green Papers, folder 354. On the day after the play opened, the UNC student newspaper had announced that the second night's performance would be followed by "a friendly 'bull session' of professors . . . to debate over the correctness of the author's theories and their application to the University of North Carolina." "World Premiere of College Play Rebukes Schools," *Daily Tar Heel*, December 7, 1935.

14. "Argument Rages on Green's Play," *News and Observer* (Raleigh), December 10, 1935; "House Deplores Content of Play," *Daily Tar Heel*, December 10, 1935.

15. "University Groups in Row over Drama," *New York Times*, December 14, 1935.

16. Diary, December 13-19, 21-24, 26-31, 1935, January 1, 1936.

17. Diary, January 2, 1936.

18. Wynn interview, tape 2, p. 26.

19. Diary, January 3, 1936.

20. Paul Green, interview by James R. Spence, August 9, 1979, James R. Spence audio recordings relating to Paul Green, 1974-1979 (collection #5170), Southern Historical Collection (hereafter cited as Spence interview, with appropriate date).

21. Diary, January 4, 7, 1936.

22. "The Play: Being Three in One Act," *New York Times*, January 14, 1936.

23. Diary, January 15, 1936.

24. Diary, January 27, 24, 1936.

25. When he visited the Greens, Clurman brought with him actress Stella Adler, with whom he was cohabiting, although she was not his wife. Green later recalled that Elizabeth's mother disapproved of the arrangement: "Mrs. Lay, Elizabeth's mother, was very strict. We were sitting together talking, and Stella . . . every once in a while she would stand up and flounce her skirts in the air, . . . and as she sat down the wind would reveal her whole anatomy. Mrs. Lay was sort of scandalized. . . . Stella said, 'Harold, you're so sweet, sometime I think I'll marry you.'" Green shared to some degree his mother-in-law's disapproval of an unmarried couple living together; recollecting the incident led him to a diatribe on the subject. Spence interview, August 9, 1979.

26. Spence interview, August 9, 1979. Green reported that he likewise received a letter from Harvard asking if he'd be interested in teaching there; he declined the offer. And after Frederick Koch died, he also turned down an offer to head the drama department at UNC.

27. Spence interview, October 24, 1974.

28. Paul Green, *Drama and the Weather: Some Notes and Papers on Life and the Theatre* (New York: Samuel French, 1958), 153.

29. Spence interview, October 24, 1974.

30. Green, *Drama and the Weather*, 154.

31. Spence interview, October 24, 1974.

32. Ibid.

33. "Green Opposes Island Pageant," *News and Observer*, April 13, 1936; the quotations in this paragraph are from the *N&O* reporter's summary of Saunders's plans.

34. "History, Hair and Tourists," *News and Observer*, April 14, 1936; "Asserts Green Promised Help," *News and Observer*, April 16, 1936.

35. Diary, April 10-13, 1936.

36. In her autobiography, Cheryl Crawford tells the story somewhat differently: "Kurt wanted a very American subject. The most American playwright I could think of was Paul Green." Crawford, *One Naked Individual: My Fifty Years in the Theatre* (New York: Bobbs-Merrill, 1977), pp. 93-94.

37. Crawford, *One Naked Individual*, 94.

38. Wynn interview, tape 3, pp. 29-30.

39. Diary, May 13, 1936.

40. Crawford, *One Naked Individual*, 94.

41. Wynn interview, tape 3, p. 33. *Johnny Johnson: The Biography of a Common Man* (New York: Samuel French, 1937). In 1940 French published a vocal score edition. Green revised the play for a 1971 edition.

42. Wynn interview, tape 3, p. 32.

43. Wynn interview, tape 3, pp. 31-32.

44. Diary, June 8, 1936. See also Donald Spoto, *Lenya* (Boston: Little, Brown, 1989), 128.

45. Crawford, *One Naked Individual*, 94.

46. Wynn interview, tape 3, pp. 36, 37.

47. Wynn interview, tape 3, p. 38.

48. When Cheryl Crawford and Dorothy Patten visited them in Chapel Hill in May 1936, the Greens had been in the process of selling their house in the glen, and they completed the transaction during the week of the visit. After having an architect create a plan for a new house, they decided to abandon the plan, instead specifying a large study as the center of the residence and two wings projecting out from it. They were not entirely satisfied with the new plan but thought it was the best they could afford. Diary, May 1-13, 1936.

49. Diary, June 21-28, 1936.

50. Spence interview, August 10, 1979.

51. Diary, July 5, August 2-9, 1936.

52. Crawford, *One Naked Individual*, 96.

53. Wynn interview, tape 3, p. 43.

54. Spence interview, April 29, 1978.

55. Harold Clurman, *The Fervent Years: The Story of the Group Theatre and the Thirties* (New York: A. Knopf, 1945), 188-189.

56. Clurman, *The Fervent Years*, 189.

57. Telegram, Clurman to Green (among other telegrams), November 19, 1936, Paul Green Papers, folder 381.

58. Diary, November 20-26, 1936.

26: *The Lost Colony*

I̤n October 1936 a Chicago component of the Federal Theatre comprised exclusively of black actors prepared to perform Paul Green's *Hymn to the Rising Sun*. Richard Wright, the group's publicity director, had suggested the play to the Chicago group; Wright later achieved fame as the author of, among other books, *Native Son*, of which Green would write a dramatization. While Green was in New York working on *Johnny Johnson*, he received a telegram from actor Charles Desheim dated October 13, 1936:

CHICAGO FEDERAL NEGRO THEATRE PRODUCTION HYMN TO RISING SUN BANNED BY ROBERT DUNHAM STATE ADMINISTRATOR WPA . . . CHICAGO TRIBUNE QUOTES DUNHAM QUOTE I STOPPED THE PLAY . . . OF SUCH A MORAL CHARACTER THAT I CAN'T EVEN DISCUSS IT WITH A MEMBER OF THE PRESS UNQUOTE WHAT CAN YOU DO.[1]

The mayor of Chicago had banned the play *Tobacco Road* the year before, but in this case no one seemed to know where the pressure to censor had come from—although both Hallie Flanagan and Brooks Atkinson quote the state WPA administrator identically to what was in the foregoing telegram.[2] Dunham was apparently offended by a reference in the play to the reason the character Runt had been thrown into the sweatbox: the guard had caught him "playing with himself" (the word "masturbation" was not used). The Federal Theatre Project of New York produced the play the following year without any mention of censorship. Atkinson attended, even though he had already seen the earlier production at the Civic Repertory Theatre. According to Flanagan, "Atkinson referred to it as Mr. Green's beautifully written case history in penal brutality" and called it "a stunning play."[3] No reviewer suggested that the material was objectionable. The Indiana Federal Theatre produced Green's *The House of Connelly* at Indianapolis the first week of January 1937.

That same month, the Greens went to Washington to confer with Hallie Flanagan about the Roanoke Island project. A delegation from Dare County had come to Chapel Hill just after the New Year's holiday to enlist Green's help again, so he and Elizabeth met with Flanagan in the McLean mansion, the national office for the Federal Theatre, and found her receptive to lending some assistance to the project. Green also spent two days doing research on the Roanoke Island colony in the Library of Congress but hurried to New York on news that *Johnny Johnson* was closing. He had dinner with Crawford, Weill, and Lenya and found them disappointed and depressed.[4] The play had struggled along for sixty-eight performances. All of those involved believed that they had developed a fresh form of musical in which they had achieved the ultimate fusion of story, music, mime, and dance, but the theater-going public had not responded enthusiastically enough. Cheryl Crawford could see the Group Theatre coming apart. It was in fact the last play on which Harold Clurman, Lee Strasberg, and Cheryl Crawford worked together. They had begun with a Paul Green play and now were ending with another.[5]

Years later Green looked back on his experience with the Group Theatre with a more appreciative feeling than he had expressed during some of his time associated with it: "I learned a lot from those dedicated people. Yes, true, I was always skeptical about their devotion to The Method, as they called it, derived out of Stanislavsky and especially remembering how that great teacher hated any kind of dogma and said so. But I found myself enjoying the Group actors' acting better than other actors. I found that those people who wept against a tree or wall were in many ways wonderful. . . . And of course the fervor of the Group Theatre acting, the lyrical power in it, was usually above average."[6] Green concluded, "I believe the Group Theatre with all its failings was one of the two best things that ever happened to American Theatre—the other being Eugene O'Neill."[7] Although Green believed that a writer does his best work alone, he missed the discussions with Crawford, Clurman, and Strasberg following the breakup of the Group. Working with them on a project such as *Johnny Johnson* had been somewhat like his student days, when the Carolina Playmakers used each other as sounding boards in the course of their writing.

Johnny Johnson was later produced in Chapel Hill, Los Angeles, and Boston, but the size of the cast and the expense of producing it have discouraged many theater groups. In the 1970s there was new interest in the play, mostly because of its anti-war theme. It was produced in Germany in 1974 and at the National Theatre in Helsinki in 1975, with the riddles of "shoes-untied" Johnson of Pleasant Union being spoken from the respective stages in German and Finnish. While Green was in New York in January 1937 he met with officials of the publishing firm Samuel French, which was proceeding with the publication of *Johnny Johnson*. He hoped that publishing the work would bring in some modest royalties. Up to that point his expenses related to the play had exceeded his income by $300.[8]

The same evening on which he computed that deficit, Green also recorded going with Barrett Clark to see Reinhardt's *The Eternal Road*. (Perhaps the extravagance of that production inspired his figuring out his own largesse with his play.) On January 8, 1937, Green sat with Clark in the Manhattan Opera House, eagerly anticipating the performance of *The Eternal Road*. The production was huge, as Green had expected, and featured more than three hundred actors. The composer and conductor Isaac Van Grove was in the orchestra pit conducting Kurt Weill's music. Green recalled that

the climax, the end of the play, [was] one of the most beautiful endings I've ever seen. The light came up, and there was a chorus of angels ascending up and up and up—far upstage into the sky, beautifully lighted, and what a heavenly chorus. . . . [But] nothing could save the play. I knew the man who had put a lot of money into it, and sometime months later I met him on the street in New York and I said, "Well, hello, how are you doing?" . . . He says, "I live in one room in the hotel. I'm broke. That *Eternal Road* broke me."[9]

At the conclusion of the production Green and Clark went to Reinhardt's apartment. They found him "feeling pretty sad," Green wrote in his diary, adding, "Wonder if Reinhardt is finished inside.

Don't know. Maybe he can ride on form for a few more years, and then he'll be able to rest with 'formal' ease being old."[10] The diary entry suggests that Green's admiration of the man may have waned; in any case, he seems to have been less enthusiastic about collaborating with his former idol. During the year since his last encounter with Reinhardt the previous January, the two men had corresponded some and had met a couple of times, but a joint project had not gotten very far. At the first meeting Reinhardt indicated that they would keep things simple, but when he took out his pencil and started sketching, it was quickly a very large production. Green soon worked out the basis of a play, with plot and characters. Reinhardt later sent Green a notebook of his ideas and plans. With both men working on major projects, however, only limited progress had been made during 1936. Green remembered Reinhardt as a patient and talented man, but they never finished their project together. Much later Reinhardt established a school in Hollywood for actors and writers and asked Green to come teach, but the offer was another that Green declined.

Reinhardt was not the only one of Green's friends who had fallen on less successful times. Not long after Barrett Clark sat with Green to watch Reinhardt's production fiasco, he visited Green in Chapel Hill. Green recalled the visit with sadness, knowing that he had disappointed one of his best friends: "Barrett came down here and we sat out in the car, I remember, and he said, 'Paul, I have been at French so long and I want to get a share in the business.'"[11] On behalf of Clark, Green went to the head of the company but was told that it was "a family business" and that there was no real opportunity for Clark to become a part owner. Green continued,

Later he said that "Sidney Howard and some woman and I . . . are starting a separate organization, and [we'll] get playwrights to join us, and we're calling it the Dramatists' Guild. And Paul," he said, "I expect you to join us." Well, I had a struggle, because Barrett had no money. It was just an organization trying to start, and I had a relation with French that any time I needed money just ask him—[like when] we were building this house and ran out of money. . . . So when Barrett proposed my joining this firm with no money at all, I had a hard struggle, but I finally told him, "I can't do it." . . . There began a separation from Barrett that I regret very much.[12]

In contrast to his friends, Green was still in his own heyday. On January 15, 1937, the Greens, Proff Koch, and Bill Couch drove to Manteo to meet with the pageant committee. The committee had received a commitment from the WPA to build an outdoor theater, and Congressman Lindsay Warren had pushed through Congress a bill to mint 25,000 memorial coins, which would be sold to help finance the project.[13] Green walked out to the site and immediately drew new plans for the theater, later recording in his diary, "I am in time to keep too much of a monstrosity from being built."[14] Perhaps he was thinking about Reinhardt's recent failure, largely the result of overproduction.

Soon after the Greens returned to Chapel Hill, Thomas Wolfe visited the town. He had been in New Orleans and had decided to visit his alma mater for the first time in seventeen years.[15] On a Saturday night in January he came out to the Green home and talked until four o'clock in the morning. A large group of faculty and friends were eager listeners. Green's diary entry of the following day suggests that he had begun to have reservations about Wolfe's continued popularity, too, perhaps a consequence of having recently witnessed evidence of the transient nature of success with other friends. Green worried that the source of Wolfe's talent might also be his downfall (as it was for Reinhardt): "Where is the staying power of our American writers? Tom Wolfe will stay as long as he himself stays for he is his own subject and photographer. But what will happen if his public grows tired of his confessions? Or will it or can it grow tired? I would be surer if he could create and fashion complete and rounded separate works of art to stand alone—cut loose from the matrix of his own emotive-self. But how thankful we should be for what we have."[16]

A few nights later Jonathan Daniels was to host a dinner for Wolfe in Raleigh. Green went with his sister Caro Mae and her husband, Phillips Russell, and they picked up Wolfe from Chapel Hill. Caro Mae recalled that Wolfe came out carrying a suitcase that was dangling a shirtsleeve, that he complained about hitting his head on a door entrance a few moments before, and that he occupied the entire back seat of the Model A Ford as they drove to Raleigh.[17] Paul Green added, "The image I have is that it was pouring rain. . . . Riding along . . . we did talk about [him] going out to the Northwest or the West somewhere, and we did talk about his future writing. I said, 'Tom, there's so much poetry in what you write; wouldn't you be interested in doing a real American epic in the style of Whitman—go the whole hog . . . a great hymn to America, to democracy?'"[18] Sadly, Green's concern about how much more Wolfe could find to write about from his own autobiography would become a moot issue, inasmuch as Wolfe died less than two years later.

Green was called upon to help entertain other famous visitors to Chapel Hill during this period: that same month David Stevens of the Rockefeller Foundation came to meet with University of North Carolina officials. Following a luncheon, Green wrote of Stevens: "A quiet gentle man. The weight of money behind him, and the spectacle of begging professors everywhere. Sometimes I want to kick Proff K. out of doors."[19] Then, in March the Greens entertained Countess Alexandra Tolstoy in their new home. Green pumped her for anecdotes about her father as she ate her vegetarian meal. She was now living on her small farm in Connecticut. She told the Greens, "I put out the—what do you say?—manure with my own hands." She had given up raising chickens because she became so attached to them.[20]

In April, and perhaps to his surprise, Green received notification that *Johnny Johnson* had won an award given annually by the Drama Study Club of New York. At the urging of Cheryl Crawford, he journeyed to New York to receive the award at a large gathering in the ballroom of the Waldorf Astoria Hotel on April 9.[21] While there Green learned that even though the Group Theatre had disbanded, Crawford wanted to produce *The Enchanted Maze* with another company she was forming. Green was interested, but "Right off we didn't agree but hope we shall."[22]

Again back in Chapel Hill, he needed to complete *The Lost Colony*, but there was also work to be done for the university. During April he wrote letters to David Stevens at the Rockefeller Foundation and to Robert B. House of the university administration about establishing a writers workshop course, a program involving eight creative writing fellowships at a cost of $500 each, with ten invited lecturers at $100 each.[23] Pulling Green in still another direction was a telegram from Kurt Weill proposing that they work together on an adaptation, as well as a telegram from MGM about doing a single film script, but Green turned them both down for the moment. After several weeks, he did take time out to go to New York and work with Sidney Howard, Maxwell Anderson, and others on a drama convention, but he came directly back to *The Lost Colony* script. During the weeks that followed he spent a great portion of his time in the North Carolina Collection of the university library studying the church music, popular airs, and folk music, as well as the history, of sixteenth-century England and America.[24]

From the start, Green knew that he wanted *The Lost Colony* to be another symphonic drama, bigger and better than *Roll, Sweet Chariot* had been. Since the theater in Manteo was outdoors, he had room to do things that even Reinhardt had never dared. He could have a sailing ship approach the Waterside Theatre in the audience's view. He could have the clash between Indians and colonists take place both onstage and in the surrounding underbrush and trees. He had designed and would use three stages that would allow scene changes without interruption. There was off-stage space for a large chorus.[25] He found new ways to integrate music into the production. For example, when the colonists were in prayer, rather than have them speak the prayer, he used the chorus to chant their thoughts. "These means are for the extension and power of the characters on the stage," he explained.[26]

When all of the music had been selected, he got his friends Lamar Stringfield and Adeline McCall to arrange the score. Green wrote the words to many of the tunes.[27] Samuel Selden, a man Green had first met with the Provincetown Players in 1926 and who had later come to the university, was named director of the production, with Koch as advisory director. Soon after the spring term was over, Selden and Green went to Roanoke Island and worked steadily for several weeks to get ready for the production. Hallie Flanagan was giving all the support she could. The Federal Theatre was paying the salaries of thirteen actors and actresses who were playing key roles. Other members of the cast included drama students Selden had recruited from the university, as well as local people. Young men from the Civilian Conservation Corps became the play's Indians. A chorus was brought in from Westminster Choir College of Princeton, New Jersey.[28]

The Lost Colony's 1937 Premiere Souvenir Program cover, courtesy of the Roanoke Island Historical Association.

All this was blended with the mystique of place—this is where the subject of the drama really happened. The production opened on the night of July 4, 1937, as another turning point in Paul Green's life.

NOTES

1. Telegram, Desheim to Green, Paul Green Papers (collection #3693), folder 375, Southern Historical Collection, Wilson Library, University of North Carolina at Chapel Hill.

2. Quoted in Hallie Flanagan, *Arena: The History of the Federal Theatre* (New York: Benjamin Blom, 1940), 136. The quotation likewise appears in Brooks Atkinson, *Broadway* (New York: Macmillan, rev. ed., 1970), 250. See both volumes for discussions of the censorship of this play.

3. Flanagan, *Arena*, 137.

4. Paul Green Diary, January 8, 9-10, 1937, Paul Green Papers (hereafter cited as Diary, with entry date).

5. After spending a year in Hollywood, Clurman returned to New York, reorganized the Group Theatre, and kept it going for a few more years, but Strasberg and Crawford never returned to the company.

6. Paul Green, *Plough and Furrow: Some Essays and Papers on Life and the Theatre* (New York: Samuel French, 1963), 55.

7. Green, *Plough and Furrow*, 56.

8. Diary, January 11, 1937.

9. Paul Green, interview by Rhoda Wynn, February 1974, tape 2, pp. 25-26, Southern Oral History Program Collection, Southern Historical Collection.

10. Diary, January 11, 1937.

11. Spence interview, August 10, 1979.

12. Ibid.

13. Paul Green, *The Hawthorn Tree: Some Papers and Letters on Life and the Theatre* (Chapel Hill: University of North Carolina Press, 1937), 99.

14. Diary, January 16, 1937. In this same diary entry, Green likewise noted, "It is finally decided that I with Elizabeth's help will write the pageant and Mr. Koch will see that it is produced." Elizabeth Green had frequently been involved not only in the editing of her husband's work but also as a trusted adviser and sounding board. As mentioned previously, Paul had called upon his wife to help with the lyrics of the songs in *Johnny Johnson*. She did the same for *The Lost Colony*, as well as a substantial amount of research for her husband.

15. For a discussion of Wolfe's visit to Chapel Hill, see Elizabeth Nowell, *Thomas Wolfe, A Biography* (New York: Doubleday, 1960), 371.

16. Diary, January 24, 1937.

17. Caro Mae Green Russell told the author this story during an unrecorded conversation in Chapel Hill on September 29, 1978.

18. Spence interview, August 9, 1979.

19. Diary, January 25, 1937.

20. Diary, April 1, 1937.

21. The more prestigious Critics Award had gone to Green's friend Maxwell Anderson for the play *High Tor*.

22. Diary, April 9, 1937.

23. The proposed program was not implemented in full, but the Rockefeller Foundation did provide some grants for fellowships and lectures. Green and House got along fine, in spite of the publicity surrounding *The Enchanted Maze* censorship incident. Green's letter to House, a copy of which Green sent to Stevens, is dated April 13, 1937. Paul Green Papers, folders 412, 425. The letter indicates that Green is following up on a conversation he had with House on April 12 and that he had spoken with Stevens two weeks earlier about the literary conference.

24. Agatha Boyd Adams, *Paul Green of Chapel Hill*, University of North Carolina Library Extension Publications, vol. 16, No. 2 (Chapel Hill: University of North Carolina Library, January 1951), 79.

25. During June Green supervised the completion of the amphitheater, which was situated on a naturally sloping site that required a minimum of earth-moving. "We built that whole thing with one mule and a scoop . . . and the C.C. Camp boys, but we could've never done it without Mr. Roosevelt and the Federal Theatre." Spence interview, October 24, 1974.

26. Diary, July 23, 1937.

27. Adams, *Paul Green of Chapel Hill*, 82.

28. Paul Green, *Drama and the Weather: Some Notes and Papers on Life and the Theatre* (New York: Samuel French, 1958), 32.

Afterword

The public liked *The Lost Colony*, and other towns and cities wanted outdoor dramas depicting their history. Paul Green wrote fifteen others that were produced, including *Wilderness Road* for Berea, Kentucky; *Cross and Sword* for St. Augustine, Florida; and *Texas* for Palo Duro Canyon, Texas.[1] These dramas have involved thousands of people since 1937, providing jobs, giving theatrical experience in every phase of production, launching careers and marriages, and teaching history to Americans. They have become the people's theater of which Green always dreamed. *The Lost Colony* itself has become the longest-running play in American theatrical history.

In spite of the fact that outdoor symphonic dramas seemed to dominate Paul Green's life after *The Lost Colony*, he had time for innumerable other works and activities. In 1941 he dramatized Richard Wright's novel *Native Son*. He moved his family to California during World War II and wrote additional screenplays for Hollywood. Five volumes of his short stories were published in the three decades after World War II. In 1951 he wrote an adaptation of *Peer Gynt* for the American National Theatre and Academy, which was headed by Cheryl Crawford. In 1954 he created an adaptation of Bizet's *Carmen* for the Central City Opera Festival in Colorado.[2] Five volumes of his essays were published between 1943 and 1963. He remained always an active fighter against capital punishment, against segregation, and against injustice. He died May 5, 1981, at the age of eighty-seven.

Thomas Aquinas said you must believe the unbelievable in order to have true faith, because it's so easy to believe in the miracle that outrages reason. . . . To me, reason, science . . . is the way forward.

—Paul Green, in an interview with James Spence
October 23, 1976

NOTES

1. *Wilderness Road: A Symphonic Outdoor Drama* (New York: Samuel French, 1956); *Cross and Sword: A Symphonic Drama of the Spanish Settlement of Florida* (New York: Samuel French, 1966); and *Texas: A Symphonic Outdoor Drama of American Life* (New York: Samuel French, 1967).

2. *Native Son (The Biography of a Young American): A Play in Ten Scenes*, with Richard Wright (New York: Harper, 1941), produced at the St. James Theatre in New York in 1941 and directed by Orson Welles; *Ibsen's Peer Gynt: American Version* (New York: Samuel French, 1951), produced at the American National Theatre and Academy Playhouse in New York in 1951; "Bizet's Carmen" (unpublished manuscript), produced for Opera Festival, Central City, Colorado, in 1953.

Bibliography

Interviews

Gold, Erma Green. Interview by James R. Spence, October 2, 1976.

Green, Paul. Interview by Billy E. Barnes, March, May 1975. Southern Oral History Program Collection, Southern Historical Collection, Wilson Library, University of North Carolina at Chapel Hill.

_____. Interview by Jacquelyn Hall, May 30, 1975. Southern Oral History Program Collection, Southern Historical Collection, Wilson Library, University of North Carolina at Chapel Hill.

_____. Interview by James R. Spence, October 24, 1974. Audio recordings relating to Paul Green, 1974-1979 (collection #5170), Southern Historical Collection.

_____. Interview by Rhoda Wynn, February 1974. Southern Oral History Program Collection, Southern Historical Collection.

Johnson, Mary Green. Interview by James R. Spence, May 8, 1976. James R. Spence audio recordings relating to Paul Green, 1974-1979 (collection #5170), Southern Historical Collection.

Russell, Caro Mae Green. Interview by James R. Spence, October 2, 1976. James R. Spence audio recordings relating to Paul Green, 1974-1979 (collection #5170), Southern Historical Collection.

Works by Paul Green

Aunt Mahaly's Cabin (play). Collected in Paul Green, *In the Valley and Other Carolina Plays.*

Blackbeard (with Elizabeth Lay). Collected in Paul Green, *The Lord's Will and Other Carolina Plays.*

Blue Thunder (play). New York: Samuel French, 1928.

"The Devil's Instrument." *Atlantic Monthly* 134 (July 1924): 81-92.

"Dimes vs. Art." *News and Observer* (Raleigh), February 7, 1934.

Drama and the Weather: Some Notes and Papers on Life and the Theatre (essay collection). New York: Samuel French, 1958.

Dramatic Heritage (essay collection). New York: Samuel French, 1953.

End of the Row (play). Collected in Paul Green, *Lonesome Road: Six Plays for the Negro Theatre.*

"Evening on the Farm" (essay). *Carolina Magazine* [old series] 47 [new series 34] (May 1917).

The Hawthorn Tree: Some Papers and Letters on Life and the Theatre (essay collection). Chapel Hill: University of North Carolina Press, 1937.

Home to My Valley (short story collection). Chapel Hill: University of North Carolina Press, 1970.

The Hot Iron (play). Collected in Paul Green, *Lonesome Road: Six Plays for the Negro Theatre.*

The House of Connelly and Other Plays (collection). New York: Samuel French, 1931.

Hymn to the Rising Sun (play). New York: Samuel French, 1936.

In the Valley and Other Carolina Plays (collection). New York: Samuel French, 1928.

"James Whitcomb Riley" (poem). *Carolina Magazine* [old series] 47 [new series 34] (November 1916).

Johnny Johnson: The Biography of a Common Man (play). New York: Samuel French, 1937.

The Laughing Pioneer (novel). New York: R. M. McBride and Company, 1932.

Last of the Lowries (play). Collected in Paul Green, *The Lord's Will and Other Carolina Plays.*

Lonesome Road: Six Plays for the Negro Theatre. New York: R. M. McBride and Company, 1926.

The Lord's Will (play). Collected in Paul Green, *The Lord's Will and Other Carolina Plays.*

The Lord's Will and Other Carolina Plays (collection). *New York: H. Holt and Company, 1925.*

The Man Who Died at Twelve O'Clock (play). Collected in Paul Green, *In the Valley and Other Carolina Plays*.

The Miser, a Farm Tragedy (play). Collected in Paul Green, *The Lord's Will and Other Carolina Plays*.

"The Mystical Bernard Shaw" (essay). Collected in Paul Green, *Dramatic Heritage*.

"The New Theatre." Preface to *One-Act Plays for Stage and Study*, fourth series. New York: Samuel French, 1928.

"Of Course" (poem). *Carolina Magazine* [old series] 47 [new series 34] (May 1917).

Out of the South: The Life of a People in Dramatic Form (collection). New York: Harper, 1939.

"A Playwright's Notes on Drama and the Screen" (essay). *New York Times*, February 4, 1934.

Plough and Furrow: Some Essays and Papers on Life and the Theatre. New York: Samuel French, 1963.

Potter's Field (play). Collected in Paul Green, *The House of Connelly and Other Plays*.

The Prayer Meeting (play). Collected in Paul Green, *Lonesome Road: Six Plays for the Negro Theatre*.

Roll, Sweet Chariot: A Symphonic Play of the Negro People (play). New York: Samuel French, 1935.

"Salvation on a String" and Other Tales of the South (short story collection). New York: Harper, 1946.

"Sienkiewicz" (poem). *Carolina Magazine* [old series] 47 [new series 34] (May 1917).

"Symphonic Outdoor Drama: A Search for New Theatre Forms" (essay). Collected in Paul Green, *Drama and the Weather: Some Notes and Papers on Life and the Theatre*.

"The Theatre and the Screen" (essay). Collected in Paul Green, *The Hawthorn Tree: Some Papers and Letters on Life and the Theatre*, and in *Drama and the Weather: Some Notes and Papers on Life and the Theatre*.

This Body the Earth (novel). New York: Harper, 1935.

"To a Lady" (poem). *Carolina Magazine* [old series] 47 [new series 34] (November 1916).

Tread the Green Grass (play). Collected in *The House of Connelly and Other Plays*.

Trifles of Thought by P.E.G. (volume of poetry). Greenville, S.C.: privately published, 1917.

"Under a Window at Dawn" (poem). *Carolina Magazine* [old series] 47 [new series 34] (November 1916).

"White Dresses" (play). Collected in Paul Green, *Lonesome Road: Six Plays for the Negro* Theatre.

Wide Fields (short story collection). New York: R. M. McBride and Company, 1928.

Words and Ways: Stories and Incidents from My Cape Fear Valley Folklore Collection. Raleigh: North Carolina Folklore Society, 1968.

Books

Adams, Agatha Boyd. *Paul Green of Chapel Hill*. University of North Carolina Library Extension Publications, vol. 16, No. 2. Chapel Hill: University of North Carolina Library, January 1951.

Atkinson, Brooks. *Broadway*. New York: Macmillan, rev. ed., 1970.

Atkinson, Brooks, and Albert Hirschfeld. *The Lively Years, 1920-1973*. New York: Association Press, 1973.

Avery, Laurence G., ed. *A Southern Life: Letters of Paul Green, 1916-1981*. Fred W. Morrison Series in Southern Studies. Chapel Hill: University of North Carolina Press, 1994.

Blotner, Joseph, ed. *Selected Letters of William Faulkner*. New York: Vintage Books, 1978.

Clark, Bennett H. *Paul Green*. New York: R. M. McBride and Company, 1928.

Clurman, Harold. *The Fervent Years: The Story of the Group Theatre and the Thirties*. New York: A. Knopf, 1945.

Crawford, Cheryl. *One Naked Individual: My Fifty Years in the Theatre*. New York: Bobbs-Merrill, 1977.

Davis, Betty. *The Lonely Life: An Autobiography*. New York: G. P. Putnam's Sons, 1962.

Ellison, Ralph. *Shadow and Act*. New York: Random House, 1953.

Flanagan, Hallie. *Arena: The History of the Federal Theatre*. New York: Benjamin Blom, 1940.

Fowler, Malcolm. *They Passed This Way: A Personal Narrative of Harnett County History*. N.p.: Harnett County Centennial, 1955.

Green, Elizabeth Lay. *The Paul Green I Know*. Chapel Hill: North Caroliniana Society, 1978.

Koch, Frederick H. *Carolina Folk Comedies*. New York: Samuel French, 1931.

_____. *Carolina Folk-Plays*. New York: H. Holt and Company, 1922; second series, New York: H. Holt and Company, 1924; third series, New York: H. Holt and Company, 1928.

_____., ed. *American Folk Plays*. New York: D. Appleton-Century, 1939.

Mantle, Burns. *Best Plays of 1926-27*. New York: Dodd, Mead, 1927.

Nowell, Elizabeth. *Thomas Wolfe, A Biography*. New York: Doubleday, 1960.

Pearce, J. Winston. *Campbell College: Big Miracle at Little Buies Creek, 1887-1974*. Nashville, Tenn.: Broadman Press, 1976.

Powell, William S. *Higher Education in North Carolina*. Raleigh: State Department of Archives and History, 1964.

Sadler, Lynn Veach, ed. *Paul Green's Celebration of Man, with a Bibliography*. Sanford, N.C.: Human Technology Interface, Ink, 1994.

Selden, Samuel, with Mary Tom Sphangos. *Frederick Henry Koch, Pioneer Playmaker: A Brief Biography*. University of North Carolina Library Extension Publications, vol 19, No. 4. Chapel Hill: University of North Carolina Library, July 1954.

Spoto, Donald. *Lenya*. Boston: Little, Brown, 1989.

Walser, Richard. *Thomas Wolfe Undergraduate*. Durham: Duke University Press, 1977.

Wilson, Louis R. *The University of North Carolina, 1900-1930: The Making of a Modern University*. Chapel Hill: University of North Carolina Press, 1957.

Wolfe, Thomas. *Look Homeward, Angel: A Story of the Buried Life*. New York: Scribner's, 1929; reprint, New York: C. Scribner, 1957.

Sayward, Dorothy Steward. Comfort *Magazine, 1888-1942: A History and Critical Study*. University of Maine Studies, second series 75. Orono: University of Maine, 1960.

Zanuck, Darryl F. *"Habit" and Other Short Stories*. Los Angeles: Times-Mirror Press, 1923.

Articles and Essays

Adams, J. Donald. "Paul Green's Novel about Sharecroppers." *New York Times Book Review*, Novenber 10, 1935.

"Argument Rages on Green's Play." *News and Observer* (Raleigh), December 10, 1935.

"Asserts Green Promised Help." *News and Observer*, April 16, 1936.

Basso, Hamilton. "Nemesis in the Cotton Belt," *The New Republic*, November 13, 1935.

"Charting the American Drama's Drift." *New York Times*, February 19, 1928.

Clark, Barrett H. Introduction to Paul Green, *Lonesome Road: Six Plays for the Negro Theatre*. New York: R. M. McBride and Company, 1926.

"Conviction of Six Defendants in 'Dynamiting' Case Is Upheld by Decision of Supreme Court." *Greensboro Daily News*, November 21, 1935.

D. W. C. "Two Strikes on the Bard." *New York Times*, February 17, 1935.

"Daughters' Story Brings Death Nearer to Father." *News and Observer*, July 4, 1934.

"Green Opposes Island Pageant." *News and Observer*, April 13, 1936.

"Green's College Drama Appears again Tomorrow." *Daily Tar Heel* (Chapel Hill), December 8, 1935.

H. N. L. "Self Justification." *Daily Tar Heel* (Chapel Hill), January 3, 1934.

Heymann, Curt L. "Herr Reinhardt Likes the Movies." *New York Times*, July 7, 1935.

"History, Hair and Tourists." *News and Observer*, April 14, 1936.

"House Deplores Content of Play." *Daily Tar Heel*, December 10, 1935.

Isaacs, Edith J. R. "Critics' Pleasure: Broadway in Review." *Theatre Arts Monthly* 18 (November 1934): 813.

Krutch, Joseph Wood. "Drama: A Folk-Tragedy." *Nation* 4 (May 1927): 510.

Madry, Robert W. "Paul Green Plans to Continue to Live in State; Not to Teach." *Charlotte Observer*, August 6, 1933.

Meade, Julian R. "Paul Green." *The Bookman* 74 (January-February 1932): 505.

"Mill Dynamiters Start Sentences." *News and Observer*, January 4, 1936.

"The Play: Being Three in One Act." *New York Times*, January 14, 1936.

"Reinhardt Fete at Fair Is Urged." *New York Times*, October 9, 1935.

"Reinhardt Is Here to Produce Play." *New York Times*, October 4, 1935.

"Reinhardt Tribute is Led by Einstein." *New York Times*, June 29, 1935.

"See Parallel in Paul Green Play: Playwright's Defense of Spice Bittings Recalls 'In Abraham's Bosom.'" *News and Observer*, March 5, 1934.

"Six 'Dynamiters' to Serve Terms, One Wins Appeal." *News and Observer*, November 21, 1935.

"A Tale of the Southland." *Saturday Review of Literature* 9 (September 24, 1932): 123-124.

Tinker, Edward Larocque. "Grim Novel of the Southern Farmer." *New York Herald Tribune*, Books section, November 3, 1935.

"University Groups in Row over Drama." *New York Times*, December 14, 1935.

Walser, Richard. "Paul Green Undergraduate." *Pembroke Magazine* 10 (1978): 29-38.

"World Premiere of College Play Rebukes Schools." *Daily Tar Heel*, December 7, 1935.

Private Collections

Green, Paul, Papers (collection #3693). Southern Historical Collection, Wilson Library, University of North Carolina at Chapel Hill.

Plays (other than by Paul Green)

Bailey, Loretto. *Cloey*. Collected in Frederick H. Koch, *Carolina Folk Comedies*. New York: Samuel French, 1931.

———. *Job's Kinfolks*. Collected in Frederick H. Koch, *Carolina Folk-Plays*, third series. New York: H. Holt and Company, 1928.

Lay, Elizabeth. *Trista*. In Frederick H. Koch, *Carolina Folk-Plays*, second series. New York: H. Holt and Company, 1924.

Russell, Caro Mae Green. *Jumping the Broom*. Collected in *One-Act Plays for Stage and Study*, fifth series. New York: Samuel French, 1929.

Index

Z

About the Author

James Robert Spence (b. 1928), the oldest of nine children, grew up on a twenty-five-acre farm near Lillington in rural Harnett County, North Carolina. He graduated from the University of North Carolina (UNC) in Chapel Hill in 1949 and from the UNC School of Law in 1953. Spence practiced law in Lillington and in Fayetteville, North Carolina, and worked in insurance and banking in Greensboro, North Carolina. He was active in the Democratic Party and served as director of the North Carolina Rural Rehabilitation Corporation and member of the Governor's Emergency Planning Task Force in the administration of Gov. Terry Sanford and later as a member of Gov. Dan K. Moore's Study Commission on the Public School System. In 1968 Spence published a book titled *The Moore-Preyer-Lake Primaries of 1964: The Making of a Governor*; the volume reflects his abiding interest in the workings of the North Carolina Democratic Party.

Spence is likewise the author of *Portrait of a Place and Time: Recollections of a Farmer's Son* (1991), an autobiographical account of three decades (from about 1925 to 1955) of history in rural North Carolina and, more specifically, the hardships and challenges he encountered and ultimately overcame on the farm on which he grew up. The volume provides a vivid and realistic picture of that life and of Spence's eventual enrollment in college, his military service, his working tobacco in Canada to help with the family finances, and his graduation from law school. Spence moved to Orlando, Florida, in 1971. There he turned some of his attention to libraries and served as chairman of the State Library Council of Florida and as a trustee of the Orlando Public Library. He and his wife, Marilyn, had three children—Helyn, James, and Louise. James R. Spence died in 1995.

—Excerpted and adapted from the entry on James R. Spence in the serialized "Dictionary of North Carolina Writers," by Lorraine Hale Robinson with NCLR staff (including, for this entry, editor Margaret D. Bauer), North Carolina Literary Review 14 (2005): 207; additional information from Charles P. Younce's eulogy of Spence, August 21, 1995

About the Editor

Louisiana native Margaret D. Bauer is the Ralph Hardee Rives Chair of Southern Literature, professor of English, and editor of the *North Carolina Literary Review* at East Carolina University. She is the author of two monographs: *The Fiction of Ellen Gilchrist* (1999) and *William Faulkner's Legacy* (2005), both published by the University of Florida Press. Her articles on southern writers have appeared in such journals as the *Mississippi Quarterly*, the *Southern Literary Journal*, *Crossroads*, *Pembroke Magazine*, *Southern Studies*, the *College Language Association Journal*, and *Studies in Short Fiction*, as well as in collections of essays on Kate Chopin, Ellen Glasgow, Flannery O'Connor, and Alice Walker. Her current book projects include a volume on Louisiana's Tim Gautreaux for the University of South Carolina Press's Understanding Contemporary American Authors Series. Bauer is the 2004 Thomas Harriot College of Arts and Sciences recipient of the East Carolina University Scholar-Teacher Award, and she was named one of ten Women of Distinction at East Carolina University in 2007. Also in 2007, she received the Parnassus Award for Significant Editorial Achievement from the Council of Editors of Learned Journals for her work as editor of the *North Carolina Literary Review*. She is currently serving as president of the North Carolina Literary and Historical Association, and she has been a member of that organization's executive board since 1998.